GREAT MOUNTAIN DAYS
IN
SCOTLAND

ABOUT THE AUTHOR

Is there more to life than mountains? Not much, according to outdoor journalist, photographer and guidebook writer Dan Bailey, who has made a career out of his obsession. He enjoys every aspect of the game – from winter mountaineering and rock climbing to hillwalking and long-distance backpacking, but he's as keen simply to be in wild landscape as on any particular activity. Although he has climbed and walked in many of the world's mountain ranges, Dan reserves his greatest passion for the mountains of Scotland. A refugee from southern flatlands, he is based on the Fife Riviera, where a wonderful wife and daughter try their best to keep him on the right path. Dan is a regular contributor to print and online media, and the author of Cicerone guidebooks *Scotland's Mountain Ridges* and *The Ridges of England, Wales and Ireland*, and Pocket Mountains guides *Kingdom of Fife* and *West Highland Way*.

Dan Bailey, 2012

GREAT MOUNTAIN DAYS

IN

SCOTLAND

50 CLASSIC HILLWALKING CHALLENGES

by

Dan Bailey

2 POLICE SQUARE, MILNTHORPE, CUMBRIA LA7 7PY
www.cicerone.co.uk

First edition 2012
ISBN: 978 1 85284 612 1
© Dan Bailey 2012

Printed by KHL Printing, Singapore
A catalogue record for this book is available from the British Library.
All photographs are by the author unless otherwise stated.

 This product includes mapping data from the Ordnance Survey® © Crown copyright and
database right 2011. Cartography by Lovell Johns Ltd www.lovelljohns.com

THANKS AND ACKNOWLEDGEMENTS

As ever the team at Cicerone deserve praise for all their hard work behind the scenes, without which there'd
be no book. Thanks to Brasher, Harvey Maps, Ordnance Survey, Pacerpoles, POD, Rab, Suunto and Terra Nova
for their support. And cheers to Wilderness Scotland for the loan of two sea kayaks. Thanks, too, to everyone
I've shared great mountain days with during the long research period for this book, including Patrick Cadell,
Jan Coggins, Steven Hanton, Alan Hudson, Ross Kinghorn, Fiona Lowrie, Lorraine McCall, Steve Perry, Tom
Rimmington, Clare Wilkie, Joe Williams and others. And, of course, much love to Pegs and Daisy for their end-
less patience, and for making me always appreciate coming home.

WARNING

Mountain walking can be a dangerous activity carrying a risk of personal injury or death. It should be
undertaken only by those with a full understanding of the risks and with the training and experience to
evaluate them. While every care and effort has been taken in the preparation of this guide, the user should
be aware that conditions can be highly variable and can change quickly, materially affecting the serious-
ness of a mountain walk. Therefore, except for any liability which cannot be excluded by law, neither
Cicerone nor the author accept liability for damage of any nature (including damage to property, personal
injury or death) arising directly or indirectly from the information in this book.

To call out the Mountain Rescue, ring 999 or the international emergency number 112 – this will
connect you via any available network. Once connected to the emergency operator, ask for the police.

ADVICE TO READERS

While every effort is made by our authors to ensure the accuracy of guidebooks as they go to print,
changes can occur during the lifetime of an edition. If we know of any, there will be an Updates tab on
this book's page on the Cicerone website (www.cicerone.co.uk), so please check before planning your
trip. We also advise that you check information about such things as transport, accommodation and shops
locally. Even rights of way can be altered over time. We are always grateful for information about any
discrepancies between a guidebook and the facts on the ground, sent by email to info@cicerone.co.uk or
by post to Cicerone, 2 Police Square, Milnthorpe LA7 7PY, United Kingdom.

Front cover: An Sgurr from Sean Bhraigh's summit (Walk 6)
Back cover: Stob Coire Easain from Sgurr Choinnich Mor (Walk 26)
Contents page: Beinn a' Bhuird from Carn Eas (Walk 41)

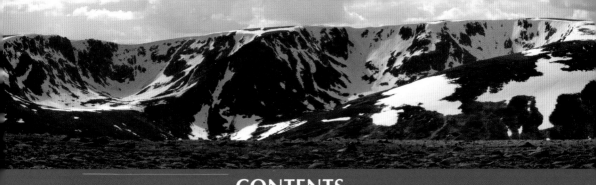

CONTENTS

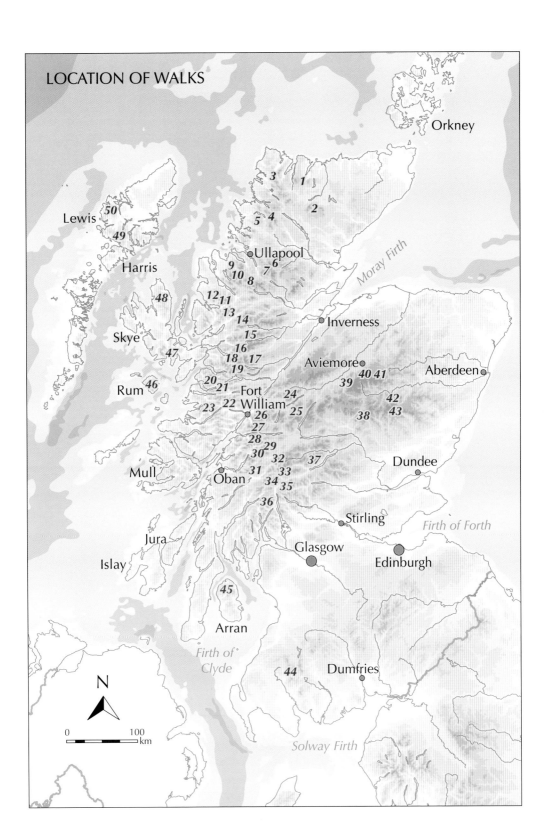

LOCATION OF WALKS

Orkney

Lewis

Harris

Skye

Rum

Mull

Jura

Islay

Arran

Ullapool

Inverness

Aviemore

Aberdeen

Fort William

Oban

Dundee

Stirling

Glasgow

Edinburgh

Dumfries

Moray Firth

Firth of Forth

Firth of Clyde

Solway Firth

N

0   100
                  km

PREFACE

I'm a Londoner by birth (well, no one's perfect). Naturally I took my early steps in hillwalking down south. Snowdonia's rugged grandeur and the manageable idyll of the Lake District both felt familiar before I'd ever ventured north of the border. At the age of 15 or so my first trip to the Highlands didn't just expand my horizons – it blew them away. Here were the hills I'd always dreamed of – elemental, austere and just a bit hostile. Their scale was liberating. Roadless empty spaces splayed across map after map, offering the limitless scope of a blank canvas.

As I recall we climbed only five or six Munros that week. We spent a lot of the time knee-deep in bogs or stumbling through low cloud; we hardly set foot on a decent path, and I don't think we met another walker on the hills the whole trip. We really earned those summits – and that's the way it should be. I instinctively feel that the less accommodating a hill, the greater its rewards; and by that measure Scotland's take some beating.

From the Alps to the Andes, I've been lucky to spend time in the major ranges of most continents, yet some of my most memorable days have been enjoyed closer to home. There remains something uniquely special about the Highlands and Islands, and 20-odd years after that first trip they still give me a thrill every time.

Working on this book has been a pleasure and a privilege, taking me the length and breadth of Scotland and even unearthing some hitherto unfamiliar gems along the way. I'm gradually filling in my canvas; but, happily, more blank space still remains than I'll ever have time to cover. Whether you follow the descriptions in this guide to the letter or simply use them as a springboard for other things, I hope these 50 routes inspire you to enjoy many great days of your own in Scotland's very special mountains.

Dan Bailey 2012

← *Beinn nan Eachan from Meall Garbh on the Tarmachan Ridge (Walk 37)*

↑ *View northeast from Goatfell.*
Left to right: Cir Mhor, Caisteal Abhail, the deep notch of the Witch's Step and North Goatfell (Walk 45)

INTRODUCTION

Scottish hill walks offer some of the greatest mountain days of their type to be found anywhere. The Highlands and Islands make an exceptional destination – rugged and remote, yet conveniently compact. This is a small nation full of big country, with a diversity of precious landscapes. The Cairngorms' subarctic magnificence; the lush green of the Southern Highlands; Sutherland's mind-cleansing emptiness; the western seaboard and islands, a dazzling interlocking of mountain and water – all these are part of Scotland's natural heritage, and each one is unique. Spanning the whole of the country, this book seeks out quality walks from every upland area, a collection that shows off Scotland's mountains in all their variety.

Scottish hills are notable for their uncompromising character, if not their height, and however straightforward they may be in climbing terms (via the easier routes at least) they may demand a lot from walkers. Summit elevations look modest compared to the Alps or the Rockies, but this can be misleading, particularly on the west coast, where tough terrain generally starts at sea level. Maritime position and northerly latitude combine to give the landscape a distinctive harshness.

When rain hoses horizontally or the winter plateaux are engulfed in 'white noise', the Scottish hills are no soft option, but the weather is also one of the country's great assets. If landscape is a visual spectacle, then it is climate that gives it kinetic energy, turning snapshot into movie. Clear northern light plays across rock and water, its sun spears and cloud shadows adding tension and a sense of movement.

With the sea's dominant influence, mercurial changeability is the one climatic constant, and no two days' weather are ever likely to seem quite the same. Although at times a curse, such unpredictability is also a source of endless novelty. Downpour, sunshine, wind and snow can come in rapid succession – or all at once. Moist air means copious cloud – often curling in tatters around the peaks or blotting out the world in an all-pervasive fuzzy dampness; sometimes sinking into the glens to leave the hills standing proud like islands.

This rigorous environment offers an earthy, authentic brand of walking that demands a certain level of self-reliance. In contrast to the situation typical on the European mainland there are no manned huts linked by waymarked trails here, and no hot meals and warm beds are laid on in the hills. Roads are few and far between, and towns, ski centres and other developments thin on the (generally boggy) ground.

The scale of the country makes it ideally suited to long testing journeys on foot, strenuous peak-bagging missions over all the major tops in a range, or

← Sgurr Mór (right), Loch Quoich and Gleouraich from Ben Aden's northeast ridge (Walk 21)

↑ Demanding terrain from sea level to summit – Sgurr na Stri (Walk 47) from Elgol, Skye

11

Backpacking on Beinn Dearg Beag (Walk 9) – hard work, but worth the effort

forays far into the backcountry to climb an isolated mountain. *Great Mountain Days* is built around such big ventures. Popular challenge walks, such as the Cairngorms 4000-ers and the Lochaber Traverse, are described alongside others less widely known but of similar merit; the common thread is size and toughness. Despite their demands these walks are aimed at a broad hill-going demographic, from superfit fell runners racing the clock to overnight backpackers in search of solitude, and from fair-weather summer walkers to seasoned winter mountaineers.

The author makes no apologies for the emphasis on difficulty and distance, but the desire to challenge should not be confused with exclusivity or elitism. With a little determination and a following wind these routes are achievable by any reasonably experienced and averagely robust hillwalker, and there's no imperative to run around them with your head down, ignoring the scenery. If it ever looks a bit much, most routes can be shortened or broken into separate smaller chunks, and there are suggestions for short cuts in the walk chapters.

The rewards of going the extra kilometre are many. A quick there-and-back summit dash may fill a spare afternoon, but why climb one peak when

you can do several? If the half-day quickie is a three-minute pop song – over before you've got stuck in – then the epic slog is more like a symphony – daunting, hard work, but richly complex and of deeper, longer-lasting significance. The cares of daily life tend to diminish when considered from a great height and distance, so the further we travel and the longer we go for the better.

The route to a truly great mountain day is through extended effort, with mud, sweat and maybe even a few tears along the way. The more improbable something may look on paper, the greater the satisfaction on completion; the harder and more prolonged the exercise, the bigger the buzz. Scotland's mountaineering and hillwalking pioneers understood all this. The distances casually covered by doughty Victorians and Edwardians such as Naismith (of Naismith's rule fame) might dwarf a typical 21st-century hill day – and all without the benefit of lightweight gear and nutritionally balanced (if barely edible) energy gels. It's amazing how far a little grit will go.

Following a cross-country through-route is a fulfilling way to travel among mountains, but it's not what this book is about. These routes are hill walks, wedded to the high ground and mostly circular (with one or two exceptions); they are not extended journeys from A to B. Any of the walks described in this book can be knocked off in a single (if in some cases rather stretching) day, but they might equally be spread over two or three – a change in pace, weight and emphasis that brings its own rewards. The divide between day trips and overnight backpacking routes is porous, and can be passed through at will. The information box at the start of each walk includes notes on wild camping and bothies.

Bigger might be better in some cases, but a key premise of this book is that the pleasure that a hill can offer is not proportional to its altitude, and that neither Munros (peaks over 3000ft) nor Corbetts (2500ft–2999ft) have cornered the market in quality. Among the chosen 50 walks, worthwhile trips at lesser elevations include the edge-of-the-world Uig hills of Lewis (Walk 50) and Skye's uniquely eccentric Trotternish Ridge (Walk 48), both in a different league from any number of duller Munros.

The Scottish guidebook canon is already well loaded with tomes on the popular hill lists. This guide is not another to add to the pile. Although you would accrue many Munro scalps (and Corbetts, and the rest) working through this book, scores of them are omitted too. The aim is not to tick through lists, but rather to present coherent and satisfying walks on the 'best' mountain groups, letting topography call the shots and adding a minimum of contrived wiggles. In some cases the neatest big route on a massif will just happen to miss a couple of peripheral Munros; those who feel obliged to climb every mountain can then choose to follow the relevant detours.

Writing a selective guidebook means making hard choices, distilling the finest quality of hills and routes out of the baffling number of possible candidates to produce a blend with a fair flavour of the country as a whole. The collection is a personal 'best of'. Not everyone will agree with all the choices, and inevitably some fantastic and popular hills have been omitted. For instance, neither Stac Pollaidh nor Schiehallion are overlooked through any fault of their own, but simply because they aren't ideally incorporated into a round of sufficient scale. A collection of big walks needs a bottom line, however arbitrary, and in this book it's roughly 20km. There is no particular upper limit placed on distance, although things have been kept within the bounds of challenging-but-achievable in one day.

Cloud-pleasing atmospherics over Glen Nevis, from Stob Bàn (Walk 27)

A sense of wilderness

Britain is an urban island tethered to a teeming continent, its landscapes and ecology shaped in large part by human hand. If wilderness is a place untouched, then few (if any) remnants are left in Europe. But at times the hills of Scotland feel close to that ideal. However, most of the remaining areas genuinely unaffected by human activity are found only above about 700m. Elsewhere the impression of wilderness is generally false. This is an environment degraded by deforestation and managed, in effect, as a giant deer farm.

But the feeling of Scotland's wildness remains. When confronted with the vast, the untamed, the ancient and the other, our feelings may evade neat definition; but we know them when we feel them. The Highlands and Islands are a rarity in modern Europe – a place where such experiences remain the norm; a sparsely populated area of significant size left largely uncluttered and uncultivated, influenced more by the elements than by industry.

Ironically, even the emptiness is to some extent a man-made desolation. Most of today's deserted glens once supported subsistence communities, and although it would be tedious to romanticise the bleakness of former times we should at the very least acknowledge the brutal economics that bled the uplands of their people during the Clearances of the 18th and 19th centuries. Born of past injustice it may have been, but its emptiness is now the area's unique selling point, making it an exceptional resource for wilderness tourism and a boon to us all in an overused world.

Getting around

Public transport in the Highlands is patchy – in some parts reasonable, but elsewhere limited or non-existent. Hubs such as Fort William and Kyle of Lochalsh are linked to the cities of Scotland's south and east by rail or long-distance bus route (sometimes both), making them accessible overland (given time) from places as exotic as Paris, Brussels or even London. Intermediate points along the main transport arteries are, of course, equally accessible, and those with hills on the doorstep make good bases for car-free walkers – such as Crianlarich, Glencoe

The amphibious assault – Sgurr na Lapaich (Walk 15) from Loch Mullardoch on the approach to Walk 16

or Aviemore. The ferry ports for the western isles are Ullapool, Oban and Uig on Skye (itself served by ferry from Mallaig and road from Kyle), while Rum and the other Small Isles are reached from Mallaig. In remoter parts of Scotland buses may be few and far between, especially in the northwest. Public transport information is provided in the box at the start of each walk in this book. See also Appendix 4 for details of the main transport providers.

By car

Walkers generally drive to the hills. Given the freedom, flexibility and kit-carrying capacity of a car it's easy to see why – particularly if the cost and carbon footprint is shared between several people. Many of the walks described in this book are simply inaccessible by public transport alone.

By bike

Quieter Highland roads are ideal for cycle touring, and this is a satisfying way to spend a holiday, ticking off a walk here or there along the way. A train/bike combination is also worth considering, as many hills are in easy cycling distance of

rail-friendly centres. Drivers can also get in on the fun, as routes that involve significant tarmac walking can be made more convenient with a cunningly pre-stashed bike.

And biking doesn't have to end at the road-head. The profusion (some would say excess) of 4WD estate tracks in Scotland makes a pedal-powered approach a realistic option for many of the walks described in this book, even for those averse to full-on mountain biking. Saddling up is arguably the most enjoyable way to negotiate long low-level track approaches such as Seana Bhraigh (Walk 6) and the end-of-day downhills can be particularly fun. The walk information box includes notes on approaches where two wheels are a good option.

High-spec full-suspension mountain bikes are unnecessary for the gentle variety of off-road cycling found in this book, but a sturdy frame, fat tyres, front suspension, mud guards and a rear pannier may all prove welcome on pedal-powered hill forays. Go armed with a basic tool kit, spare inner tubes and a pump. It's better to carry all this and end up not needing it, than to take your irreparable steed for an unintended long walk.

← On some approaches it's 'two wheels good, two legs bad' –
Sgurr na Lapaich (Walk 15) from Glen Strathfarrar (Walk 14)

Loch Quoich from Sgurr na Ciche, 4.20am (Walk 21)

By boat

Water makes up a large part of the Highland landscape, so it's worth making practical use of it. Lochs – both salt and fresh – can serve as highways, stretching far into remote country to give access to the hills. Where possible, paddling is much more enjoyable than plodding along bulldozed tracks, and somehow it feels more adventurous than cycling too. To follow in the wake of Polynesian island-hoppers, Inuit hunters and Yukon pioneers – if only for a weekend – is the yarn from which dreams are braided.

Long journeys by paddle power are the aquatic equivalent of backpacking, the meditative dip of blades echoing the rhythm of a hiker's footfall. Approach a big hill route by water and you should have the best of both worlds – a trip on which the first part of the journey is at least as memorable as the high-level destination at the end of it.

A handful of the walks in this book can be accessed amphibiously, and if a practical water-borne option exists this is noted in the walk information box. Although a boat on a loch might be more romantic than a slog through a bog, none of the paddles described are strictly necessary; there is always an alternative – in some cases taking more time and effort, and sometimes wetter. In most cases

paddlers will want to make a weekend of it – and here's where boats excel, since their generous load-carrying capacity permits more luxurious camping, from disposable barbecues to wine boxes (as long as you take them back out with you, of course).

The most suitable vessels are sea kayaks and open canoes, each of which have their adherents. Specialist equipment differs between them, but the two essential bits of kit common to both are dry bags in which to store all spare clothing and bedding, and a buoyancy aid. Boat-handling skills are different in each case too, and best learned on a course or with a club. Safe sea kayaking, for instance, requires a broad set of skills and a familiarity with currents, tides and other nautical mysteries. No open sea crossings are suggested in this book, and only a very few trips in salt water are mentioned at all. But even freshwater lochs can be unforgiving. Wind, waves and extremely cold water are all things to be wary of, and the best advice for the less experienced is go in a group and wait for ideal conditions. Even then be cautious.

Camps, bivvies, bothies and howffs

It was tempting to title this book 'Great Mountain Days and Wild Nights Out', since the latter are integral to a hill-walking life fully lived. The roar of rutting stags echoing through empty evening glens; ridges rolled out under a starry sky free of light pollution; dawn tinting frosted slopes pink and gold – walkers who habitually forsake hills for the nocturnal comfort of valleys miss out on so much.

To **camp** wild is to take temporary refuge from the everyday, deepening awareness of nature and landscape by making yourself at home within it. With silence and solitude comes freedom simply to be. From high cols and sheltered lochans to remote sea shores, potential camp sites are as diverse as Scotland's wild landscapes. Thanks to liberal access legislation we are officially entitled to pitch up at will, although the usual caveats about responsibility and discretion still apply. Camping wild is an activity best conducted far from roads and houses.

Bivvying is more flexible than camping, as a reclining body needs a smaller floor space than even the most compact tent. Because less gear is generally involved, the bivvy is a true lightweight option. With a roof of sky instead of nylon there's a sense of unmediated immersion in the environment; isn't this what we go to the hills for? However, the two biggest drawbacks of going tent-less are rain and

midges, and too much immersion in either is miserable. Hooped bivvies and tarps are a middle ground between tent and bag, but as with most such compromises there are disadvantages – less comfort than camping, and less of the specialness of lying outside on a starry night that is bivvying's strongest draw.

Tent-free walkers often resort to some kind of shelter, be that a laboriously excavated snowhole or a cave-like **howff** secreted under boulders. Snowholes are an excellent winter option, but constructing them properly and using them safely takes more time and knowledge than might be supposed. The best howffs have generally been improved by hand to afford a relatively salubrious, moderately weatherproof residence. The location of some is a closely guarded secret, while others – such as Loch Avon's Shelter Stone – are part of hillwalking folklore and rarely without a weekend occupant.

If a damp cranny under a boulder or a camp in a storm sound rather too close to nature, then consider something with four solid walls and a (more or less watertight) roof. While not entirely unique to Scotland, **bothies** are a big part of the country's hillwalking scene. Dotted across the land, these remote

Tent versus bothy – Corrour (Walk 40), dwarfed by the Devil's Point   17

huts range from the most spartan mud-floored biers to well-appointed cottages with such mod cons as glazed windows, bunk platforms and fireplaces. There are even a couple of bothies with sit-down toilets, although facilities more typically consist of a bog and a spade.

Bothies are free to use and open to all comers, an admirably inclusive ethos, but with the downside that well-known huts in popular areas may fill to capacity (and beyond) at peak times. Bothy culture is very accepting of high spirits (generally lubricated with spirits of the liquid kind), so those seeking guaranteed peace in busy locations such as Shenavall (Walks 9 and 10) or Culra (Walk 25) probably ought to consider camping instead.

Many Scottish bothies are maintained by volunteers from the Mountain Bothies Association (MBA) (see Appendix 4), a charity that exists to look after remote buildings for which estate owners typically have little use, but which remain important to walkers. Although they are keen to point out that there are no actual rules, the MBA does offer guidelines for visitors. In essence the Bothy Code is to keep the building and its surroundings clean and tidy, extinguish fires before leaving, respect other users and restrict groups to six or fewer.

Maps and guidebooks

Even GPS users should carry a map and compass (and know how to use them) in case of electronic gremlins or battery failure. The Ordnance Survey (OS) produce comprehensive mapping of the whole country in a range of scales, the most useful for walkers being Explorer maps at 1:25,000 and Landranger sheets at 1:50,000. The latter are generally better for long hill walks since they cover more ground per sheet at sufficient (but not excessive) detail. Popular mountain areas are also covered by the small independent cartographer Harvey, their Superwalker (1:25,000) and British Mountain Map (1:40,000) series having been designed to contain only information pertinent to outdoor users. The relevant maps are given in the information box for each walk.

Scotland's hills must be among the best documented anywhere, covered by a library of guidebooks in a thriving 'literary' tradition dating back to the 19th century. Activity-specific guides are available for every mainstream outdoor activity

Ben Loyal from a tarp bivi on Ben Hope (Walk 1)

Dramatic – and unavoidable – scrambling on the east ridge of Lurg Mhòr (Walk 14)

– post-lunch glen strolls, long-distance hikes, serious hill walks, scrambling, climbing, paddling, and cycling in its various sub-genres. Regional guides provide detail on a given area; national guides take a broad-brush approach or (like this book) they cherry pick. There are too many books to list, but for some specific recommendations see Appendix 3.

Scrambles

This book does not go out of its way to find steep rock, and none of the walks involves graded climbing (in summer at least). For this reason the traverse of Skye's Cuillin ridge has been omitted, although it is the greatest of all Scottish hill challenges. But in these rugged mountains scrambling can't always be entirely avoided. In some cases the best walker's route to a summit happens to involve some gentle clambering, such as the famous Carn Mòr Dearg (CMD) Arête onto Ben Nevis (Walk 26) or the prow of The Stuic on Lochnagar (Walk 42).

For easy grade 1 scrambles such as these rock climbing skills and gear are unnecessary, but a head for heights is essential. Even the simplest scrambles need respect in wet, windy or icy conditions. Despite the non-climbing caveat, there are a few walks in this book that err towards mountaineering. After all, no collection of great Scottish mountain walks would be complete without the traverse of Aonach Eagach (grade 2), Liathach (grade 2) or the formidable An Teallach (grade 3). If there is a way to

avoid the harder hands-on sections of a walk (and there usually is), then the description will mention it.

Scrambling grades are expressed numerically in ascending order of difficulty.

Grade 1
Where hillwalking gets hands-on. In good weather these are routes that walkers with no scrambling experience should be capable of, given a reasonable tolerance for heights. Very limited technical difficulty in climbing terms, although there will be some exposure and a fall could be nasty.

Grade 2
Steeper rock, generally bigger drops, less easily escaped from and perhaps with less intuitive route finding. The harder steps may feel extremely daunting, although they'll usually be short lived. Potentially very unpleasant in poor weather. Prior scrambling experience highly advised.

Grade 3
Committing, serious and technically challenging, routes of this grade are tantamount to climbing proper. Best left to competent and suitably equipped mountaineers.

Summer scrambles become winter mountaineering routes (Aonach Eagach, Walk 28)

Seasonal variations

Hillwalking is a year-round activity. The chief advantages of late spring or early summer are almost endless daylight – at the best, over 18hrs a day in the far north – and relatively few midges. Mid-summer may be less ideal than expected, being high season for both crowds and midges. The weather, too, is often wet and humid at mid-summer; but don't let that spoil things. Early autumn can be lovely on the hills, but November is often the opposite.

The approaching tread of winter brings dwindling daylight and worsening weather, and big hill routes are correspondingly harder to pull off. Summer seems a distant memory in the chill gloom of mid-winter. Life was once cheerily described by Nabokov as 'a crack of light between two eternities of darkness'; he could as easily have been talking about a Scottish winter day. Around the winter

solstice in the far north, daylight hours dwindle to a little over 6 in 24. During this period hill walks routinely start and finish in the dark, and a determined pace is needed for tricky ground to be safely negotiated before sunset.

Winter walking is an activity defined not by the calendar, but by the state of the ground. If a January thaw has stripped snow cover to the grass, then the hills may feel barely more challenging than in June; but, conversely, full-on 'winter' conditions can often be encountered in spring and autumn. Blame it on Scotland's unpredictable temperate maritime climate.

In whatever month snow and ice are encountered, they transform Scotland's mountains, giving them a serious arctic/alpine edge and placing big demands on a walker's skills, fitness and equipment. If winter conditions are expected, then an ice axe

Climbing into the sun on the north ridge of Ben Starav (Walk 30),
with the peaks of Buachaille Etive Mòr (Walk 28) prominent behind →

Midsummer moisture – Croit Bheinn (right) and the Beinn Odhar hills from Druim Fiaclach (Walk 23)

and crampons should be considered essential – and they're naturally no good without the ability to use them safely. Other winter must-haves include ski goggles, headtorch and spare batteries, spare hat and gloves, and a bivvi bag or group shelter.

There's a hoary old cliché that winter hillwalking is actually a branch of mountaineering. In snow, scrambly summer ridge walks certainly become exciting mountaineering routes, genuine climbs with their own grading system (expressed in Roman numerals), for which climbing equipment and skills are essential. Non-climbers should avoid any of the walks in this book given a winter grade of I or II in the Seasonal notes section of the information box. On even the least craggy peaks walkers might encounter steep icy slopes, cornices and the lurking threat of avalanche (see Avalanches, below). Ploughing through deep snow is slow and tiring, and in such conditions big walks might stretch from day trips into rigorous overnighters. Skis or snowshoes sometimes prove handy to cover meaningful distances, and occasionally verge on essential in a really snowy spell. Even driving to your chosen route can become an adventure; check road conditions before departure, and consider investing in snow chains or winter tyres.

At its worst winter weather is ferocious, with any combination of crippling wind speeds, stinging hail and rain, blizzards, spindrift and thick mist reducing visibility to as little as a few metres. When there's less margin for error navigation has to be that bit sharper, an ability that is only developed through repeated practice. Could you navigate confidently across a featureless snowy plateau in a white-out, with invisible cornices out there somewhere and darkness fast approaching? In the heaviest conditions even basic mobility on exposed ground may be reduced to a crawl, and it's a struggle just to get off the hill. When the weather forecast is bad consider downgrading your ambitions; if it's really horrendous, then the sofa might be a better place to be.

But all this extra effort brings proportionate rewards – and while winter's lows are cavernous,

Stob Coire nan Lochan, Aonach Eagach and distant Ben Nevis from Bidean nam Bian (Walk 28)

the highs are correspondingly stratospheric. On any true adventure success must occasionally be in doubt; there are certainly few guarantees in the Scottish winter hills. Here we are thrown onto our own resources, and plans made in the comfort of the pub may have to be adapted on the hoof to suit the changing demands of the day.

Winter hills are a world apart from the ordinary, so harsh and so elementally beautiful that their existence on an overdeveloped island can at times seem barely credible – ranks of white-capped peaks jostling to the horizon; wind-carved abstractions on the snow's crust, each shadow stretched in the low-slung mid-day sun; dark clouds boiling in ice-streaked corries; Gothic gloom and moments of uplifting joy. Winter trips are the most rigorous of all hill walks, and arguably the most memorable. Just take nothing for granted.

Hazards

Avalanches

Walkers disregard the possibility of avalanches at their peril, and avoidable accidents sadly occur. Daily avalanche forecasts for five popular mountain areas are provided by the sportScotland Avalanche Information Service (SAIS) www.sais.gov.uk. Although a handy weapon in the hill-going armoury, these forecasts are a supplement to knowledge, not a substitute for it. Snow can fall outside the SAIS forecast season, and many mountain areas are not covered by the service at all. Besides, even the best forecasts are only a rough guide. Personal responsibility is integral to all mountain activities, so it pays to learn a little about avalanches and to cultivate a weather eye for likely trouble spots.

The necessary preconditions for an avalanche are simply sufficient snow cover and an incline. The snowpack builds in layers over time, each of which may have different properties depending on the weather when it was laid and subsequently. Contact between layers of different consistency can be a point of weakness – windslab lying on ice, for instance. In such a situation a 'surface avalanche' may be an accident waiting to happen, just wanting an appropriate trigger to release – perhaps a passing walker. In the hairiest conditions avalanches don't even need an identifiable trigger. Slides may also occur to the full depth of the snowpack, and here the underlying ground surface may be implicated – smooth grass or rock slabs, perhaps.

Consider the weather. Rapid thaws are obviously risky. Be vigilant during heavy snowfall, too, and for a day or two afterwards while things settle. All loaded snow slopes may be considered suspect, but there will always be particular danger areas. Winds scour lying snow from windward slopes, depositing it on sheltered leeward aspects to build as cornices at the tops of gullies and corrie headwalls and as windslab on the slopes below; either may mean trouble. Wise walkers scan the weather for several days before a trip, noting both the amount of snowfall and the strength and general direction of the wind. A route can then be planned that avoids likely lee slopes, always bearing in mind, of course, that topography may channel winds in unpredictable directions.

Here are a few more general rules. Slopes between about 25° and 45° are the most at risk – precisely the sort of angles that walkers tend to encounter. Stress fractures occur more readily where the underlying ground is convex. Ridge crests are generally safer than open slopes, although they might carry substantial cornices, the possible fracture line for which may be surprisingly far from the edge.

These brief paragraphs inevitably raise more questions than they answer. If there's no choice but to travel a suspect slope, how should you proceed? How might a victim increase their survival chances while falling with hundreds of tons of snow? In a Scottish context, what are the pros and cons of transceivers, probes and shovels? As a bare minimum some further reading is highly recommended – see Appendix 3; better still would be to take a course on avalanche awareness.

Cold

Continental mountains may be much colder than Scottish ones in absolute terms, but they tend to be drier too. The combination of wind and wet for which Scotland is renowned can drain body heat very rapidly, creating a felt temperature far lower than the actual thermometer value. Walkers who are inadequately dressed, soaking wet, tired, hungry or slowed by disorientating weather may risk hypothermia, and not just in winter.

Shivering is an early danger sign. With a drop in core body temperature of only a couple of degrees from the optimum average 37°C the blood begins to drain from the extremities to conserve heat in the core, making manual tasks difficult and exposing hands and feet to the possibility of frostnip (or even in, extreme cases, frostbite). Coordination and brain function begin to be impaired, resulting in slower progress and poorer decision making. If heat loss is unchecked a downward spiral may set in, eventually leading to unconsciousness and ultimately death. As ever, prevention is better than cure, so eat plenty through the day and carry a spare warm layer and a bivvy bag or group shelter for unforeseen stationary periods.

River crossing

Runoff from large areas of high ground may channel into a single water course lower down. As the hills drain during thaws or heavy rainfall, the level of burns and rivers can rise dramatically. After a rainy day's walk a trickle that was crossed with a simple hop from rock to rock that morning might have risen to a torrent. On meeting a swollen river, a long tiring detour to a safer crossing point is preferable to an accident.

Treat fast-flowing water greater than knee depth with circumspection. If you're intent on crossing, never do so immediately upstream of waterfalls or boulders into which you might be swept. Ensure that spare dry clothes and other essentials are sealed in a waterproof bag; undo hip and chest straps so that your rucksack doesn't drag you under. Wear boots or shoes to protect feet from rolling rocks (a pair of 'Crocs' or lightweight trainers can be carried for this purpose). Crossing tactics vary, from linking arms in a mutually supportive team shuffle (largest body upstream) to a no-holds-barred diagonal downstream dash (not recommended). A rope can in

*Crossing the Abhainn Gleann na Muice below An Teallach (Walks 9 and 10) –
the following day this was waist deep and impassable*

theory be used, although done badly it's a sure way to drown your friends. If things have got to this stage, it's probably better to think again.

Biting beasties

Midges (midgies) are the bane of the Highlands. In season these blood-sucking pests swarm wherever there are bogs and lush vegetation (in other words, most places), their tininess more than compensated for by strength in inconceivable numbers. Some people react worse than others to their bites, which can itch for days, but nobody reacts well to the maddening onslaught, the skin-crawling torment of being relentlessly feasted upon en masse. Who could stand still and stoic in the face of a midge cloud? Perhaps this explains the origin of the Highland fling.

Summer is midge high season, with a spike in July and August, but it is the weather that really dictates their numbers. Warm wet conditions suit them best, while strong sunlight or a slight breeze both tend to keep them at bay. Sheltered hollows in the hours around dawn and dusk are to be avoided at all costs. Lotions and potions may have a placebo effect on the wearer, but nothing short of napalm can really quell a midge's fervour. Invest in a head net, tuck trousers into socks, and think twice before camping in the glens in summer.

Horse flies (clegs) may be less numerous, but they inflict more painful bites. On balance these vicious delinquents are perhaps preferable to the midge hordes, but only just.

When walking through vegetation, particularly in steamy summer glens in areas with high sheep or deer numbers, consider the **tick**. These tiny crab-like blood suckers are hard to spot, and their bites painless. They latch onto a human or animal host by burrowing into the skin and may remain attached for many days slowly feeding and expanding.

While their parasitic tendencies are a cause of squeamishness, the major concern is that ticks can carry and transmit Lyme Disease, among other nasties. This debilitating condition may go unrecognised and untreated, although it is thought that cases are increasing in the UK. Early symptoms that may develop within weeks include tiredness, fever, muscle or joint pain and a characteristic bull's-eye rash at the site of the bite. Long-term effects are nastier still – recurrent arthritis, nervous system disorders, memory problems, meningitis and heart arrhythmia.

Lyme Disease can be treated, but only if identified early. But here's the catch. Knowledge of tickborne diseases is not generally good in medical circles, so if there's reason to suspect a case you may have to be proactive about getting tested and treated.

Avoidance is the best cure. Try not to loll about in thick vegetation; walk in the middle of paths to avoid brushing past bushes; tuck trousers into socks or wear gaiters; consider treating your clothing with insect repellent. After a day out it's worth having a rummage through clothing (ticks show up best against light colours), and thoroughly examining

yourself – particularly armpits, neck, head and groin. Once engorged with blood their presence is more likely to be felt, but removing a well-established tick takes some deftness (see Lyme Disease Action, Appendix 4).

Access – the legal situation

Scotland enjoys some of the most liberal access legislation in the world. Since the Land Reform (Scotland) Act 2003 a principle of unfettered public access to the countryside has been enshrined in law, but that right comes bound up with responsibility. The Scottish Outdoor Access Code provides guidance both for those exercising their rights and for land managers. Provided walkers behave responsibly they are free to roam at will over all open ground, forests, rivers and lochs, at any time of day or night, while pre-established public rights of way continue to exist as before.

However walkers cannot just trample absolutely everywhere. While the grounds or 'policies' of large estate houses are generally accessible, the garden immediately adjacent to any private house is quite

The Skye Cuillin (Walk 47) from Loch Scresort, Rum (Walk 46) – Rum's midges are renowned for their ferocity   27

Left to right – Beinn Eighe (Walk 11) and Spidean a' Choire Leith from Mullach an Rathain (Walk 12). Torridon has not (yet) been deemed worthy of National Park status.

reasonably deemed off limits; so too are farmyards, industrial sites, paying visitor attractions and fields planted with crops. 'Responsible behaviour' means, among other things, treating the environment and wildlife with care, leaving no litter, respecting the needs and privacy of those who live and work on the land, taking pains not to obstruct activities such as farming and stalking, damaging no fences or walls, abiding by reasonable detours suggested by those felling trees or shooting things, and keeping dogs under strict control near livestock or ground-nesting birds.

If carried out in the spirit of the law wild camping is permitted more or less everywhere, except one small area beside Loch Lomond, where at the time of going to print local seasonal bylaws are in force. There are no rights to hunt, fish or use motorised vehicles under access legislation. In other words, common sense and courtesy go a long way.

The annual red deer stag stalking season runs from 1 July to 20 October, generally increasing in intensity as the season progresses. Stalking activities rarely if ever encompass an entire range at once, and

estates should be able to suggest alternative routes that avoid areas of activity. In many cases estates post details of their movements at popular access points to the hills, while the most enlightened are members of the Hillphones scheme, which provides daily pre-recorded telephone messages (see Appendix 4). Often, however, it is necessary to phone an individual estate in person (the Hillphones service is the best source for contact numbers) – either that or take pot luck on the day.

The hill environment

The big issues

Scotland's uplands are a priceless resource that few European countries are fortunate to match – places of great symbolic, recreational and (dare I say it) spiritual significance that can be enjoyed by all. But the industrialisation of this environment continues apace. The preservation of wild places lies further down the political agenda than the rush to renewables, a policy imbalance that can have regrettable results. According to Scottish Natural Heritage the area in Scotland unaffected by visual intrusion from built development decreased from 41 to 31 per cent between 2002 and 2008, an ongoing trend for which wind farm development is largely responsible.

An insensitively sited wind farm will damage large areas of peat bog (a carbon store if left undisturbed), but wider than the physical footprint is its visual impact, a long-range intrusion that can reach far into otherwise unspoilt mountains. The value of wild land decreases in inverse proportion to the spread of industry, and wind farms now feature in the views from many of our most iconic peaks. In each case a little something has been lost. It seems likely that the current extent of development represents only a fraction of what's to come.

Under a more responsible planning regime renewable energy and conservation of our best landscapes could coexist, but at present Scotland's statutory landscape protection is a patchwork of inadequate designations, with only two national parks in the entire country (compare that to England's ten). Strategy is needed at the national level for zoning industrial development, the presumption being to minimise its impact on core hill areas. No amount of 'green' energy will compensate for their continued degradation.

Industrialisation is just one conservation issue among many; another is vehicle tracks. Track construction with heavy machinery leaves scars miles long, damages peat, affects hydrology and compromises long term the wild quality of entire ranges. The spread of new tracks is effectively unchecked thanks to a planning loophole. Outside protected sites tracks can currently be built without planning consent or notification to the local authority if they are claimed to be for agricultural or forestry

Only a minority of Scotland's wild landscape is protected – the Cairngorms National Park is one of just two in the entire country; Carn Etchachan and Beinn Meadhoin from Coire an t-Sneachda (Walk 40)

purposes. However, in many cases sporting estates seem to have other uses in mind, namely vehicle access for deer stalking and grouse shooting. It may be difficult for councils to distinguish between stated and actual purpose, and many tracks are so remote that the temptation may exist to ignore the issue. Left largely unchallenged, estates, self-styled custodians of the land, currently remain free to damage swathes of countryside that ought to be protected for the nation.

A still more serious charge is often levelled against Scotland's sporting estates – that they obstruct the regeneration of natural woodland. The reasoning is straightforward. Most estates are managed to maximise return from commercial stalking, and this requires plenty of deer. Dense deer populations mean overgrazing, the result being the traditional denuded Highland habitat or 'green desert'. In contrast, public opinion increasingly favours the restoration of thriving natural habitats. Where deer are tightly controlled or excluded, native trees soon return – and with them biodiversity. Case closed?

Personal environmental impact

It would be hypocritical to rail about big issues without also examining the personal.

How should we travel to the hills, for instance, for minimum impact? Although little use for many hill areas, public transport remains a viable way to access some, and it's worth considering by anyone serious about reducing their personal tyre print. Some walks in this book have been tailored with public transport in mind; see Getting Around, above, for more ideas.

Obligations don't come to an end once we set foot on the hill; every walker has a small but significant impact on their treasured environment. Soil erosion is an ongoing problem in many areas, particularly on the popular Munros, where thousands of footfalls are concentrated on a few key paths. As overused path surfaces are reduced over time to rubble or deep mud the natural inclination is for walkers to follow firmer ground along the edges, trampling delicate upland vegetation that binds the soil. Where everyone does this, busy paths can spread

↑ *Seana Bhraigh from the Creag an Duine ridge (Walk 6)*

Hallival and the Skye Cuillin (Walk 47) from Askival (Walk 46) →

into broad scars that become channels for surface runoff, further compounding the damage.

The most eroded paths are a chore to walk on and visible from afar. Short of restricting access, the long-term solution is to engineer a new path surface, an expensive and labour-intensive process favoured only by conservation-minded landowners. If the work is done intrusively, there can be something over-manicured and park-like about these snaking trails of gravel or flagstone steps; but sensitive methods do exist, and on the crowded hills these may be the least bad option. Where paths are still in a more 'natural' (messy) state, damage can be minimised by sticking to the middle of the trail and avoiding cutting corners at zigzags.

It seems barely credible that litter on remote mountains is an issue worth mentioning, but sadly even the hillwalking community has its idiots. Large visitor numbers inevitably mean more rubbish, with pride of place going to Ben Nevis, the highest dustbin in Scotland. But discarded beer cans, cigarette butts and food packaging can be found almost anywhere in the hills. The responsible course is to pack out everything that you've carried in, including fruit peel that does not readily biodegrade in the hilltop environment; bonus 'greenie' points for anyone willing to pick up other people's rubbish (I draw the line at bog roll).

Toilet waste is another problematic environmental issue. No one wants to encounter human leftovers halfway up their scramble or next to the summit cairn at which they've sat for lunch (this really happens). The most responsible course is to carry out everything you produce in a biodegradable flushable bag enclosed in an airtight, waterproof canister; in some wilderness areas in the United States this is now compulsory. Next best is to bury solid waste at least 15cm deep, for which a trowel comes in handy. This can be hard to achieve in snowy conditions, but simply hiding the evidence in the snow to be revealed at the next thaw is a loathsome ruse. Never defecate close to burns and lochs – an exclusion zone of 30m is a bare minimum – and ensure you are downstream of anywhere people are likely to collect drinking water, close to bothies for instance. Used toilet paper

North Goatfell from a camp on The Saddle (Walk 45)

should be packed out or carefully burned, although note that the environmental benefit of doing the latter is cancelled out if you inadvertently start a forest fire. Female sanitary products are not biodegradable and should always be carried home.

Using this guide

All the walks in this book require a degree of fitness and the endurance to maintain a steady – if not necessarily athletic – pace from dawn to dusk (or beyond). The **walk times** are loose suggestions only, indicating roughly how long an experienced hillwalker of normal ability might expect to take in favourable weather. Committed fell runners could conceivably halve the time estimates, although they are not primarily intended as performance targets to foster competitive or inadequate feelings (delete as applicable). Timings do not allow for mid-route siestas or the progress-slowing properties of heavy loads, high wind, poor visibility or deep snow. If a given walk is quoted as 16hrs, that means 16hrs of solid walking; whether to do the lot in a single rigorous day or spread it over a more leisurely two is up to you. Obvious places to break for the night are mentioned in every walk description.

Overall **ascent** and **distance** figures are provided in the information box at the start of each walk. These have been measured from OS maps, so it is worth remembering that they may not fully reflect the intricate ins and outs walked on rough ground, nor those little zigzags on steep slopes, nor the cumulative height gain of the many ups and downs too slight to be represented by contour lines at 10m intervals. In the walk description distance is further subdivided to give figures for the approach, on the hill and the return (where such a division is applicable). Approaches and walk-outs are usually at a low level and tend to follow clear paths. While these legs might be done sensibly in darkness or poor weather, the harder ground on the hill itself will usually be better left for daylight. Knowing the length of each stage should help with route planning at times of year when light is in short supply.

Major points at which the nature of a walk might significantly change in **winter conditions** or very

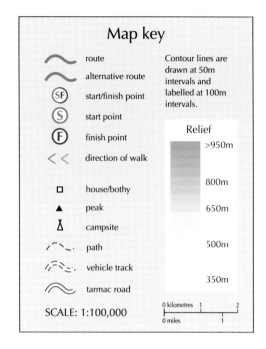

Map key

~	route	Contour lines are drawn at 50m intervals and labelled at 100m intervals.
~	alternative route	
(SF)	start/finish point	
(S)	start point	
(F)	finish point	Relief
< <	direction of walk	>950m
□	house/bothy	800m
▲	peak	650m
Ⅺ	campsite	
path		500m
vehicle track		350m
tarmac road		

SCALE: 1:100,000

wet weather are mentioned in the information box under Seasonal notes.

The more obvious points at which a walk can be curtailed are listed under **Short cuts** in the information box. These are get-out options for bad weather or tiredness, and in some cases can also be used to split the single long day's walk described into two more manageable separate trips.

In walk descriptions 'left' and 'right' are relative to the direction of travel, while compass directions (NE, SW and so on) are always approximate unless precise numerical bearings are given. Key navigational features along the route that appear on the map in the guide are shown in the walk description in **bold**. The maps throughout this guide are adapted for the book from Ordnance Survey data and are at a scale of 1:100,000 (1cm = 1km). For navigation on the routes, it is recommended that you use the relevant Ordnance Survey or Harvey maps, details of which are given in the introduction box for each route.

Ben Hope
and Ben Loyal

B ens Hope and Loyal are peaks on the edge, with the expanse of the Flow Country rippling out
to the east, and northwards the cold open sea. Next stop, the Arctic. Both stand tall among the
great hills of the far north, each rising in magnificent independence – Hope a precipitous wedge,
Loyal a remarkable multi-topped mass bristling crags and tors. These rugged individuals tend to be
tackled separately, and their standard routes are fairly short outings. However, the two can also
be combined in this extended loop, a logical and compelling challenge for the more ambitious.
The peaks themselves may be the obvious highlights, but the emptiness between them has its own
unique atmosphere too. Some tolerance for bogs is required.

Approach 9.5km
North of Kinloch Lodge is an unoccupied house
just above the road; take the track past this, and
at a junction in gorse thickets go right. Climb over
a slight rise, and having crossed a burn make a
long gradual ascent across open moorland. This
approach follows the **Moine Path**, an excellent
well-drained historic route linking the Kyle of
Tongue with Loch Hope. Ben Loyal's multiple rocky
summits form a remarkable backdrop, while the
sharp wedge of Ben Hope rises out of the moor
ahead. After several kilometres the path begins a
steady descent towards Loch Hope; leave it here
and strike S over the bogs to reach the outflow of
Loch na Seilg below the rugged, secretive eastern
flank of Ben Hope.

↑ *Ben Loyal from Ben Hope*

ROUTE INFORMATION

Start/finish	Track entrance off the Tongue–Kinloch road (NC 554 526); limited parking in laybys N and S of here
Distance	33.5km (21 miles)
Ascent	1800m
Time	12hrs
Terrain	The Moine Path gives an easy start, but thereafter the low ground is predominantly boggy and pathless. The north ridge of Ben Hope is steep and rocky with some modest grade 1 scrambling higher up; the infamous Bad Step (a rock climbing pitch) is easily bypassed. Ben Loyal is gentler and grassier underfoot, although several of its summit tors provide optional scrambling.
Summits	Ben Hope 927m ('hill of the bay', Norse); Ben Loyal 764m (possibly 'law mountain', Norse)

Maps	OS Landranger (1:50,000) 9 & 10; OS Explorer (1:25,000) 447
Public transport	Bus from Thurso to Tongue; no public transport to the start of the walk
Accommodation	Tongue YH (01847 611789)
Sleeping out	Good camping beside any of several lochans under the east flank of Ben Hope, and also near the ruined cottage at Dithreibh (NC 541 469)
Seasonal notes	The north ridge of Ben Hope needs some care in winter conditions, but there are no other particular difficulties. The low-level bogs are best in a dry spell or when frozen solid.
Short cuts	The good track running between the hills permits either mountain to be done on its own as a shorter circuit

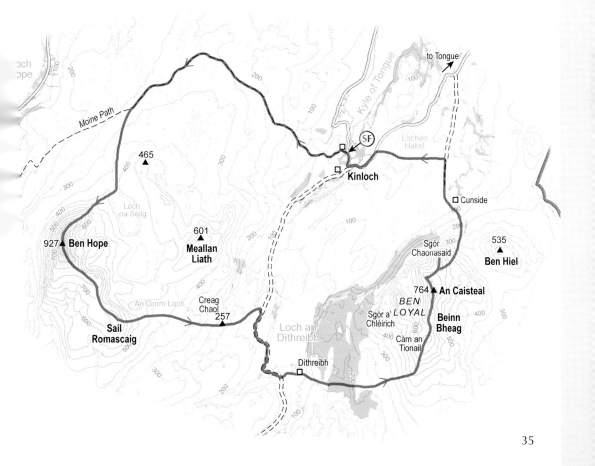

On the hill 20km

Head WSW, where steepening stony slopes give strenuous access to Ben Hope's north ridge, the best walkers' route up the mountain. Follow the ridge onto a grassy levelling. The direct continuation is barred by an intimidating rock barrier, or Bad Step. Tackled on its right side this gives a short pitch of VDiff grade climbing in a serious position above the full height of the mountain's huge northwest face. Most people will want to avoid it, and this is easily done via an obvious gully well to the left – a very basic but slimy scramble. Above this regain the crest of the ridge, where some enjoyable blocky scrambling leads airily to **Ben Hope**'s table top. With steep ground on three sides and a vast expanse of emptiness all around, the summit has a great sense of open space.

From the summit trig point and wind break follow the edge of the eastern corrie, An Garbh-choire. Skirt just right of an unnamed top to descend rolling slopes of grass and rocks, then climb a little onto the outlying summit **Sail Romascaig**, which is marked with a cairn. Here bear E, descending carefully through a band of little crags then down a steep boulder-strewn slope onto a knobbly shoulder overlooking idyllic **An Gorm Loch**.

Continue E through a deserted wilderness of bogs, rocks and pools (confusing in mist). Bear just right of the summit of **Creag Chaol** to pick up a quad bike track; this trends left as it descends to cross the Allt na Luibe Moire in a little flat-bottomed glen. Here gain a more distinct estate track, which is followed S to the shore of **Loch an Dìthreibh**, a lovely spot overlooked by the peaks of Ben Loyal. Stay with the track past a private estate bothy, and at a junction by the head of the loch go left to the ruined cottage of **Dìthreibh**.

Beyond the cottage leave the track, cross a burn, then climb E onto a pathless pool-pitted bog land. Aim for the south ridge of **Càrn an Tionail**, Ben

An Gorm Loch and the east side of Ben Hope

Sgòr Chaonasaid and the Kyle of Tongue

Loyal's southern top, where the low-lying bogs soon give way to steep slopes. Follow the broad ridge to the summit. Head N over **Beinn Bheag**, a delightful stroll on springy turf, then climb to **An Caisteal**, Loyal's well-named main top. From the south the massive summit tor looks impregnable; skirt left to scramble up its more manageable north side.

Two further tors are worth exploring, first Sgòr a' Bhatain, then the dramatic promontory peak of **Sgòr Chaonasaid**, the south ridge of which gives some optional scrambling. From the saddle south of Sgòr Chaonasaid descend ENE; at first it's steep and rough, but a path soon takes shape. The lower slopes are dominated by the huge front face of Sgòr Chaonasaid. Pass left of the cottage at **Cunside**.

Return 4km

Beyond the Allt Lon Malmsgaig the path continues N across heather moorland, soon becoming a track. Here strike W over open boggy ground, passing south of **Lochan Hakel** to reach the single-track road. This leads downhill to a bridge over the Kinloch river and the start point.

Ben Klibreck

*C*aithness and Sutherland share a waterlogged nothingness unmatched in scale, yet the apparent desolation belies a rich habitat of international botanical and ornithological significance. This is Europe's largest blanket bog, the least mucked-up ecosystem of significant size remaining in the British Isles. Commercial forestry wreaked great damage here as a 1980s tax break, but the Flow Country's unique value is now recognised – not least as a natural carbon sink. The lone massif of Ben Klibreck rises as a rounded wave on the western side of this great moorland sea.

From the A836 at its foot this gentle hump promises little, its sole attraction seemingly the ease of ascent for Munro baggers; but a linear dash from the road does neither the hill nor the hillwalker justice. This full circuit of Ben Klibreck has a sense of scale and isolation more worthy of the surroundings. Little-frequented Bealach Easach leads to the obscure lochs stretched below the mountain's hidden eastern flank, a post-glacial landscape of unexpected grandeur.

Approach 11km

This drawn-out approach permits a return along the full stretch of Klibreck's high, grassy spine. The A836 is fairly close but this does little to dent the sense of remoteness; after all, it's a single-track A-road on which a dozen cars per hour would count as significant traffic. Even the walk's starting point has a back-of-beyond feel, the Crask Inn being almost the only habitation for miles (and a good place for seeing a spectacular night sky without braving the elements).

↑ *Ben Klibreck from Ben Hope*

ROUTE INFORMATION

Start/finish	Layby opposite the Crask Inn (NC 523 247)
Distance	26km (16 miles)
Ascent	1200m
Time	9½hrs
Terrain	A lengthy approach on a clear track, then a steep pathless ascent. Open grassy ground lacking the boulders and heather so common elsewhere on Scottish hills. Attentive navigation is needed in poor visibility.
Summits	Ben Klibreck (possibly 'hill of the speckled cliff', Gaelic; or possibly 'cliff slope', Norse); Meall nan Con 961m ('hill of the dogs')
Maps	OS Landranger (1:50,000) 16; OS Explorer (1:25,000) 443
Public transport	Daily post bus from Lairg to Altnaharra on A836 – you won't miss your stop, there's literally nothing to confuse it with

Accommodation	The Crask Inn (01549 411241)
Sleeping out	The shores of Loch a' Bhealaich and Loch Choire are ideal for wild camping
Seasonal notes	There are no particular difficulties in winter, although it might be sensible to reverse the direction of the walk so that the hill stage is done in daylight. The distance could be reduced significantly, too, by incorporating Meall an Eòin into the round instead of the more distant Meall Ailein. Bear in mind that the steep grassy slopes of Meall nan Con present a potential avalanche hazard.
Short cuts	Climb Meall nan Con from the Bealach Easach, then return over Cnoc Sgriodain as described

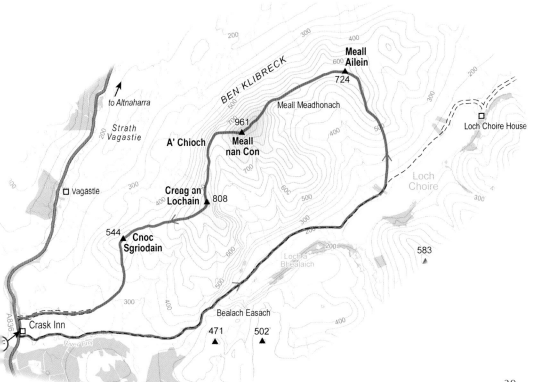

Loch Choire from Meall Ailein

Park opposite the Crask Inn, then walk a short way S along the road until level with a cottage. Go left through a little gate and follow a track roughly E alongside the **River Tirry**, which runs almost dead straight past two big pine plantations. Once level with the second plantation the path climbs the left flank of a vague corrie to reach the remote **Bealach Easach**, a historic cross-country through-route.

Hitherto gentle and rolling, the terrain to the east now becomes more rugged. Ahead stretches a broad crag-rimmed trough cradling two connected lochs. The fine old track descends gently into the glen, following the north bank of **Loch a' Bhealaich** to reach the shore of the larger **Loch Choire**. With sandy beaches, crags and scatterings of native woodland, this is an attractive spot. Beyond a patch of tall pines by the shore and an adjacent forestry enclosure is a wooden bridge over a gorse-flanked river.

On the hill 13km

Beyond the bridge split left from the track, climbing N up a seemingly never-ending grassy slope.

Looking east into the Flow Country from Meall Ailein

There is no path, but since the hillside is also free of the usual Scottish duo of tussocks and heather the going is fairly easy. Pass a small cairn to reach a broad rocky ridge, and a while later a stone memorial to the victims of an air crash. This long ascent eventually gains the little rugged peak of **Meall Ailein**, a grand viewpoint from which to survey the enormous emptiness that stretches to every horizon. To the north is Loch Naver; to the west the distant peaks of the Atlantic seaboard; to the east nothing much at all.

Follow the ridge W. At first the going is gentle, then a rougher climb through peat hags leads over **Meall Meadhonach**. From here it's grassy again, the well-defined crest of the main peak's northeast ridge rising airily to **Meall nan Con**, Klibreck's sole Munro summit. Descent requires care in the mist;

drop steeply almost due W to the crest of **A' Chioch**, which then swings southward to a broad col (spot height 688m).

Continue S on the gradual ridge climb to **Creag an Lochain**. From here briefly head S before bearing SW and then, lower down, W, descending a steady slope cut with peat hags to reach a low col – there is a path, although it's easily misplaced. A last climb now gains the minor summit of **Cnoc Sgriodain**. Descend the vague south spur, bearing rightwards across the tussocky lower slopes to pick up a wide 4WD track.

Return 2km
The track blazes through the peat, leading (muddily in parts) back to the A836 just north of the **Crask Inn** – a welcome sight.

Meall nan Con from Strath Vagastie

Foinaven

*F*oinaven is a mysterious hill, a complex range-in-miniature (not that miniature) with an almost primeval feel. High point Ganu Mòr was long a borderline case for Munro status, but a recent survey has shaved a fraction from its erstwhile 914m altitude, sparing it from the list-ticking hordes. Secreted away in its eastern folds, the hill's most impressive corners take effort to reach, and a full traverse of the mountain is a strenuous and memorable expedition. Geological decay is writ large everywhere, the shattered crests crumbling into vast, stark scree skirts. Add the long miles of approach, the serious emptiness and the occasional scrambly moment, and it's clear that this is no ordinary hill walk. Of several possible angles of attack perhaps the best (and least popular?) is this route starting from sea level at Loch Eriboll. This has a satisfying aura of obscurity, leading through glens and passes walked by few.

Approach 7km
Head S into **Srath Beag** on a farm track running below rambling crags. This soon dwindles to a boggy path leading to **Strabeg**, a spacious bothy in a scenic setting. Continuing up-glen the going gets tougher, and the path is sketchy in places as it weaves through woods and giant boulders at the foot of the cliffs of **Creag Shomhairle**, an under-appreciated climbing venue. About 1.5km beyond the bothy cross the river at a gravelly shallows (may prove interesting in spate) and head W across the glen-floor marsh to pick up a path along the foot of the far slope. At a sheep

↑ *Cranstackie (left) and Foinaven from the Kyle of Durness*

Start/finish	Junction of the Srath Beag track and the scenic A838 Tongue–Durness road; parking space is limited (NC 393 539)
Distance	27km (17 miles)
Ascent	1600m
Time	11hrs
Terrain	Hard walking from start to finish, with a mix of rough paths and long stretches of pathless ground. With its angular rocks Foinaven itself is hard going, and there is some short-lived easy scrambling. The lower glens and passes tend to be boggy, while major river crossings in Srath Beag and Srath Dionard require care in wet weather.
Summits	Foinaven ('wart mountain'); Ganu Mòr 911m ('big head')
Maps	OS Landranger (1:50,000) 9; OS Explorer (1:25,000) 445 covers most but not quite all the route
Public transport	There is no public transport provision beyond the Lairg–Durness bus
By bike	Bulldozed vehicle tracks up Srath Dionard and the Bealach Horn may

be regrettable from the point of view of wild land conservation, but they do facilitate quick approaches to Foinaven by mountain bike. Srath Beag is not bike friendly, however.

Accommodation	Tongue YH (01847 611789); Durness YH (01971 511264)
Sleeping out	Strabeg bothy (NC 392 518) is excellent, but too close to the road to be of much advantage as a base for Foinaven. A wild camp near Loch Dionard or on the Bealach Horn would seem more logical, although the ground is either hummocky or boggy, or both.
Seasonal notes	Winter walkers would be unlikely to complete this entire route in daylight, but the first/last 4km could be done in the dark. Under snow Foinaven's ridges offer challenging walking, nudging towards winter mountaineering.
Short cuts	A linear out-and-back dash is the quickest way to bag Ganu Mòr, although it's missing the point somewhat

fank (stone-walled enclosure) turn diagonally uphill, climbing the now-faint trail onto rocky **Bealach na h-Imrich**, where an inspiring view of Foinaven's complex eastern side is revealed.

From a cairn overlooking Srath Dionard descend rough pathless slopes W into the glen, with the huge wall of Creag Urbhard ahead to spur you on. Ford the major river at some braided shallows just north of **Loch Dionard** (in wet weather a safe crossing might require a detour south of the loch).

On the hill 10km

Cross the 4WD track (its construction here was controversial), then strike NW up a long, grassy pathless incline passing below the formidable prow of A' Ch'eir Ghorm. The ascent leads to a broad saddle between **Cnoc Dùail** and Ganu Mòr. Follow the corrie rim leftwards, climbing rocky ground above the crags. As it ascends, the slope narrows into a steep scree-covered spur which cuts SW onto the top of **Ganu Mòr**. The first cairn reached is the official high point – note that the previously estimated height of

*Approaching Stob Cadha na Beucaich
from Lord Reay's Seat*

914m has been revised down to 911m.

Keep going W along the summit ridge to a second cairn and turn left, descending the mountain's south ridge to pass over a mini-peak and a slight saddle before climbing onto an unnamed **869m summit**. Here it is possible to detour along the narrow scrambly crest of **A' Ch'eir Ghorm**, a scree-draped

Below Creag Urbhard, one of the great crags of the far north

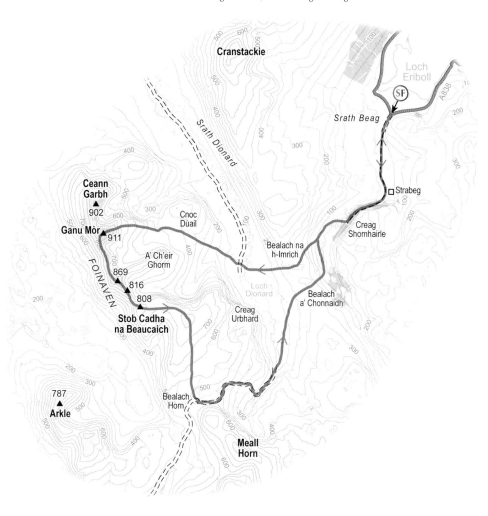

Srath Coille na Fearna from Creag Shomhairle

offshoot from the main ridge, although it is a dead end and involves extra effort.

From point 869m continue SE along the main ridge to the rugged minor peak of Lord Reay's Seat (**spot height 816m** on 1:25,000 maps; not named on any map) overlooking the deep notch of Cadha na Beucaich. Leave the crumbling crest here, descending steep unstable scree on its right flank to reach the pass. The next summit is **Stob Cadha na Beucalch** (unnamed spot height 808m on OS maps), a strenuous rocky climb with some simple scrambling. From the summit head roughly E down gentle stony slopes, which soon become grassy underfoot. Either pass over the next easy-angled summit (An t-Sàil Mhòr according to the maps) or skirt just right of it, then descend a long boggy slope roughly S into a bowl just east of the **Bealach Horn**.

Return 10km

Where there was once a simple stalker's path a vehicle track has recently been scored into the hillside – an ugly mess. The worst scars will gradually heal, but the mere fact of its existence compromises the wild character of these hills. Vehicles can now go to places they have never before been able to. The proliferation of new tracks in remote landscapes is an indictment of the conservation credentials of sporting estates.

Turn left onto this track, which leads down among impressive crags into **Srath Dionard**. About 1.5km shy of the loch peel off NNE, fording the river and climbing over a hummocky slope. Cross yet another vehicle track and continue onto the **Bealach a' Chonnaidh**, a pass immediately adjacent to the one that you crossed at the beginning of the day. Descend the far side carefully, looping right to skirt a crag, to reach the flood plain beneath **Creag Shomhairle**. From the sheep fank retrace your steps to the road.

Ben More Assynt, Conival and Breabag

*T*he highest summits and only Munros in Assynt, Ben More Assynt and Conival, are less immediately striking than their freakish neighbours on the western seaboard, but closer inspection reveals a range of remote and unexpected grandeur. The standard bagger's route from Inchnadamph has the benefit of directness but misses out many interesting corners. This route, a meatier offering by far, approaches from the south to make a circuit of the high ground ringing the lonely head of Glen Oykel.

The round starts with Breabag, an extensive and eccentric Corbett. Conival is next, climbed by its southeast ridge – an exciting scramble, but not too tricky. The circuit then continues in classic ridge-walking vein, with a narrow shattered crest to Ben More Assynt, from where more easy but atmospheric scrambling leads on over the South Top to Càrn nan Conbhairean. Finish with a quick nip up Eagle Rock – not many people come this way.

Approach 6.5km

Take the track past **Loch Ailsh** to reach the houses at **Benmore Lodge**. Beyond the big house the track becomes rougher, following the River Oykel upstream for roughly 2.5km and crossing a bridge over the Allt Sail an Ruathair along the way (cyclists should leave bikes here). The 1:50,000 map shows a bridge over the River Oykel east of Black Rock,

46   ↑ *Conival from Loch Assynt*

ROUTE INFORMATION

Start/finish	Where the Benmore Lodge track joins the A837 (NC 296 082) – limited parking	**By bike**	Cycling the approach track can save about 12km of walking; as far as Benmore Lodge it's a mix of hard-packed gravel and tarmac sections, although the final stretch from there is a bit rougher
Distance	34km (21 miles)		
Ascent	1660m		
Time	12hrs	**Accommodation**	Hostel at Inchnadamph Lodge (01571 822218); Achmelvich Beach YH (01571 844480); Achininver YH (01854 622482)
Terrain	Long easy track approach. Rough and largely pathless on Breabag. More signs of passage on the higher hills, but also more scrambling. The southeast ridge of Conival has some exposed grade 1/2 ground and needs caution in the wet, while the south ridge of Ben More Assynt is easier at grade 1 but feels similarly airy at times.		
		Sleeping out	The grassy hollows around Breabag's summit give novel camping spots sheltered from many wind directions. The shores of Dubh Loch Mor under Ben More Assynt are an obvious lower-level alternative.
Summits	Breabag 815m ('little height'); Conival 987m ('joined-on or adjoining hill', possibly); Ben More Assynt 998m ('big hill of assynt')	**Seasonal notes**	In snowy conditions the southeast ridge of Conival becomes a grade I/II winter climb, and the south ridge of Ben More Assynt is grade I – taken together, a spectacular mountaineering round. It may be hard to ford the River Oykel in a wet spell.
Maps	OS Landranger (1:50,000) 15; OS Explorer (1:25,000) 440 & 442; Harvey Superwalker (1:25,000) Suilven covers most but not quite all of the route		
Public transport	Postbus service 123 from Lairg; explain you're getting off at the Benmore Lodge track	**Short cuts**	The traverse of Breabag takes nearly as much effort as all the other hills combined, so missing it out is the simplest short cut

The towers on Conival's southeast ridge

but this does not exist; instead ford the river where it shallows at a gravel island. In spate it may be wiser to cross on a footbridge much closer to Benmore Lodge.

On the hill 18.5km

Breabag is a sprawling, complex hill and needs close navigation in poor visibility. Head W, climbing quite steeply to skirt right of **Black Rock**. Cross a boggy area beyond, and continue WNW beside a burn (occasional traces of path) up to a broad whalebacked shoulder. From here take a more or less direct line to **Breabag's** summit up a mix of grass and scree, staying a little right of the Bealach Choinnich and the minor top of Meall Diamhain. The summit is merely the highest of several knolls, set a little back from the cliff edge of Coirean Ban.

Descend roughly NNE to a col above the glen of the Allt nan Uamh, which cuts through the limestone of Breabag's lower slopes. Downstream are

*On the slippery south ridge
of Ben More Assynt*

Breabag from the ford on the River Oykel

the fascinating Bone Caves, where the remains of pre-historic animals have been found; they're a detour too far from here, but easily reached from the A837. Climb through a moonscape of quartzite pavements onto **Breabag's** north top (again, just the highest of several knobbles), crossing a striking square-cut fissure and enjoying impressive views of the mountain's rock-walled eastern corries. Continue over Breabag Tarsuinn (point 649m), then bear right to the col between Breabag and Conival.

The latter looms huge and craggy above. To out-flank this steep face cut right along a pronounced terrace to two tiny pools. From here head directly uphill, weaving among outcrops and scree; **Conival's** southeast ridge takes shape as height is gained. The upper ridge sports a series of blunt towers. Clamber through a heap of boulders then scramble up rough slabby sandstone onto the top of the first tower – it's pick-your-own ground, generally easier slightly left of centre. Continue directly over the second and third towers, then make a very exposed step across a gap (unavoidable – extreme caution in the wet). Now climb more easily through broken crags to reach the summit.

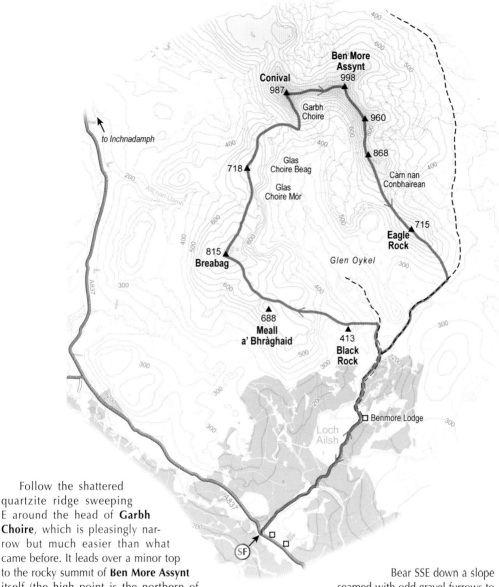

Follow the shattered quartzite ridge sweeping E around the head of **Garbh Choire**, which is pleasingly narrow but much easier than what came before. It leads over a minor top to the rocky summit of **Ben More Assynt** itself (the high point is the northern of two bumps). In descent head SE down a narrower crest, where a couple of slabby rock steps are encountered en route to the South Top – awkward and airy rather than genuinely difficult, but you wouldn't want to slip. From the South Top (unnamed **point 960m** on the OS Landranger map) the ridge continues southwards, still narrow and with the odd scrambly moment, to arrive at the grassy summit of **Càrn nan Conbhairean**.

Bear SSE down a slope seamed with odd gravel furrows to the col below **Eagle Rock**; it's as well to go over this little-visited dome as to try outflanking it. From the summit trig point descend ESE down grass and scree to meet a well-used quad bike track.

Return 9km
Turn right onto this track to return to the main Glen Oykel track and the footsore trudge (or joyous cycle) back to the **A837**.

49

Suilven and Canisp

A *ssynt/Inverpolly is a composite landscape – equal parts water, rock and peat. Each free-stand-ing peak has a unique organic form, sculpted by millions of years of weather. It is easier here to make the imaginative leap over the giddying gulf of geological timespans than perhaps anywhere else in Scotland. Suilven is the area's headline mountain and among the best in the country, an improbable sandstone galleon riding a rippling sea of moorland and gneiss. Seen end-on it looks pillar-like, but a broadside view shows it as a long multi-topped ridge.*

Suilven is a big day out from any starting point, and while a full traverse of the ridge gives some exciting scrambling, the highest summit alone can be reached almost hands-free. The hill is most often climbed from the coast, but the eastern approach is equally attractive, particularly if, as described here, Suilven is combined with neighbouring Canisp, a higher if less charismatic summit that offers stunning views of the other Assynt peaks.

Approach 4km
At the car park a signpost shows the path to Lochinver (19km). Follow this trail (wrongly marked on the 1:50,000 map) to the southeast end of **Cam Loch**, then through a deer fence and along the east shore, where steep slopes drop into the loch. The

path soon peels away from the loch, climbing NW and then N on a low ridge.

On the hill 13km
Once close to Loch a' Chroisg leave the path and head NNE over bogs, climbing rough slopes to

↑ *Suilven from Canisp*

ROUTE INFORMATION

Start/finish	Car park between Elphin and Ledmore Junction (NC 233 122)
Distance	25km (15½ miles)
Ascent	1790m
Time	10hrs
Terrain	The low ground is invariably boggy and to a large extent pathless. Canisp gives an easy ascent, but the full traverse of Suilven involves short sharp bursts of exposed grade 3 scrambling; there's a non-scrambler's alternative described taking in just the principal peak.
Summits	Canisp 846m ('white hill', possibly); Suilven 731m ('pillar mountain', possibly, though obscure)
Maps	OS Landranger (1:50,000) 15; OS Explorer (1:25,000) 442 & 439; Harvey Superwalker (1:25,000) Suilven
Public transport	Postbus service 123 from Lairg; alight at Elphin or Ledmore Junction
By boat	The 7km paddle down Loch Veyatie to Suilven is one of the classic waterborne approaches to a Scottish hill, with stunning surroundings but no notable difficulty. Put in at Cam Loch, near Elphin, from where a short portage around a waterfall gains freshwater Loch Veyatie.
Accommodation	Hostel at Inchnadamph Lodge (01571 822218); Achmelvich Beach YH (01571 844480); Achininver YH (01854 622482)
Sleeping out	Loch-shore wild camping pretty much anywhere – try Loch na Gainimh or Loch a' Choire Dhuibh. Bothy at Suileag (NC 150 211).
Seasonal notes	Low coastal mountains not best suited to reliable winter conditions, but in a cold snowy spell the full traverse of Suilven is a grade II winter climb
Short cuts	For a more manageable single-peak day simply omit Canisp

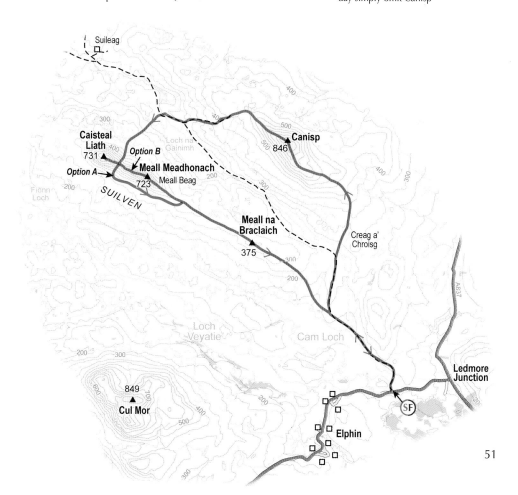

51

reach a slight shoulder, marked by a large cairn. Continue uphill, bearing gradually left, to climb onto the broad southeast spur of **Canisp**, where a path appears. Views of Suilven and its surrounding peaks become increasingly impressive on the final climb to the stone-scattered summit, where there are two windbreak cairns.

Descend the well-defined northwest ridge, and where the angle markedly eases just above a lochan at about 500m trend left down boggy slopes to pick up a quad bike track. This heads roughly west, winding down a pronounced burn-cutting to meet the Elphin–Lochinver track in the glen bottom near **Loch na Gainimh**. Turn right onto this to cross a bridge over the loch's outflow. Having done so leave the track and head roughly SW towards Suilven.

The main hillwalker's path up the hill is soon met, but this doesn't bring any improvement underfoot, since it is falling to bits on the steep sections and very boggy on the flat. The path climbs to a lochan-studded

Approaching Meall Bheag

shelf beneath Suilven's huge north wall, passing the idyllic Loch a' Choire Dhuibh. Suilven's formidable ramparts are breached by a steep scree gully running to the Bealach Mór, a col between the main summit, Caisteal Liath, and the lesser tops strung along the east ridge. The gully gives an unpleasant climb on an eroded path. On reaching the col a sudden view opens to the south over the wild watery heart of Inverpolly to the quirky peaks of Cul Mor and Stac Pollaidh.

Suilven (left), Canisp and Cul Mor from Stac Pollaidh

Turn right, passing through a gap in an incongruous stone wall to follow the dramatic but easy ridgeline over a minor top and on to the grassy dome of **Caisteal Liath**. This promontory summit is circled by steep cliffs, giving it a feeling of island-like isolation and spaciousness; the sea dominates the western outlook. The only safe way off is back the same way to the Bealach Mór. There are now two options.

Option A Non-scramblers could retrace their steps to the Lochinver–Elphin track, but it's better to head SW down an eroded scree gully path, similar to the ascent route, to reach the shelf below Suilven's south wall. Vague traces of path now lead along this, running below Suilven's eastern summits to join Option B on the shoulder ESE of Meall Meadhonach.

Option B Scramblers are in for a treat. Follow Suilven's spine eastwards over a minor summit with occasional light scrambling, then descend quite steeply into a pronounced notch. Suilven's second highest summit, **Meall Meadhonach**, looms above; a worn path leads up broken ground and rocky steps to an unavoidable rock band that bars access to the summit. This is climbed via a series of ledges and steep walls, and although there's a choice of lines none are easy. From the east end of Meall Meadhonach another steep broken descent leads into another tight notch. The lower final peak, **Meall Bheag**, is the most intimidating of all, a leaning rock tower sprouting from the side of the mountain. Cross a short arête to reach the base of the tower. Make an unnerving step left, then pick your own line up airy ledges and tricky rock steps on the tower's north flank – serious ground that needs a cool head. The broad summit marks the end of the major difficulties. A path descends its far end (steep at first, but only slightly scrambly) to reach the easy-angled shoulder below, where Options A and B rejoin.

Return 8km
Follow the high ground ESE to the minor top of **Meall na Braclaich**. Hold roughly the same line down boggy slopes to meet a sketchy path near the shore of **Cam Loch** at a burn. This climbs to a shoulder overlooking the loch, where the approach path is rejoined.

Canisp (left) and Suilven's eastern summits from the ascent of Caisteal Liath

Seana Bhraigh
and Càrn Bàn

F *ew places are as wild as the Freevater Forest, a deserted upland of bog and heather with the spacious feel that's such a defining characteristic of Scotland's far north. At its heart are Seana Bhraigh, famously one of the Munros furthest from a road, and Càrn Bàn, which holds a similar status among Corbetts. These plateau summits sprawl wide, their rolling flanks gouged by deep corries. The cliff-rimmed bowl of Luchd Choire is particularly impressive. Despite their remoteness the hills can be reached quite quickly on estate tracks, especially if bikes are used. Of several possible approaches the Strath Mulzie route described here is best, the upper glen dominated by the striking pyramid of An Sgurr. For anyone willing to get hands-on, the traverse of this sharp peak on the north ridge of Creag an Duine is the most exciting route onto Seana Bhraigh. A non-scrambler's alternative is also given.*

Approach 8km

From the signed car park the Strath Mulzie track continues, passing through the lodge grounds then following the Corriemulzie river upstream. About 4km beyond the lodge is a track junction; go left. Roughly 2km further on the track fords a side-burn (stepping stones), and soon after it fords the main river too. It then continues parallel with the opposite bank, climbing a little and then descending to the outflow of **Loch a' Choire Mhòir**. The peak of An Sgurr now towers overhead. For the Coiremor/ Magoo's bothy complex stay with the track along the loch shore; for Seana Bhraigh leave the track here and ford the river at its shallowest point.

↑ *The Seana Bhraigh massif (left) and the distant hills of Assynt from Càrn Bàn*

ROUTE INFORMATION

Start/finish	Car park near Corriemulzie Lodge (NH 327 952), 9km down a potholed track from the A837 at Oykel Bridge. Access by car is tolerated, but please don't jeopardise this.
Distance	31.5km (19½ miles)
Ascent	1350m
Time	12hrs
Terrain	Easy access on an estate track. The ascent of Seana Bhraigh's northeast ridge is straightforward, but the other ascent via Creag an Duine's north ridge involves some exposed scrambling at grade 1/2. The boggy ground between Seana Bhraigh and Càrn Bàn is hard going, and needs good navigation in mist.
Summits	Seana Bhraigh 927m ('old height'); Càrn Bàn 845m ('white cairn')
Maps	OS Landranger (1:50,000) 20; OS Explorer (1:25,000) 436 & 437
Public transport	Postbus service 123 from Lairg to Oykel Bridge – from here it's a long walk-in
By bike	For those who don't want to knock the bottom out of their car the Corriemulzie Lodge track gives a fun cycle through the woods. Bikes can be taken as far as Coiremor/Magoo's Bothy too, to save a couple of hours' walking.

Accommodation	Carbisdale Castle YH (01549 421232)
Sleeping out	Great camping in Seana Bhraigh's Luchd Choire, and on the Coire Mòr col. Three excellent bothies are handy for this walk –The Schoolhouse (NH 340 975) is passed on the track to Corriemulzie Lodge, while the other two stand by Loch a' Choire Mhòir at the mountain's foot (the MBA-maintained Coiremor and, directly adjacent, Magoo's Bothy, for which the RAF is responsible) (NH 305 888). Both have stoves.
Seasonal notes	Seana Bhraigh is a serious hill in winter, with plenty of snow-holding potential; corrie rims may be heavily corniced. In full conditions the north ridge of Creag an Duine gives some climbing up to grade II; there are no other technical difficulties. River crossings in Strath Mulzie may be dicey in very wet weather.
Short cuts	Most people will do Seana Bhraigh and Càrn Bàn as separate trips. From the Seana Bhraigh plateau the only straightforward descent route is the northeast ridge, and the mountain's cliffs extend to the Coire Mòr col, making an early descent from here a little tricky too.

An Sgurr from the continuation ridge to Creag an Duine

On the hill 15km

Head SW, then follow the obvious burn uphill into the mouth of **Luchd Choire** (faint path), where the huge cliffs at its head are suddenly revealed. Now there's a choice of route.

Option A The easy way. Head W, climbing quite steeply onto the northeast ridge of **Seana Bhraigh**. Follow this over a broad minor top and past a lochan for the final steeper ascent around the cliffs to the mountain's summit cairn, perched on the rim.

Option B The spectacular way. Turn left for the relentless climb onto the north ridge of **Creag an Duine**. Now follow the crest, where brief airy sections of scrambling are encountered. Signs of wear generally indicate the best line, and the harder steps can be outflanked. The ridge leads quite steeply onto a short level arête, then up again to the sharp top of

An Sgurr, one of the few mainland summits with an obligatory scramble. The col beyond is blocked by a bad step. The most direct descent of this goes via a loose and very exposed path just on the left flank, but it's more sensible to backtrack briefly from An Sgurr and then contour across its eastern face at a lower level to the col. From here the scrambling rapidly eases, leading to the summit of **Creag an Duine** on the Seana Bhraigh plateau. Follow the edge of Luchd Choire over a domed minor top (point 906m) and on up to **Seana Bhraigh**.

Both options rejoin on the summit of **Seanna Bhraigh**. From here head to point 906m then skirt south of Creag an Duine, going E down a gentle slope into the shallow boggy scoop of Coire Mhic Mhathain (OK the bogs aren't shallow). The next few kilometres are fraught with complex knolls and

An Sgurr from Coiremor/Magoo's bothy

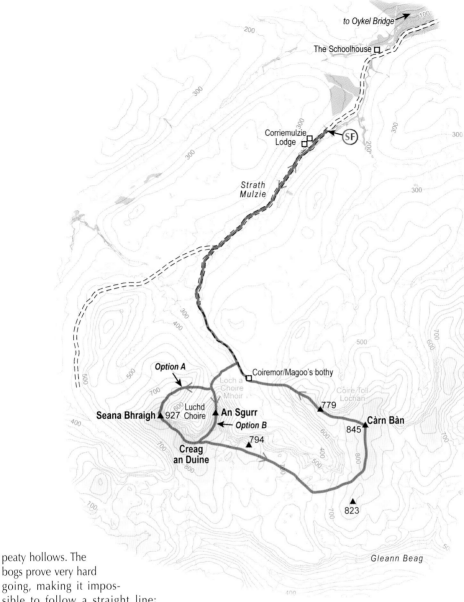

peaty hollows. The bogs prove very hard going, making it impossible to follow a straight line; navigation needs close attention in poor visibility. Stay just S of the high ground that rims Coire Mòr, heading roughly ESE across the wastes to reach a lochan on the rocky bealach above the head of the corrie. The whaleback of **Càrn Bàn** rises ahead; climb ENE across its sprawling slopes. Mercifully, the ground gets drier and easier the higher you go. Pass over a minor top to reach the cairn on the marginally higher main summit.

Descend WNW to pick up the cliff edge of the remote **Coire Toll Lochan**, which is followed over a minor summit (**spot height 779m**). Now keep descending WNW towards **Loch a' Choire Mhòir**. The ground soon steepens, breaking into a series of rock outcrops that are best bypassed on the left. Cross the bogs of the lower slopes to reach the lochshore **bothies**.

Return 8.5km

Take the track back down Strath Mulzie.

The Beinn Dearg four

*T*he Beinn Dearg range dips its western toe into tidal Loch Broom, while from its inland flanks the ground rolls out into Easter Ross, a sprawling emptiness of lonely glens and huge skies. There's nothing higher north of the Dingwall–Ullapool road, from where Beinn Dearg and neighbouring Cona' Mheall are well seen, divided by Coire Ghrànda. This spectacular glacial scoop is a compelling feature, but access to it from the south is fraught with wet pathless ground and burns that turn nasty in spate. Less problematic – so more popular – is this approach from the west, where forest tracks and an excellent stalker's path give a quick route up Gleann na Sguaib. The four central Munros of the range (Beinn Dearg, Cona' Mheall, Eididh nan Clach Geala and Meall nan Ceapraichean) form a tight group, with high intervening cols and minimal reascent between each peak. It's an easy enough walk, but in a wild setting.

Approach 7km

Take the track past the house, heading E into forestry. Follow signs for Beinn Dearg, sticking with the main track at any junctions, then crossing a bridge. Pass a ruin at **Glensguaib**, taking the track alongside the River Lael to reach a gate at the upper forest edge. The route up **Gleann na Sguaib** continues as an excellent stalker's path, an efficient eater of ascent and distance that climbs parallel to but some way above the river. Beinn Dearg and Meall nan Ceapraichean rise precipitously ahead; prominent are the deep gullies of Beinn Dearg's northern crags, which give some of the best winter climbing in the area. At a trail junction just beyond an impressive waterfall go left, climbing towards the col between Meall nan Ceapraichean and Eididh nan Clach Geala.

↑ *Beinn Dearg (left) and Cona' Mheall beyond Loch Glascarnoch*

ROUTE INFORMATION

Start/finish	Car park beside A835 at Inverlael (NH 182 852)
Distance	24.5km (15 miles)
Ascent	1600m
Time	9½hrs
Terrain	Rough and stony up high, but not excessively so, with easy low-level access on forest tracks and stalker's paths
Summits	Eididh nan Clach Geala 928m ('nest/web of the white stones'); Meall nan Ceapraichean 977m ('hill of the stubby hillocks'); Cona' Mheall 980m ('joined-on or adjoining hill', possibly); Beinn Dearg 1084m ('red hill')
Maps	OS Landranger (1:50,000) 20; OS Explorer (1:25,000) 436
Public transport	Inverness–Ullapool buses on the A835 give access to the start of this walk
By bike	Bike-friendly forest tracks in lower Gleann na Sguaib, but cycling won't save much walking

Accommodation	Ullapool YH (01854 612254)
Sleeping out	Excellent camping potential beside Lochan a' Chnapaich and on the Bealach an Lochain Uaine. The nearest bothy is Glenbeg (NH 313 834), not convenient for the western walk-in to Beinn Dearg but an ideal overnight location if the range is tackled via the much longer and wilder eastern approach from Strathcarron (not described here – bike recommended).
Seasonal notes	Long stretches at low altitude and a comparatively short time spent up high make this route ideal as a single winter day. No technical difficulties under snow, although winter increases the air of isolation.
Short cuts	Possible to omit any particular summit, with quick escapes into Gleann na Sguaib from the cols between the peaks

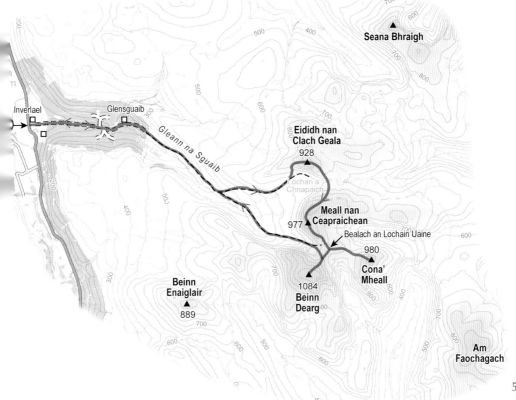

Approaching Eididh nan Clach Geala

Cona' Mheall from the northeast flank of Beinn Dearg

Meall nan Ceapraichean (left) and Beinn Dearg from Gleann na Sguaib

On the hill 9.5km

A little way short of **Lochan a' Chnapaich** leave the path at will. Climb N onto **Eididh nan Clach Geala's** broad western spur, then easily to the summit cairn. This is a fairly nondescript hill, but makes up for it with views of the Easter Ross interior and north-west to the free-standing peaks of Assynt (Walk 5). Descend ESE, skirting the rim of a crag to reach a col. Ascend steeply towards the minor summit of Ceann Garbh, picking a line among scattered outcrops; pass over this rounded top to reach **Meall nan Ceapraichean** itself. Drop easily SE to the lochan-pitted Bealach an Lochain Uaine (not named on 1:50,000 map), which forms a central hub between Meall nan Ceapraichean, Beinn Dearg and Cona' Mheall, giving a spectacular outlook into Coire Ghrànda.

Pass over or right of a knoll (spot height 886m), then climb scree slopes to **Cona' Mheall's** little summit cairn. Return to the bealach to attack Beinn Dearg's northeast flank, following a dilapidated drystone wall up the steep lower slopes. Once up on the gentler summit dome the wall kinks right; here part company with it, heading almost S to the sizeable cairn on top. Since **Beinn Dearg** rises high above its neighbours the views are uninterrupted – An Teallach (Walk 9) and the Fannaichs (Walk 8) are among the many hills visible on a clear day.

In descent an attractive option is to follow the wall along Beinn Dearg's west ridge, staying above the cliffs until they fizzle out about 1km beyond the minor top of Meall Breac (not named on 1:50,000 map). From here cut NE into **Gleann na Sguaib**, crossing the River Lael near the waterfall mentioned in the approach description. However, this river crossing may be difficult in wet conditions, so the surer alternative is to backtrack NE down to the Bealach an Lochain Uaine, as shown on the accompanying map.

Return 8km

From the bealach go W to pick up a stalker's path that descends into the corrie between Meall nan Ceapraichean and the cliffs of Beinn Dearg, zigzagging a little before passing a tiny lochan. A while later rejoin the approach route, and follow this back to **Inverlael**.

Traverse of
the Fannaichs

A grassy range of multiple summits and rugged hidden corries, the Fannaichs offer quality ridge walking in a lonely setting, with a sense of openness and impressive views of the mountain-crowded western seaboard. To visit all nine Munros in the range in a single go would be logistically and physically taxing, and that is probably easiest done as a round trip from Loch Fannich – itself far from the nearest public road. Luckily not all the summits are equally worthwhile, and some can be safely omitted. The range is more accessible from the north, and its best bits can all be trod in this logical east–west route incorporating just five of the Munros, plus a possible two extra for those keen enough to add detours to an already demanding day. It finishes with a long roadside slog – less onerous if travelling by bike or thumb.

Approach 3km
Walk SE along the A835 verge for a few minutes. Once level with an old shed by a bend in the **Abhainn Droma** turn S off the road, ford the river, pass left of the building and pick up a path through the bogs.

Having crossed a footbridge over the **Allt a' Mhadaidh** the path climbs beside the burn's west bank to join a vehicle track in a little over 1km. Continue upstream on this for another 1km, passing a little stone shelter, then head S off the track where it runs close to the burn.

↑ *Sgùrr Mòr and the distant Beinn Dearg group (Walk 7) from Sgùrr nan Clach Geala*

ROUTE INFORMATION

Start/finish	Parking beside A835 on an old stretch of road at roughly NH 228 765
Distance	28km (17½ miles), including 7km of potentially avoidable road walking
Ascent	2200m
Time	11hrs
Terrain	Rough and occasionally boggy ground, steep in places but largely on clear paths
Summits	Beinn Liath Mhòr Fannaich 954m ('big grey hill of Fannaich'); Sgùrr Mòr 1110m ('big peak'); Sgùrr nan Clach Geala 1093m ('peak of the white stones'); Sgùrr Breac 999m ('speckled/dappled peak'); A' Chailleach 997m ('the old woman')
Maps	OS Landranger (1:50,000) 20 and a snippet of 19; OS explorer (1:25,000) 436 & 435
Public transport	Inverness–Ullapool buses on the A835 give access to the start of this walk
By bike	Stash a bike beside the A832 to make short work of the final footsore tarmac trudge. The alternative

southerly approach to these hills follows a long private road from Lochluichart to Loch Fannich, and is best cycled.

Accommodation	Ullapool YH (01854 612254)
Sleeping out	Lochivraon bothy (NH 117 733) is a good pre- or post-hills option, although a detour from the walk as described. The various lochans, grassy cols and corries of the Fannaichs offer many camping possibilities.
Seasonal notes	An ambitious walk for a single winter day, but not technically problematic. Beware cornices, particularly rimming the east faces of Sgùrr Mòr and Sgùrr nan Clach Geala. If the Abhainn Droma is difficult to ford in wet weather cross the Loch Droma dam instead.
Short cuts	A low bealach divides the main Fannaichs group from the western outliers, Sgùrr Breac and A' Chailleach, carrying a well-used path from Loch Fannich to Loch a' Bhraoin; this allows the route to be easily split into two shorter walks

Sgùrr nan Each and Loch Fannich

Braemore Junction

SF

A835

Abhainn Dròma

Allt a' Mhadaidh

Loch a'
Bhraoin

Abhainn Cuileig

Druim
Rèidh

Meall a'
Chrasgaidh
▲
934

Carn na Criche

Beinn Liath
Mhòr Fannaich
▲
954

Sròn na
Goibhre

Toman
Còinnich

997 ▲
A'
Chailleach

999 ▲
Sgùrr Breac

1093 ▲
Sgùrr nan
Clach Geal

▲1110
Sgùrr
Mòr

▲
Sgùrr
nan Each

Meall
Gorm

An
Coileachan

Loch
Fannich

Fannich Lodge

On the hill 18km

Re-cross the Allt a' Mhadaidh and ad-lib up the steep northern slopes of **Beinn Liath Mhòr Fannaich** on rough wet ground with no path to speak of. Reach a level shoulder, then a second, passing some cairns before the final short pull to the summit. Descent directly towards the connecting ridge to Sgùrr Mòr is precipitous and rocky; a gentler stalker's path can be found by first dropping NW. From the col below Beinn Liath Mhòr Fannaich continue over or just left of a minor top and pass another stone shelter.

Now climb the steep east ridge of **Sgùrr Mòr** on odd grass 'terraces', staying close to its impressive east face. The name 'big peak' might be prosaically literalistic, but then this is the highest point in the range and the conical summit has a suitably airy feel,

its substantial cairn sitting right on the cliff edge. The view spans a great arc of the mountain northwest from the Beinn Dearg group (Walk 7) and Assynt (Walk 5) to Fisherfield (Walks 9 and 10) and Torridon (Walks 11, 12 and 13). Across the remote trench of Coire Mòr towers the crag-buttressed giant Sgùrr nan Clach Geala, most imposing of the Fannaichs. After a steep stony descent NW the path passes over the minor hump of **Carn na Criche**, looping the head of Coire Mòr to reach a pool on a broad bealach. On the way the unprepossessing Munro **Meall a' Chrasgaidh** could be bagged with a brief detour.

Climb to the edge of **Sgùrr nan Clach Geala's** rugged eastern corrie and follow a short sharp ridge

Meall a' Chrasgaidh (left), the Beinn Deargs (Walk 7) and An Teallach (Walk 9) from Beinn Liath Mhòr Fannaich

to the summit. Pass the shattered trig point and briefly stay with the corrie rim before descending S on steep grass beside the cliff edge to a col. The pointy Munro of **Sgùrr nan Each** is a worthwhile detour from here, but if that seems a ridge too far then drop W from the col down a steep pathless slope with many tiny burns to gain the low bealach that divides the main Fannaich group from its western outliers. A path offers an optional escape to the A832 here, but those made of sterner stuff will head back uphill for the final two Munros, charismatic mountains with perhaps the best westward views of the day.

From the bealach a well-trodden trail climbs the east-southeast ridge of **Sgùrr Breac**, steeply at first and with some rock outcrops to negotiate, and then more gently along the rim of a craggy corrie. From the little summit plateau descend W and continue over the grassy hump of **Toman Còinnich**. The north ridge of this top, Druim Rèidh, offers the quickest way off these hills, but don't take it just yet; instead descend W above the deep scoop of Coire Toll an Lochain, then climb the east ridge of **A' Chailleach** to the summit.

A short steep descent now gains the north ridge, **Sròn na Goibhre**, with a vague path and occasional rusty fence posts to follow. Beyond a rocky mini-top peel right down rough ground into the base of the corrie near the outflow from Loch Toll an Lochain. Hop the burn and make a rising traverse onto **Druim Rèidh** to meet a path on its broad peaty crest, leading N to a cairn at the lip of a steep drop. The muddy path weaves down through the rocks, then crosses the boggy lower slopes to reach a bridge over the Abhainn Cuileig at the outflow from beautiful Loch a' Bhraoin near a boathouse and a ruin. A track cuts through the edge of a forestry plantation to a junction just N of the buildings; follow the forest boundary track to the **A832**.

Return 7km

A long but scenic road walk now takes you past the wooded Corrieshalloch Gorge to **Braemore Junction** and the A835.

An Teallach
and the Beinn Deargs

*F*ew mountains can match the grandeur of An Teallach, a multi-topped fortress walled with gully-seamed crags, rising in tiers to castellated crests that glow in the sunrise. Its Gaelic name is poetically apt – 'the forge' fires the imagination and puts iron in a mountaineer's soul. The famous Corrag Bhuidhe Pinnacles are the most daunting scrambling traverse on the Scottish mainland and the hardest described in this book; but there are walker-friendly ways to outflank the towers. An Teallach stands guard at the northern fringe of the untamed Fisherfield Forest, and although the customary shortish circuit from the nearby A832 cannot be faulted, incorporating the mountain into this more ambitious route allows a greater insight into its remote hinterland.

Secretively sequestered beyond the broad trough of the Strath na Sealga, Beinn Dearg Bheag and Beinn Dearg Mòr are spectacular hills in their own right and less visited than their neighbour. A long scenic approach from Gruinard Bay gives access to a circuit over both mountain groups, a testing wilderness expedition with intricate scrambling and two major river crossings. Runners might knock it off in a single summer day; others will welcome the midway bothy at Shenavall.

↑ *An Teallach, Loch na Sealga and Loch Toll an Lochain from the Beinn Dearg Bheag/Mòr col*

ROUTE INFORMATION

Start/finish	Verge parking on A832 at the Gruinard river (NG 961 911)		post-walk bike retrieval would involve fording the Gruinard river, only worth considering in a dry spell.
Distance	37km (23 miles)		
Ascent	2610m	**Accommodation**	Sail Mhor Croft hostel, Dundonnell (01854 633224)
Time	17½hrs		
Terrain	Long stretches pathless and rough. Amenable grade 1 scrambling on the northwest ridge of Beinn Dearg Bheag and the east ridge of Sgùrr Creag an Eich. Sustained grade 3 ground on the Corrag Bhuidhe Pinnacles of An Teallach – paths on the SW flank avoid most difficulties. Two major river crossings in Strath na Sealga need care; may be impassable in flood.	**Sleeping out**	Shenavall bothy (NH 066 810) is the obvious choice, so often crowded; may be unavailable in the stalking season. If cut off by rising rivers there's an emergency shelter behind the private stone house at Larachantivore (NH 052 801). Grassy camp sites in Gleann na Muice and Strath na Sealga.
		Seasonal notes	A stunning winter mountaineering walk with an expeditionary feel. The traverse of An Teallach via the Corrag Bhuidhe Pinnacles is a serious and technical grade II climb, and the avoiding path may be unsafe if banked with snow. The northwest ridge of Beinn Dearg Bheag merits at least grade I, as does the east ridge of Sgùrr Creag an Eich.
Summits	Beinn Dearg Bheag 820m ('little red hill'); Beinn Dearg Mòr 910m ('big red hill'); An Teallach ('the forge'); Sgurr Fiona 1060m ('white peak or wine peak'); Bidein a' Ghlas Thuill 1062m ('peak of the grey-green hollow')		
Maps	OS Landranger (1:50,000) 19; OS explorer (1:25,000) 433 & 435; Harvey Superwalker (1:25,000) An Teallach and Fisherfield	**Short cuts**	Strath na Sealga cleaves the hills, offering a long low-level return to Gruinard Bay should one be needed. A rough soggy path runs along the south side of Loch na Sealga. A quicker escape is the path from Shenavall to the A832 at Corrie Hallie (see Walk 10), although this is far from your start point.
Public transport	Infrequent bus service between Gairloch and Ullapool		
By bike	The rough stony track from Gruinard Bay to Loch na Sealga suits a bike with good suspension. However		

Approach 8km

Follow the track up the west bank of the **Gruinard river** through craggy hummocks and scattered birch woods, with Beinn Dearg Bheag becoming ever more prominent. The track ends by the shingle beach at the outflow from **Loch na Sealga** ('Loch na Shellag' on Harvey maps). The boat house marked on OS maps has long vanished. Pick up a faint path along the south bank of the loch, beneath steep wooded hillsides. After approximately 1km the path climbs slightly to avoid wooded crags on the loch shore; look out for a small cairn here marking a right-hand turn off.

On the hill 21km

This increasingly sketchy path ascends roughly SSE over soggy moorland, heading for the distinctive cone of Beinn Dearg Bheag. Skirt below the unnamed knoll at spot height 392m to gain the col beyond. The terminal nose of **Beinn Dearg Bheag's** northwest ridge rises steeply ahead; the best route first takes a grassy depression a little left of centre before veering right onto the crest of the ridge – take care in the wet. Ascend through scrambly rock tiers with occasional hints of a path, then over a rising series of knobbly false summits leading up the narrow ridge – airy walking and some modest scrambling entertainment. The summit gives stirring views of the Fisherfield Munros (Walk 10).

There's now a more definite path in descent to the col at the head of Toll an Lochain, and on up the steep gravelly slopes of **Beinn Dearg Mòr**. This is among the shapeliest of all the Corbetts, its summit perched on the lip of an amphitheatre of monumental

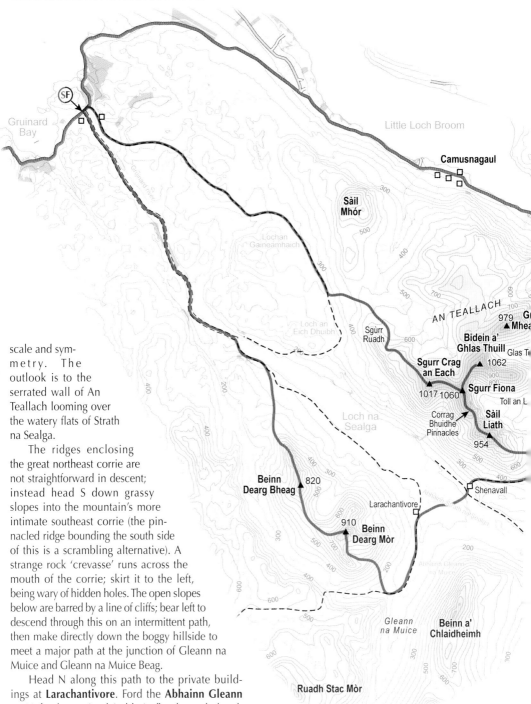

scale and symmetry. The outlook is to the serrated wall of An Teallach looming over the watery flats of Strath na Sealga.

The ridges enclosing the great northeast corrie are not straightforward in descent; instead head S down grassy slopes into the mountain's more intimate southeast corrie (the pinnacled ridge bounding the south side of this is a scrambling alternative). A strange rock 'crevasse' runs across the mouth of the corrie; skirt it to the left, being wary of hidden holes. The open slopes below are barred by a line of cliffs; bear left to descend through this on an intermittent path, then make directly down the boggy hillside to meet a major path at the junction of Gleann na Muice and Gleann na Muice Beag.

Head N along this path to the private buildings at **Larachantivore**. Ford the **Abhainn Gleann na Muice** here – inadvisable in flood – and plough across a kilometre of level bog to reach the Abhainn Strath na Sealga near **Shenavall bothy**. This, too, is a weather-dependent river crossing. Take the uphill path by a burn behind the bothy, as per Walk 10. At the burn that drains Lochan na Bradhan (not named

on Harvey maps) turn uphill to find a fainter path that zigzags steeply up the rough southeast slopes of **Sàil Liath**; the incline eventually eases on a

Beinn Dearg Mòr and the Coire Mhic Fhearchair massif (Walk 10) from Beinn Dearg Bheag

stony spur leading to the summit cairn. The cavernous bowl of Toll an Lochain yawns below, its spired skyline seeming to bar access to the Munro summits beyond. Rest assured, the tough stuff is mostly optional.

Pass over the minor summit of Cadha Gobhlach, cross a col and ascend scree below a toothed crest to reach a levelling. Climb an introductory slabby tier to the base of the first of the **Corrag Bhuidhe Pinnacles**. Here there's a choice – for minimal scrambling stay below the ridge crest, following a well-worn path along its left (southwest)

Fresh spring snow on Sgurr Fiona and the Corrag Bhuidhe Pinnacles, seen from Bidein a' Ghlas Thuill flank; but for maximum excitement go high. To start the latter option climbers might enjoy a steep and extremely exposed pitch on the Toll an Lochain side; more cautious scramblers will prefer the less airy left flank.

Once on top of the first tower the most entertaining route stays with the skyline to climb several more towers. There's generally a choice of line, the best options showing signs of wear; some difficulties may be bypassed via paths on the left. Beyond the pinnacles a straightforward descent and some brief scrambling gain the tip of Lord Berkeley's Seat, a sharp spire above a dizzying drop. From here the rocky crest leads up to **Sgurr Fiona**. Given time it's well worth detouring to the second Munro, **Bidein a' Ghlas Thuill**, for the impressive view back along the corrie wall; the connecting ridge involves a steep descent and reascent, but minimal scrambling.

To continue the circuit descend Sgurr Fiona's rough WNW ridge to a col, then take the narrow east ridge of **Sgùrr Creag an Eich**, with some pleasant easy scrambling, to reach this sharp outlying top. Descending NW, a broad ridge soon takes shape. It's rough underfoot and there's no path to speak of; keep heading NW over a plateau-like area. It's worth walking out to the airy promontory summit of **Sgùrr Ruadh** for the views, but the easiest way off is to cut N before this, descending to the peaty flat ground below this craggy headland. From here ad-lib WNW over rough boggy slopes, descending to a footpath between **Loch an Eich Dhuibh** and Lochan Gaineamhaich.

Return 8km

Follow the path along the east shore of **Lochan Gaineamhaich**, then through complex terrain of knolls and bogs, where the path is occasionally intermittent and frequently wet, to eventually reach the east bank of the Gruinard river not far from the **A832**. **Note** The obvious alternative return via the Gruinard river track entails a weather-dependent river crossing.

Sàil Mhór (right) and Gruinard Bay from Beinn Dearg Bheag's northwest ridge

Fisherfield Six

*E*xamine OS Landranger 19 – convoluted contours hedged with crags, great splashes of blue and a roadless expanse shining off the page. This is the Letterewe/Fisherfield Forest, a place of thrilling remoteness that attracts superlatives like midges to a bare arm. A complex tangle of rock and loch, empty glens and unbridged rivers, it fully deserves its breathless alias the 'Great Wilderness'. The six peaks at its heart are famously among the least accessible of the Munros, and this isolation is both their biggest challenge and chief attraction. This horseshoe linking all six is testingly long, of course, with ascent and rough ground to match; but most notable is the atmosphere of uncompromising rawness. Among the hills A' Mhaighdean takes top billing, a rocky bastion rising at the head of the remarkable mountain trench of Carnmore to offer some of the most inspiring views of any Scottish summit. Although the route is possible in a single hefty day, most walkers make a weekend of it, typically basing themselves at Shenavall bothy.

↑ Left to right – Mullach Coire Mhic Fhearchair, Beinn Tarsuinn, Ruadh Stac Mór and A' Mhaighdean from Beinn Dearg Bheag (Walk 9)

ROUTE INFORMATION

Start/finish	Layby on A832 at Corrie Hallie (NH 113 851)
Distance	37km (23 miles)
Ascent	3000m
Time	16hrs
Terrain	Rough rocky hills with several steep ascents and descents and occasional very basic scrambling. Bogs abound, and two major river crossings in Strath na Sealga need care – in a wet spell they may be impassable.
Summits	Beinn a' Chlaidheimh 914m–916m ('hill of the sword', height under dispute at the end of 2011); Sgurr Bán 989m ('white peak'); Mullach Coire Mhic Fhearchair 1019m ('peak of the corrie of Farquhar's son'); Beinn Tarsuinn 937m ('transverse hill'); A' Mhaighdean 967m ('the maiden'); Ruadh Stac Mór 918m ('big red stack')
Maps	OS Landranger (1:50,000) 19; OS explorer (1:25,000) 435 & 433; Harvey Superwalker (1:25,000) An Teallach and Fisherfield
Public transport	Infrequent bus service between Gairloch and Ullapool
By bike	Mountain bikes could be used part-way up the Corrie Hallie track, but it's hardly worth the effort
Accommodation	Sàil Mhór Croft hostel, Dundonnell (01854 633224)

Sleeping out It would be almost a crime to visit the Great Wilderness without spending a night or two. A comfortable bothy in a stunning location, Shenavall (NH 066 810) is the obvious choice; often crowded, and may be unavailable in the stalking season. For those cut off by rising rivers there's an emergency shelter behind the private stone house at Larachantivore (NH 052 801). Grassy camp sites can be found by the Abhainn Gleann na Muice. There's a fairly pokey but well-located howff under a boulder on the A' Mhaighdean / Ruadh Stac Mór col.

Seasonal notes In winter conditions the Great Wilderness really lives up to its billing and needs a well-prepared team. Even from a base at Shenavall this round would be an achievement in a single winter day. Although steep in places the ground is largely non-technical under snow, except a short avoidable passage of easy mountaineering on Beinn Tarsuinn's craggy west ridge.

Short cuts A major col divides the four Munros of the Mullach Coire Mhic Fhearchair massif from the A' Mhaighdean two, so for a shorter day either group can be done separately, with Gleann na Muice providing low-level access back to Shenavall.

Beinn Dearg Mòr (left, Walk 9) and Beinn a' Chlaidheimh from Sgurr Bán

Approach 6km

From **Corrie Hallie** take the burn-side track up wooded Gleann Chaorachain. Beyond waterfalls at the head of the glen the track climbs onto open ground. Cyclists might stay with the track as far as **Achneigie**, but walkers heading for Shenavall should turn onto a path at a cairn roughly 3km from the road. The path runs around the foot of Sàil Liath (see Walk 9) before descending fairly steeply beside a burn to reach **Shenavall bothy**.

On the hill 25km

Ford the **Abhainn Strath na Sealga** at stony shallows near the bothy. In a wet spell this may range from foolhardy to impossible; note that the walk returns the same

way later, and heavy rain during the day may leave you cut off. Continue S over the bogs towards **Beinn a' Chlaidheimh**. Some advocate climbing the northeast spur, Creag Ghlas; but, although steeper, the heathery north slopes are more direct and offer some easy scrambling through crag bands. A path develops as you gain height. The summit ridge is an airy walkway with spacious views to An Teallach and Beinn Dearg Mòr (Walk 9); there are two false summits before the high point.

A steep descent, partly on quartzite scree, leads to a little saddle pitted with pools. Pass over an unnamed

73

A' Mhaighdean from Beinn Tarsuinn's west ridge

top (spot height 815m on OS maps) to descend to the low col of Am Briseadh, overlooking the loch of the same name. **Sgurr Bán** is basically a giant mound of quartzite rubble, and its gently sloping northeast spur is a tiresome trudge – a stone 'igloo' halfway up might offer shelter in an emergency. Although it's less easily accessed, the north ridge offers a grassier alternative ascent. The summit is broad and featureless, needing attentive navigation in mist.

A steep stony spur heads SSW down to the col below **Mullach Coire Mhic Fhearchair**. With yet more steep rocky ground and a sometimes faint path, the ascent of this rugged peak is almost as much of a challenge as is pronouncing its name. Follow your nose through outcrops for the slog to the summit cairn. The descent S is predictably steep and boulder-strewn, but at the next col the terrain begins to relent.

Those with spare energy can climb the minor peak of **Meall Garbh**, while for everyone else a path traverses its right flank to reach boggy Bealach Odhar beneath the grassy eastern aspect of **Beinn Tarsuinn**. A straightforward 200m ascent gains the summit, where the ground abruptly drops away into the mountain's cliffy northern corrie. Heading W, a delightful ridge takes shape, curving around the corrie rim and offering some scrambly entertainment – first over a curious flat tabletop and then a succession of little sandstone teeth. If you must, a path down on the left flank avoids all the fun. Where the ridge broadens and begins to lose height drop left, roughly WNW, where a steep rough slope runs down into the peaty bealach below **A' Mhaighdean**.

Thread through the bogs, then skirt just left of a line of outcrops to gain the long gentle climb up the mountain's grassy southeast slopes (there's a path of sorts, but it's not really needed) – the only dull side of an otherwise awesome peak. A cairn crowns the sharp top, with a stupendous outlook over crags along the wild expanse of Fionn Loch to the sea. To the south is the gully-seamed wall of Beinn Lair and the distant Torridon skyline.

Head over the plateau towards the mountain's lower north top, then bear right to descend a steep path onto the rugged bealach below **Ruadh Stac Mór**. A band of sandstone crags seems to bar access to this peak; the rocks are breached by a rough, nastily eroded path. Above is a scree plod to the summit trig. It is common to retrace one's steps from here to meet a good path above Fuar Loch Mor, but instead take the stony northwest ridge. Having made the initial descent from the summit cone bear right (NE) down rough slopes; pass between two lochs (**Lochan a' Bhràghad**) then pick up a vague trail parallel with a burn down onto the boggy ground above the head of Gleann na Muice Beag.

Here join an excellent path which runs downhill towards Loch Beinn Dearg before cutting back right to the floor of Gleann na Muice near a burn junction. The path continues downstream into the wide **Strath na Sealga**, dominated by the serrated peaks of Beinn Dearg Mòr and An Teallach. Ford the Abhainn Gleann na Muice close to the private house at **Larachantivore** (NH 053 801), then cross a kilometre of bog to return to **Shenavall** via another wading of the Abhainn Strath na Sealga.

Return 6km

Follow the path and track back to **Corrie Hallie**.

The view west from A' Mhaighdean – Beinn Lair (left), Beinn Airigh Charr and the Fionn and Dubh lochs (pick a clear day if possible)

Beinn Eighe

*T*here's nowhere like Torridon. Its great peaks each feature high in the Scottish mountain pan-
theon; taken as a group they are unrivalled. Complex, multi-topped Beinn Eighe splays elegantly
across the eastern end of the range, its crests draped in quartzite screes that shine pale in the light.
Walkers tend to tackle the hill from its more accessible Glen Torridon side, and too many focus
solely on the two Munro-listed summits. But that rather misses the point. Beinn Eighe's true scale and
character are revealed only on a full traverse, and as with neighbouring Liathach its most impressive
corners are best seen from the hard-to-access north. From Kinlochewe this rarely trodden approach
leads through uncompromising wilds, shadowing the mountain's entire length to reach Coire Mhic
Fhearchair. The route ascends beneath the grandiose rock architecture of the famous Triple Buttress,
then follows the bleached spine of the land back east on a stunning ridge walk book-ended with a
couple of brief but exciting scrambles.

Approach 11km

Head NW out of **Kinlochewe** on the A832. Beinn
Eighe is Britain's oldest National Nature Reserve
(NNR), and visitor-friendly waymarked trails have
been built in the ecologically rich Caledonian pine
woods that fringe the mountain. Pick up one such just
left of the road. At a path junction go left, crossing
a bridge to follow the Allt Sguabaidh uphill. Where
the waymarked way cuts right quit it for a rougher
trail (the so-called 'Pony Path'), which continues
alongside the burn before climbing into the upper
reaches of the Doire Daraich, a ravine sheltering a

↑ *The awesome Triple Buttress from Loch Coire Mhic Fhearchair*

ROUTE INFORMATION

Start/finish	Car park in Kinlochewe (NH 029 619)
Distance	25.5km (16 miles)
Ascent	2000m
Time	10½hrs
Terrain	Good path to start, but in Toll a' Ghiubhais this is lost among bogs and the boulder-strewn complexities of moraines, where the ground is extremely rough and navigation tricky in mist. The ridge walk is well trodden, and although the screes are slow going it is technically straightforward except for short grade 1 scrambles on Coinneach Mhor, Spidean Coire nan Clach and Sgurr nan Fhir Duibhe.
Summits	Beinn Eighe ('file mountain' or, possibly, 'ice mountain'); Sàil Mhór 980m ('big heel'); Ruadh-stac Mór 1010m ('big red stack'); Spidean Coire nan Clach 993m ('peak of the stony corrie'); Sgurr Bán 970m ('white peak'); Sgurr nan Fhir Duibhe 963m ('peak of the black men')
Maps	OS Landranger (1:50,000) 19 & 25; OS Explorer (1:25,000) 433; Harvey Superwalker (1:25,000) Torridon
Public transport	Inverness–Gairloch buses (infrequent) call at Kinlochewe
Accommodation	Kinlochewe Hotel bunkhouse (01445 760253); Torridon YH (01445 791284); free campsite in Torridon village
Sleeping out	Toll a' Ghiubhais invites a secluded camp, while for atmosphere Coire Mhic Fhearchair can't be beaten anywhere in Scotland
Seasonal notes	In wet weather it may be wise to ford the Allt Toll a' Ghiubhais quite far upstream. In deep snow the long approach might be better missed out and the traverse done as a linear route from Glen Torridon. Beinn Eighe's ridges provide spectacular winter walking, the scrambles becoming grade I climbs on which mountaineering competence is needed.
Short cuts	Sàil Mhór and the first scramble can be avoided by climbing to the col between Coinneach Mhor and Ruadh-stac Mór; ascent of the latter is also optional

Spidean Coire nan Clach from Coinneach Mhor

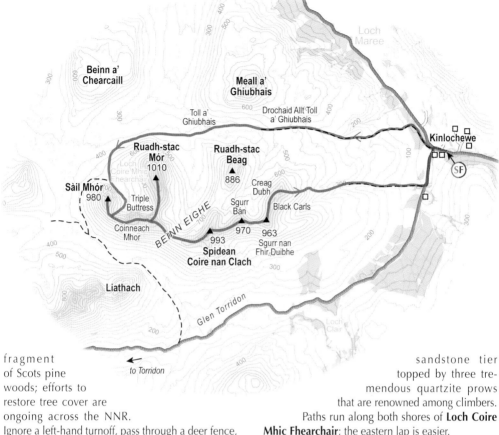

Beinn a'
Chearcaill

Meall a'
Ghiubhais

Toll a'
Ghiubhais

Drochaid Allt Toll
a' Ghiubhais

Loch
Maree

Kinlochewe

Ruadh-stac
Mór
1010

Ruadh-stac
Beag
886

Creag
Dubh

Sàil Mhór
980

Triple
Buttress

Sgurr
Bàn

Black Carls

BEINN EIGHE

Coinneach
Mhor

993
Spidean
Coire nan Clach

970

963
Sgurr nan
Fhir Duibhe

Liathach

Glen Torridon

to Torridon

fragment
of Scots pine
woods; efforts to
restore tree cover are
ongoing across the NNR.

Ignore a left-hand turnoff, pass through a deer fence, and ignore a second left-hand turnoff, following occasional cairns onto the saddle of the Drochaid Allt Toll a' Ghiubhais.

Here a sketchy path cuts right towards Meall a' Ghiubhais; instead go straight on to descend a similarly intermittent trail into remote **Toll a' Ghiubhais**, dominated by the squat craggy form of Ruadh-stac Beag. Once the path dwindles continue W through bogs north of the river to enter a wilderness of moraines, heather and boulders. Cross the river just downstream of a waterfall and keep winding W through the hummocks; views into Beinn Eighe's northern recesses repay the hard work.

Pass below the terraces of Ruadh-stac Mór, and once the craggy pyramid of Sàil Mhór has risen into view a vague path is soon met at right angles. Follow this uphill (cairns), crossing the burn flowing from Coire Mhic Fhearchair to join the popular path into the corrie. Dominated by the monumental Triple Buttress, this is perhaps the most impressive single place in Torridon – no faint praise. The cliff reflects the mountain's composite geology, a lower

sandstone tier topped by three tremendous quartzite prows that are renowned among climbers. Paths run along both shores of **Loch Coire Mhic Fhearchair**; the eastern lap is easier.

On the hill 11km

From the far end of the loch head S then SW, climbing quite steeply to a col on the skyline right of the Triple Buttress. Here the brooding bulk of Liathach (Walk 12) is suddenly revealed across the depth of Coire Dubh Mòr. The summit of **Sàil Mhór** is worth the short easy walk for its outlook over Torridon's loch-studded hinterland. Return to the col and head towards Coinneach Mhor. A level rock crest abuts a short steep crag at the western end of the **Triple Buttress** cliffs. This requires a scramble up airy ledges, easiest on the right. Stroll over the summit plateau to a cairn at its eastern end, marking the 2km out-and-back detour to **Ruadh-stac Mór**, Beinn Eighe's high point. To reach this outlier drop quite steeply NNE, then climb more gently N on a mix of stones and grass to the little nipple of the summit.

Once back on the main ridge follow the rim of Coire Ruadh-staca, where the crest narrows as it leads into a stony saddle before rising towards the ragged twin peaks of **Spidean Coire nan Clach**, Eighe's

← Fisherfield (Walk 10) from the Black Carls of Sgurr nan Fhir Duibhe

second Munro. A trig point adorns the western top, but the sharp eastern summit is higher, gained with a brief scramble. From here a rough descent and a narrow rocky ridge lead E onto the pyramid of **Sgurr Bán** above the scree-filled bowl of Toll Bàn. Descend E around the edge of shattered cliffs before climbing very steep scree, skirting the lip of **Sgurr nan Fhir Duibhe's** crumbling columnar crags to reach its dramatic wedge-shaped peak. The north ridge of this final major summit is riven into pinnacles, the infamous Bodaich Dubh or **Black Carls**.

The initial unnerving descent is the hardest section if done direct, although easier on the east side; after this, climb over or around the remaining pinnacles at will. The scramble is exposed rather than difficult, but the marble-like quartzite is slippery when wet (even when dry) and extensively loose. Much gentler ground follows, leading to the very last minor top, **Creag Dhubh**. On a clear evening this is a prime place to admire the northward outlook to Fisherfield (Walks 9 and 10). To descend take a clear path on the well-defined east ridge. To avoid the craggy lower reaches of the ridge turn N at a cairn on a tiny knoll, dropping down eroded gravel into a shallow bowl. From here the path turns E above a burn-cutting, then follows an easier-angled spur down to a burn junction in a wooded ravine.

Return 3.5km

Scramble into the ravine, cross the burn and clamber up rocks on the far side, stepping through a gate in a deer fence to gain an engineered path. This follows the tree-lined Allt a' Chuirn downstream for about 2km. On meeting a track go right to continue beside the burn. At the next junction either turn left onto a track to **Kinlochewe** or go straight on to meet the **A896** about 1km south of the village.

Sgurr nan Fhir Duibhe and the Black Carls from Kinlochewe

Liathach
and Beinn Alligin

*B*eauty and the Beast make a lovely couple. Liathach is a brute by any standards, an improbable upthrust of tiered crags, gouged into Gothic corries and ice-chiselled crests. The effect is, in equal parts, forbidding and intriguing. Nearby Beinn Alligin has a curvier, gentler grace, suiting beautifully the two possible romantic translations of its Gaelic name ('darling mountain' or 'jewel mountain').

Each of these unique hills offers two Munros and a classic ridge-scrambling traverse. They are generally done individually, but better than 'either–or' is 'both–and'. It is a rough walk with much ascent and some exciting ridge-crest clambering, and although it looks an illogically roundabout route on paper for two hills that are so close to the road and might be done in a linear day, the long return leg is one of the great low-level walks of Scotland in its own right, with a wild setting and stunning views of Liathach's craggy hidden side. The keen may note the possibility of incorporating Beinn Dearg into the round; this book may be about challenging walks, but there are limits.

↑ *Liathach from Loch Clair, early morning* 81

Start/finish	Car park by the A896 near the Ling Hut (private) (NG 958 569)
Distance	28.5km (18 miles)
Ascent	2750m
Time	13hrs
Terrain	Rough, rocky and steep throughout. Most of the day is on clear trails, but there are two boggy pathless sections. If taken direct, the Pinnacles of Am Fasarinen give exposed grade 2 scrambling, while Alligin's Horns are grade 1; optional paths outflank both.
Summits	Liathach ('greyish one'); Spidean a' Choire Leith 1055m ('peak of the grey corrie'); Am Fasarinen ('the teeth'); Mullach an Rathain 1023m ('summit of the pulley' or 'summit of the row of pinnacles'); Tom na Gruagaich 922m ('hill of the damsel'); Beinn Alligin ('darling mountain' or 'jewel mountain'); Sgurr Mhór 986m ('big peak')
Maps	Awkwardly spans OS Landranger (1:50,000) 19, 24 & 25; OS Explorer (1:25,000) 433; Harvey Superwalker (1:25,000) Torridon

Public transport	By rail from Inverness to Strathcarron; by bus from there to Torridon
Accommodation	Kinlochewe Hotel bunkhouse (01445 760253); Torridon YH (01445 791284); free campsite in Torridon village
Sleeping out	Coire Mhic Nòbuil and Coire Dubh Mòr would be very atmospheric places to camp, although the ground is invariably rough
Seasonal notes	A winter mountaineering epic with serious ground in abundance. The Am Fasarinen Pinnacles are technical grade II climbing, and Alligin's Horns grade I; in both cases the flanking paths may be precariously banked with snow. From the crest of Liathach winter escape routes are limited.
Short cuts	If transport is no issue a shorter linear route can be made, omitting the return along the Coire Mhic Nòbuil / Coire Dubh Mòr path

Approach 1.5km

Follow the Coire Dubh Mòr path (signposted) uphill into the glen separating Beinn Eighe from Liathach. At about 300m altitude look out for a cairn marking a sketchy left-hand turnoff.

On the hill 17km

Take this W through a patch of gently inclined rock slabs, climbing towards Liathach's precipitous terminal nose, **Stùc a' Choire Dhuibh Bhig**. Beyond a jumble of massive boulders the ground steepens. The path zigzags just left of a band of crags, then continues towards a cliff tier that seems to bar the skyline. The path trends right here to a point overlooking Coire Dubh Mòr where the crags are most easily breached, a short steep scramble (grade 1) leading onto the crest above. Here rounded sandstone gives way to angular quartzite blocks, the geological shift that gives Liathach its distinctive conical summits and makes for such hard going on the tops. Rough scrambly walking gains Stuc a' Choire Bhig – a taste of things to come.

The ridge now undulates W, starting with a descent to a little col (possible escape S on a clear path into Glen Torridon). Follow the crest over Stob a' Choire Liath-Mhor, then descend to another gap before making the tough slog onto **Spidean a' Choire Leith**, first of the day's Munros and a magnificent viewpoint overlooking the forbidding sandstone spires of Am Fasarinen; they are not as scary as they seem.

Descend steep scree (various paths) to the little notch that marks the start of the **Pinnacles**. The scrambling comes in short bursts, with exciting exposure and difficulties that can be varied to suit; crampon scratches give a good general guide. Less brave souls might prefer the path low on the left (S) flank of the ridge, which avoids pretty much everything of interest. Beyond the highest pinnacle the ground soon reverts to walking, with a brief descent then a long gentle cliff edge climb to **Mullach an Rathain**. Here there's a tremendous outlook over the crumbling Northern Pinnacles (a classic winter climb).

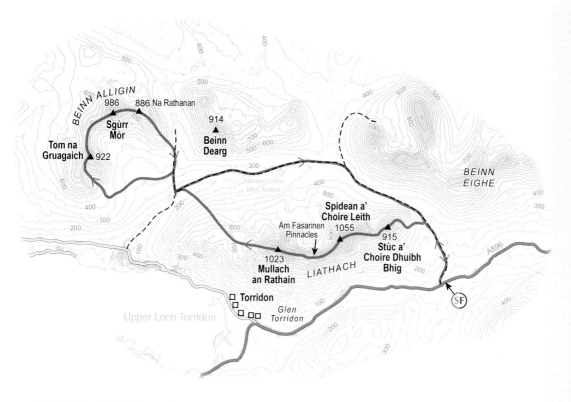

Left to right – Mullach an Rathain, Beinn Alligin and Beinn Dearg from the Pinnacles of Am Fasarinen   83

Beinn Alligin (left) and Liathach from the Coulin Forest (Walk 13)

Ignore the customary descent route S into Toll Ban and instead keep heading W down a gradual gravel slope; there's not much of a path, but if it's misty a line of cairns is a helpful handrail. Continuing all the way down this ridge to link with the Beinn Alligin path comes with a height-loss penalty. Alternatively leave the high ground a few hundred metres short of Sgorr a' Chadail and descend NW from about 700m altitude into Coire Mhic Nòbuil; it's rough, boggy and pathless but quick.

Hop over the **Abhainn Coire Mhic Nòbuil** (care in flood) to pick up the glen-bottom path. Follow this to a junction and turn right. Ascend past falls on the Allt a' Bhealaich to a footbridge. Having crossed this, quit the path and traverse rough soggy ground beneath Alligin's looming tiered walls, crossing the Allt Toll a' Mhadaidh to reach the popular Alligin ascent path.

In places quite eroded, this trail makes a brutal assault of Coir' nan Laogh to eventually emerge at a cairn. The summit of **Tom na Gruagaich** is the right of two tops a short stroll NNE, its cairn perched on the edge of the monumental curved face of Toll a' Mhadaidh. Descend N on a well-defined ridge with the odd hands-on moment, then climb to **Sgurr Mhór**, passing the top of the famous Eag Dhubh just before the summit. This dramatic rift cuts straight down the flank of the mountain, looking like one half of a gully; a huge boulder field on the corrie floor below suggests where the other half may have ended up.

A steep stony descent leads E to a low notch. Above rear **Na Rathanan** or the Horns of Alligin, three blunt towers with rock-tiered flanks. The scramble over the towers is well used and obvious, with limited technical difficulties and a memorably airy atmosphere. Non-scramblers might prefer the delightful trail that traverses the hill's steep south flank, accessed by ascending briefly towards the Horns. Both options meet up just beyond the third and lowest horn to descend quite steeply SSE, where the path negotiates a couple of minor rocky bits before reaching easy ground.

Return 10km

Only the abnormally energetic will fancy Beinn Dearg. Otherwise it's a quick descent to recross the bridge over the Allt a' Bhealaich, then on down to the path junction in Coire Mhic Nòbuil. The road may be less than 2km away to the SW, but the much tougher scenic route is well worth the effort. Turning inland, the path ascends gradually beside the **Abhainn Coire Mhic Nòbuil**, with much rough going among post-glacial moraines. Eventually pass

the lonely reed-choked pools of **Lochan a' Choire Dhuibh** in a magnificently rugged setting below the glowering precipices of Liathach, then climb to a high point and a cairned junction with a trail running from Beinn Eighe's Coire Mhic Fhearchair. Underfoot conditions are easier on the final descent to the starting point.

Beinn Alligin from the west end of Liathach

Coulin Forest

*I*n scenic terms the Coulin Forest is the southern outpost of the far northwest, a final flourish of freakish geology and ruggedly eccentric peaks before the more ordered ranks of the west take over. Bristling crags and spattered with constellations of lochans, this raw wonderland gives walking as aesthetic and challenging as nearby Torridon's. But there are no great ridges here to draw the crowds, and even Coulin's Munros can have the feel of a forgotten backwater. The stand-alone nature of each hill makes hard work of this round of all three 3000-ers, but although these are charismatic peaks no extended Coulin traverse would be complete without the further addition of Corbett Fuar Tholl, a remarkable hill by any standards and the best of this bunch.

Approach 0.5km

Follow the track signed for Achnashellach station, passing houses to cross the railway at the platform. Take a forest track uphill very briefly to a junction; turn left here, following a track through a gate into woods above the River Lair. At a marker cut left onto a path, stepping through a round gate in a deer fence to reach, and then ford, the river (see Seasonal notes).

On the hill 22.5km

Pathless heather slopes lead onto the broad shoulder of Sgurr a' Mhuilinn, from where an occasional path skirts just left of rock slabs (possible scrambling detour) to climb into the unfrequented, crag-walled southeast corrie of **Fuar Tholl**. At a tiny lochan cut right onto the rock-strewn east ridge. As the ridge ascends, it narrows dramatically and the path becomes clearer, soon leading to the summit wind

↑ *Fuar Tholl from the Bhealaich Mhoir*

ROUTE INFORMATION

Start/finish	Layby on the A890 by telephone box and sign for Achnashellach station (NH 005 483)	**Accommodation**	Gerry's hostel, Achnashellach (01520 766232)
Distance	28km (17½ miles)	**Sleeping out**	The lochan-scattered bealachs of the Coulin Forest could have been tailored for wild camping, and idyllic possibilities are everywhere. Coire Fionnaraich bothy (NG 950 480) also makes a good base.
Ascent	2150m		
Time	11hrs		
Terrain	Excellent stalker's paths in the glens, but the hills themselves are invariably steep and rocky. Particularly uncompromising are the ascent and descent of Fuar Tholl and the northern side of Maol Chean-dearg.	**Seasonal notes**	Under snow, care is needed on the ascent of Fuar Tholl's east ridge and the descent of its northwest spur, and more still on the ascent of Maol Chean-dearg described here, which becomes the grade I climb Hidden Gully. In winter conditions non-climbers should stick to Maol Chean-dearg's southeast ridge. In wet weather the safest way across the River Lair at the start of the walk may be via the railway bridge.
Summits	Fuar Tholl 907m ('cold hollow'); Sgorr Ruadh 962m ('red peak'); Beinn Liath Mhòr 926m ('big grey hill'); Maol Chean-dearg 933m ('bald red head')		
Maps	OS Landranger (1:50,000) 25; OS Explorer (1:25,000) 429		
Public transport	Start and finish at Achnashellach train station on the A890	**Short cuts**	Low cols make it easy to omit any particular hill. If Maol Chean-dearg seems a ridge too far (in winter, say), then the round of Coire Lair, taking in only its three neighbours, is a superb alternative.
By bike	Leave a bike at Coulags to ease the road stage back to Achnashellach		

Beinn Alligin (left) and Liathach (Walk 12) from Sgorr Ruadh

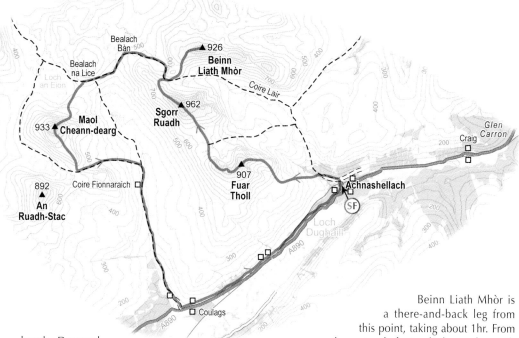

break. Descend over a slight saddle to the lower west top above the sinister tombstone of the Mainreachan Buttress, then loop around the incut corrie edge to reach the mountain's lowest top, Creag Mainnrichean. Here descend steeply NW, following an eroded path through broken crags and down scree onto the Bealach Mor, a maze of hummocks and pools. Cut across a stalker's path at right angles to reach the west end of Loch a' Bhealaich Mhoir.

Climb **Sgorr Ruadh** head on from here, linking grass between scree patches. After this sprawling southern flank the shapely summit comes as a welcome surprise, with a spacious prospect over Coire Fionnaraich to the primeval hulk of Maol Cheandearg; the line of ascent taken later in the day up a ramp/gully is clearly visible. In descent a path follows the well-defined northwest ridge before trending onto the west flank below the crest to reach a saddle that connects an unnamed top (spot height 785m) to the main mountain. Below is the bealach at the head of Coire Lair; a direct descent is all angular scree and awkward outcrops, so instead go N briefly before cutting E into the bealach. This is a major through-route across the range, with a stalker's path that offers a quick escape back to Achnashellach.

Beinn Liath Mhòr is a there-and-back leg from this point, taking about 1hr. From the east end of a tiny lochan a clear path starts towards the craggy knoll that overlooks the pass, then cuts right to skirt around it at mid-height, soon reaching another pool on the little col beyond. A well-trodden route now cuts straight up a cliff tier. Continue over a barren moonscape for the final pull up awkward quartzite screes to **Beinn Liath Mhòr's** summit, the high point of a long rubbly ridge.

Return to the bealach at the head of Coire Lair, where the old stalker's path will be met with relief. Follow this as it drops N into remote Coire Grannda (great views of the serrated Torridon skyline), then wiggles W around the northern toe of Sgorr Ruadh to the **Bealach Bàn**. At a path junction go left, downhill, cutting across the head of Coire Fionnaraich to a second junction. Here turn right for a short climb onto the **Bealach na Lice**.

Above, the looming north face of **Maol Cheandearg** seems to offer little to walkers. At a cairn on the high point of the bealach leave the path to climb over heather and rocks to a boggy levelling beneath the steep face. From here it is possible to outflank the crags by looping wide, either left onto the mountain's east spur or far to the right; both are long, complex detours. The painfully obvious alternative is a direct assault. From low on the left cut steeply right to gain a broad grassy ramp, and follow it diagonally

← *Mainreachan Buttress and Maol Chean-dearg from Fuar Tholl*

rightwards between cliffs. As it steepens the ramp funnels into a narrow gully, with grass replaced by loose scree. Care is required here, but the unpleasantness doesn't last long; scramblers may prefer to take a line just right of the gully bed. Emerge from the gully at a dip just under the mountain's summit, from where the perspective over island-studded Loch an Eion to Liathach is giddyingly bird's-eyed.

Descend SSE over the summit dome, a short steep boulder field leading to the easier-angled southeast ridge. Follow this broad crest over pale quartzite outcrops to reach another steepening above the Bealach a' Choire Ghairbh; this is best negotiated on the right, down a gravel scree like chips of builder's aggregate. At this stage in the proceedings the raw mass of An Ruadh-stac is unlikely to appeal, and at the bealach most will prefer to descend the stony stalker's path into Coire Fionnaraich instead. Continue down-glen past Clach nan Con-fionn, an upright rock to which mythical Fionn mac Cumhaill tied his hunting dogs, and then pass the **Coire Fionnaraich bothy**. A while later cross a footbridge over the Fionn-abhainn, continuing to the A890 at **Coulags**.

Return 5km
It's a pleasant (if long) road stroll back to **Achnashellach**.

Maol Chean-dearg (left) and Beinn Damh from Sgorr Ruadh

Circuit of Loch Monar

*T*he tourist-brochure tag 'Scotland's last wilderness' is commonly appended to Knoydart or the Fisherfield Forest, but they are not without rivals. Ironically such hype has helped turn these areas into hives of walking activity. For a refreshing contrast make a beeline to the expanse between glens Affric and Carron, the dark heart of the Highlands. Here sprawling strings of mountains wrap themselves around windswept lochs, and visitors are swallowed up by the land.

The Munros circling the head of remote Loch Monar are among the least accessible in the country, and each a stunner – plateau-topped, corrie-bitten Maoile Lunndaidh; the graceful crests of the Sgurr a' Chaorachain group; pointy Bidein a' Choire Sheasgaich; and knife-edged Lurg Mhòr, high above the ribbon-like loch. This walk combines the lot in a single epic trip, which can be undertaken either as an appealingly brutal one-day assault or a slower overnighter. The northerly approach to these hills is more common, but for those prepared to hitchhike or cycle this easterly alternative along beautiful Glen Strathfarrar makes a more aesthetic circuit, a high-level lap of Loch Monar that you'll long remember.

↑ *Heading east on the Lurg Mhòr ridge, with Loch Monar and the Strathfarrar hills beyond*   91

ROUTE INFORMATION

Start/finish   Cyclists should park at the end of the
public road in Struy (NH 395 405);
walk begins at the Loch Monar dam
(NH 203 394), 26km up-glen

Distance   43km (27 miles) (plus 52km cycle)

Ascent   2940m

Time   18hrs

Terrain   Tarmac, tracks, stalker's paths,
pathless bogs and stony ridges. The
scrambly ascent of Bidein a' Choire
Sheasgaich requires canny route
finding, while the traverse of Lurg
Mhòr's crest is an exciting scramble
(grade 1/2).

Summits   Maoile Lunndaidh 1007m ('bare/
bald hill of the wet place'); Sgurr
a' Chaorachain 1053m ('peak of
the rowan berries' or 'peak of the
torrents'); Sgurr Choinnich 999m
('bog peak' or 'mossy peak');
Beinn Tharsuinn 863m ('transverse
mountain'); Bidein a' Choire
Sheasgaich 945m ('pinnacle of the
corrie of farrow cattle'); Lurg Mhòr
986m ('big shin / long shank')

Maps   OS Landranger (1:50,000) 25; OS
Explorer (1:25,000) 429 & 430

Public transport   None for this circuit, although the
hills can alternatively be accessed
from Achnashellach train station in
Glen Carron

By bike   Those unable to cadge a lift to the
Monar dam are obliged to cycle Glen

Strathfarrar's 26km private road. On
the plus side it's tarmac all the way,
there are no nasty inclines, and the
surroundings are stunning.

Accommodation   BCC 'Loch Ness' Hostel, Glen
Urquhart (01456 476296); Cannich
Caravan and Camping Park (01456
415364)

Sleeping out   If the two-way cycle in Glen
Strathfarrar (see By bike, above) looks
a tall order in conjunction with the
walk, consider a pre-hike camp near
the Loch Monar dam; places are
plentiful for the discreet. Mid-walk
sites include the Bealach Bhearnais
and up on Beinn Tharsuinn. With a
detour, Bearnais bothy (NH 021 430)
could also be used.

Seasonal notes   Particularly serious and isolated
in winter. Snowbound ascents of
Sgurr a' Chaorachain and Bidein
a' Choire Sheasgaich require basic
mountaineering competence, while
the Lurg Mhòr ridge is an airy grade
I/II winter climb.

Short cuts   Maoile Lunndaidh can be omitted by
staying longer on the loch shore path

Note   Vehicle access on the private road
up Glen Strathfarrar is currently
restricted; details can be found on
www.mcofs.org.uk. There is no
overnight parking in the glen.

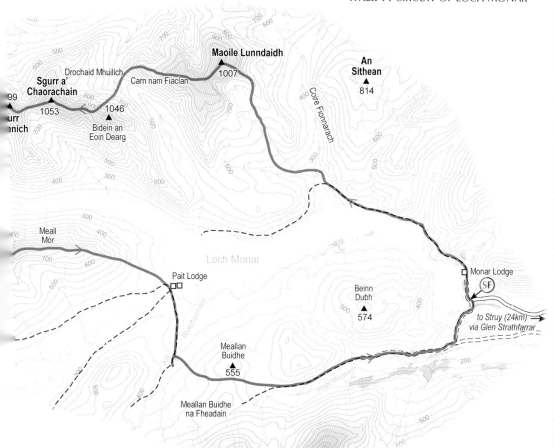

Approach 6km

From Loch Monar dam follow
the private track to **Monar Lodge**, where a footpath is signposted. After a brief climb cut left on a
path above the loch shore to go through a rocky
defile, then pass a wooded bay. Having crossed a
deep-cut burn on a wooden footbridge the path
follows the shoreline for nearly 3km, with further
bridged burns, to reach an inlet at the mouth of
Coire Fionnarach. Head inland on the east bank of
the burn, passing a sheep enclosure. At a junction of
burns hop across a line of stepping-stones.

On the hill 26km

Ascend an indistinct burn-side path towards Toll
a' Choin, and where the stream divides take the
right fork, walking up a little gorge into the corrie's
broad, boggy upper recesses. Here cut right onto
Maoile Lunndaidh's well-defined southeast ridge,
which leads to the tabletop summit. This extensive
plateau has been described as Cairngorm-like, and
with good reason. From the large summit cairn stride
WSW over a minor top at a narrow neck between

the mountain's impres-
sive deep-scooped cor-
ries, then bear roughly W along
the cliff edge to the cairn on **Carn nam
Fiaclan**. Continuing W, a stony descent leads onto
a level shoulder; from here follow the blunt spur
steeply down to **Drochaid Mhuilich**.

Above is the precipitous wall of the Sgurr a'
Chaorachain group, vaguely reminiscent of the north
side of Ben Cruachan. Three obvious ribs can be seen;
all are feasible, but the grassy middle rib is most convenient. Stay just right of the obvious burn-cutting,
where a sketchy path leads up through the knobbles,
trending right to scramble easily onto a short narrow
crest which tops out on the saddle between the ragged pyramid of Beinn an Eoin Deirg and unnamed
summit **1035m**. Stony slopes lead up the latter, for
the grassy continuation to **Sgurr a' Chaorachain**.
Descend the steep west ridge, then continue in similar vein up to the dramatic narrow summit crest of
Sgurr Choinnich. The west ridge of this hill offers
more of the same, leading steeply down to the
Bealach Crudhain, with a few scrambly moments.

93

The complex multi-summited Corbett **Beinn Tharsuinn** bars direct access to the final two Munros; it would be possible to avoid it by descending to the head of Loch Monar, but it is an attractive and natural part of the circuit. Ascent paths are indistinct, although the general gist is clear enough. Pass over several minor tops to reach the main summit, riven with little rock crevasses. The chiselled cone of Bidein a' Choire Sheasgaich ('Cheescake' to non-Gaels) looks awesome from here, perhaps even slightly unnerving for non-climbers. In descent pass just right of a lochan (idyllic camping), then bear W to a saddle. From here make a rough diagonal descent to the deeper col below the crags that seem to bar access to Cheesecake.

Care is needed in this next ascent. Step over the tumbledown wall on the col and pick up a worn path climbing through the lower outcrops, bearing right to reach the first major rock tier. This is breached via a dank groove, where care is needed with loose rock and soil. Above this, ascend to a broad terrace below the larger, more intimidating upper tier;

here cut back left and look out for a cairn marking the bottom of a grassy gully/rake, which slants up through the crags to offer a steep but non-scrambling ascent. Pleasant walking then leads through scattered outcrops, over a minor top and past a lochan before a final climb to **Sheasgaich's** airy summit – a stunning viewpoint.

Descend easily to the col below **Lurg Mhòr**. The ascent is steep and stony at first, then eases on a broad shoulder before the final pull to the summit cairn. Continuing E the mountain narrows suddenly to form a sharp and aesthetically stunning rock crest; the scramble along this is more dramatic than technically difficult, save a couple of awkward steps at about grade 2. From Lurg Mhòr's eastern top the **Meall Mòr** ridge continues E, now grassy underfoot but still with a bird's-eye view over Loch Monar. After nearly 2km of gentle descent the hillside steepens, leading down into the intractable bogland that cloaks Loch Monar's southern shore. Weave across this to **Pait Lodge**, perhaps the most isolated house in the country.

Coulin Forest (Walk 13) from Sgurr Choinnich

On Bidein a' Choire Sheasgaich, looking back at Beinn Tharsuinn (centre) and Sgurr Choinnich (right)

Return 11km

So far it has been superb hillwalking all the way; now for the payback. Pass left of the house and across the edge of the garden to pick up a gated track on the right. This heads S over the moor to meet the **Allt Riabhachain** then follows it for a little over 1km, passing a bier. Where a side-burn flows into the main channel leave the track, descend into the cutting and ford the main stream. The side-burn immediately divides; shadow the left branch uphill onto the peaty saddle between **Meallan Buidhe** and **Meallan Buidhe na Fheadain**, then descend E over challenging bogs to pick up a path with relief. This follows the **Uisge Misgeach** downstream for several kilometres, turning from trail to rough track and to full-on metalled road as height is gradually lost. Just under 2km beyond a small power station the tarmac road curves left at a track junction, climbing to **Loch Monar**. Cross the first dam, then follow the road around a headland to the second barrage. Those who cycled in now have a 26km ride back.

Loch Mullardoch hills

*T*he four Munros north of Loch Mullardoch are put together here to create a meaty ridge walk in spectacular surroundings. Sgurr na Lapaich and An Riabhachan are among the giants of the area – the 24th and 29th highest in Scotland respectively. Lapaich is a distinctive rugged peak; its neighbour a long drawn-out grassy ridge that's a joy to walk. The hills exude an air of isolation, and An Socach at the western end of the range is particularly notable for this.

But it wasn't always thus. The construction of a hydro-electric dam in the 1950s finished what the Clearances started centuries earlier, drowning old tracks and making a wilderness of the once populated upper reaches of Glen Cannich. Access remains challenging today, with the rough loch shore 'path' infamous for its tendency to disappear beneath the bracken – great fun at the end of a long day. Backpackers might consider combining these hills with those south of Loch Mullardoch (see Walk 16) in an extended circuit of the loch.

Approach 1.5km

From the house at the north end of the dam a track leads past a boathouse, then continues uphill of the loch with gentle – if muddy – ups and downs to reach a bridge over the **Allt Mullardoch**. Some might prefer to knock off the loch shore stage while still fresh, but an east–west traverse of the hills is arguably more aesthetic.

On the hill 19.5km

There are two obvious ways up the first Munro, **Carn nan Gobhar**. Either cross the bridge and ascend via the outlying summit Mullach na Maoile (not shown on the accompanying map), or take a rough path that follows the east side of the burn into Coire an t-Sith and from here bear NNE across the boggy upper corrie to a saddle east of Carn nan Gobhar,

↑ *An Riabhachan (left) and An Socach from Lurg Mhòr (Walk 14)*

ROUTE INFORMATION

Start/finish	Car park just before the north end of the Mullardoch dam (NH 222 316)		August) and reverse the hill route as described
Distance	29km (18 miles)	**Accommodation**	BCC 'Loch Ness' Hostel, Glen Urquhart (01456 476296); Cannich Caravan and Camping Park (01456 415364)
Ascent	1840m		
Time	10hrs		
Terrain	Lower ground is boggy and, in places, pathless; the long rough stretch on the north shore of Loch Mullardoch can be overgrown in summer and may feel irksome at the end of the day. The hills themselves offer generally easier going with occasional scrambly moments.	**Sleeping out**	Good camping by Loch Tuill Bhearnach under Sgurr na Lapaich, and at several points on the shore of Loch Mullardoch
		Seasonal notes	A big winter day, but feasible (conditions permitting) if the loch shore is walked in darkness. The east ridge of Sgurr na Lapaich and short stretches of ridge at either end of An Riabhachan may need modest mountaineering competence under snow. On the loch shore path note that fording the Allt Taige can prove tricky in a wet spell and might require an uphill detour.
Summits	Carn nan Gobhar 992m ('hill of the goats'); Sgurr na Lapaich 1150m ('peak of the bogland'); An Riabhachan 1129m ('the grey one'); An Socach 1069m ('the snout')		
Maps	OS Landranger (1:50,000) 25; OS Explorer (1:25,000) 430 and a snippet of 429	**Short cuts**	The western tops are easily omitted, particularly An Socach – descend the south ridge of Sgurr na Lapaich or the ridge running SE from An Riabhachan
Public transport	The closest bus stop is Cannich. To avoid the loch shore 'path' pre-book a private boat service (01456 415347) down Loch Mullardoch (available only April to early		

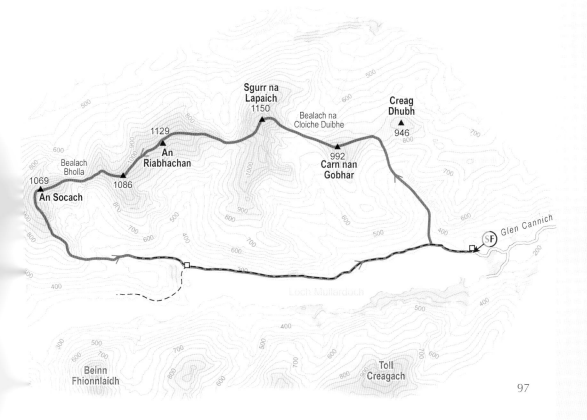

97

Sgurr na Lapaich from the east end of Loch Monar (Walk 14)

turning left here to reach the top. The mountain has twin summits, the bigger cairn sitting misleadingly on the lower. From here the rugged scale of Sgurr na Lapaich is impressive.

Descend a broad stony ridge to the Bealach na Cloiche Duibhe, and continue up **Lapaich's** east ridge, grassy at first and rougher as height is gained. A clear path stays just left of the true crest, weaving through the bouldery complexities of old land-slips with a minimum of scrambling; more hands-on entertainment can be found further right. The summit trig point is enclosed in a circular wind break; the view of An Riabhachan's craggy eastern end is spectacular.

Head roughly SW down grassy slopes, keeping safely left of the broken face overlooking Loch Mòr to reach a low bealach. Now a well-defined ridge runs along the top of Coire Gnada's crags, giving a long but enjoyable ascent to **An Riabhachan's** north-east top. A casual level stroll on springy moss leads over the fractionally higher central summit, then on along the grassy rooftop to the cairn on the minor summit at its far end (**spot height 1086m**).

Here the ridge cuts right, with a steep descent beside broken crags and then an airy but techni-cally straightforward crest. Climb a final minor top (spot height 1040m) – or skirt it on the right – then descend a final stretch of ridge, weaving through outcrops to gain the Bealach Bholla. Climb the attractive east ridge of **An Socach** to the sharp east top, from where an easier stroll gains the trig point on the true summit. A grassy ridge descends S at first and then SE, looping around the mountain's eastern corrie. Below the steep ground the path fades onto a boggy shoulder; cut E across peat hags in the mouth of Coire Mhaim to reach a wooden bridge over the burn draining the corrie. A quad bike track follows the north bank down to **Loch Mullardoch** at a pri-vate bothy on a bay.

Return 8km

Cross a bridge over the Allt Socrach to pick up the loch shore path. At first it's boggy and vague, but becomes better defined as it traverses a steep slope just above the bouldery tideline of the loch. The going is not gentle, and occasional erosion scars need a little care. When the slope eases the route becomes less distinct again, braiding into several cattle-trampled trails through thick bracken. The Allt Taige is met after nearly 5km; there's no bridge, and fording may be dicey in very wet conditions. A while later pass just above a small clump of pines, eventu-ally reaching the footbridge over the Allt Mullardoch and the track back to the **dam**.

Sgurr na Lapaich from the west end of Loch Mullardoch

Carn Eige,
Sgurr nan Ceathreamhnan
and more

*T*he 1100-ers Carn Eige, Màm Sodhail and Sgurr nan Ceathreamhnan tend to be climbed from Glen Affric, but this more exciting alternative starts at lonely Loch Mullardoch on the wilder north side of the hills, then makes a strenuous circuit of narrow ridges linking the six Munros (and several tops) that rim Gleann a' Choilich. For quality and challenge this long, logical round easily equals more famous bagging extravaganzas such as the South Glen Shiel Ridge (Walk 19), yet its remoteness suggests a degree of solitude unthinkable in Glen Shiel. These are the highest peaks north of the Great Glen, with a great sense of spacious scale. The walk is best treated as a mini-expedition, starting with either a waterborne approach or a testing loch shore hike along the considerable length of Loch Mullardoch and a wild camp at its isolated head.

↑ *Mullach na Dheiragain (centre), Carn Eighe and Màm Sodhail (right), and the distant north Loch Mullardoch hills (Walk 15) from Sgurr nan Ceathreamhnan's northeast ridge*

Start/finish	Car park either end of the Mullardoch dam (NH 222 316) or (NH 223 310); in either case boats will have to be carried some distance to the shore	**By boat**	The amphibious assault is the best way to approach this walk (non-paddlers see Public transport, above). There are no tides to worry about, of course, but the full length of Loch Mullardoch is a respectable paddle nonetheless, and strong westerly or easterly winds build up impressive waves on this 13km stretch of water. Less confident teams should save it for a settled spell.
Distance	46km (28 miles) if you approach by boat or 54km (34 miles) all on foot		
Ascent	2220m		
Time	16hrs (on foot and by boat); best over 2 days	**By bike**	No scope for cycling on the walk described, but coming in from the west along Glen Elchaig would get mountain bikers as close as Iron Lodge, 6km on foot from Gleann a' Choilich
Terrain	Approach is either by boat along the full length of Loch Mullardoch or a rough and even longer walk on the north shore. The hill stage starts with a river crossing that needs care in spate. Ascent of Beinn Fhionnlaidh is steep, rough and pathless, as is descent from Mullach Sithidh; the rest of the circuit is on clear paths.		
		Accommodation	Alltbeithe (Glen Affric) YH (0845 293 7373) is close geographically, but not well placed for this particular round; alternatively, BCC 'Loch Ness' Hostel, Glen Urquhart (01456 476296) and Cannich Caravan and Camping Park (01456 415364)
Summits	Beinn Fhionnlaidh 1005m ('Finlay's hill'); Carn Eige 1183m ('file hill'); Màm Sodhail 1181m ('rounded, breast-shaped hill of the barns'); An Socach 921m ('the snout'); Sgurr nan Ceathreamhnan 1143m ('peak of the quarters'); Mullach na Dheiragain 982m ('summit of the kestrels')		
		Sleeping out	Camp by an inlet near the west end of Loch Mullardoch, in the mouth of Gleann a' Choilich
Maps	OS Landranger (1:50,000) 25; OS Explorer (1:25,000) 414 covers the hills, but only the western half of Loch Mullardoch, as does Harvey British Mountain Map (1:40,000) Knoydart, Kintail and Glen Affric	**Seasonal notes**	These are the highest hills north of the Great Glen. In snow the full circuit of Gleann a' Choilich is a major undertaking. The northeast ridge of Sgurr nan Ceathreamhnan approaches a grade I climb in full winter conditions, although the difficulties are brief. Snowfields and cornices may last into early summer.
Public transport	The closest bus stop is either Cannich or the Cluanie Inn in Glen Shiel. Non-kayakers might like to pre-book a private boat service (01456 415347) down Loch Mullardoch (available only April to early August).		
		Short cuts	Path from Bealach Coire Ghàidheil into Gleann a' Choilich is a useful midway circuit breaker

Approach

Walk (17km)

Follow a rough and occasionally indistinct path on the north shore of **Loch Mullardoch**, initially as per Walk 15. From the private bothy in the mouth of Coire Mhaim cross the burn and climb onto a headland above the narrows in the loch before descending past a gaunt ruin to regain the shore. Continue to a trail junction 1km beyond the head of the loch. Turn S here to ford the river in the boggy glen floor; if this seems unwise then a footbridge may be found about 1km further upstream (not marked on OS Landranger map; OS Explorer map and Harvey Mountain Map differ as to the details). Head back E towards the loch. A quad bike track runs above the loch before curving into **Gleann a' Choilich**, but no map shows it. The best camping is downhill of this by the shore, near the outflow of the Abhainn a' Choilich.

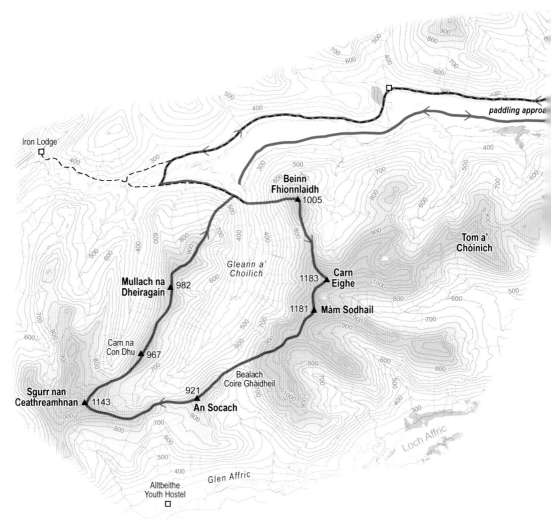

Iron Lodge

paddling approa

Beinn
Fhionnlaidh
1005

Tom a'
Chòinich

Gleann a'
Choilich

Mullach na
Dheiragain 982

1183 Carn
Eighe

1181 Màm Sodhail

Carn na
Con Dhu 967

Bealach
Coire Ghàidheil

Sgurr nan
Ceathreamhnan 1143

921

An Socach

Loch Affric

Glen Affric

Alltbeithe
Youth Hostel

Paddle (13km)

Hemmed in by high mountains, the fjord-like expanse of **Loch Mullardoch** is an inspiring place to paddle – and there's rarely anyone else on the water. Allow several hours to reach the far end of the loch. Although straightforward in calm conditions, surprisingly large waves can build up in windy weather, and powerful downdraughts gust off the slopes. With its stands of Scots pine the south shore is initially more scenic, but beyond the obvious narrows the surroundings become bleaker. Make landfall in the bay at the mouth of **Gleann a' Choilich**, just west of the river outflow.

On the hill 20km

Follow the unmapped track into **Gleann a' Choilich** and ford the river where the track does (watch out if it's in spate). Now make a merciless head-on assault of the steep, pathless west flank of **Beinn Fhionnlaidh**. It's a brutal start to the day, but at least height is gained quickly. From the summit cairn a clear path runs down to grassy Bealach Beag and on up the curving, stony north ridge of **Carn Eige**. This is the highest peak north of the Great Glen, and its northeast face has an Alpine look under snow. A quick descent and reascent then gains the top of neighbouring giant **Màm Sodhail**, the final climb needing a bit of care in icy snow. The massive circular drystone cairn on top dates from Ordnance Survey mapping in the 19th century.

Drop easily SW, passing the ruins of an old hut and then following a broad stony ridge over two unnamed minor summits. A flanking path can be found some way down on the right, but it's nicer to stay on top to pass the cairn on the second peak. Before reaching summit 1068m peel off right, descending about 50m to pick up the path, which makes a descending traverse onto the **Bealach Coire Ghàidheil** (a direct line from 1068m to the pass runs into unpleasantly craggy ground). The bealach is a useful cross-country hiker's through-route from Glen Affric to Loch Mullardoch, and offers escape options both north and south.

Next comes twin-peaked **An Socach**, a little hill with plenty of craggy charm. Although it only just scrapes Munro height, it is flanked at either end by low cols and exacts more effort than expected; the second summit is the higher. In atrocious weather the next bealach also offers get-out options – an easy path heads south to Alltbeithe Youth Hostel in the roadless upper reaches of Glen Affric; going north, steep craggy ground leads quickly into Gleann a' Choilich. A rough, steep ascent over Stob Coire na Cloiche (a minor summit, unnamed on Landranger map) gains the long east ridge of **Sgurr nan Ceathreamhnan**. This is the third of the day's trio of biggies, a complex and beautiful mountain with an enticing tapered profile when seen from this angle. The long knobbly ridge starts gently, but steepens considerably for the final summit slog.

Beinn Fhionnlaidh (right) and the north Loch Mullardoch hills (Walk 15) from Mullach Sithidh

From the cairn on the high point descend the narrow northeast ridge. This is pleasantly airy, and needs thought under snow. The next col, Bealach nan Daoine (unnamed on Landranger map), provides another get-out option – but it's worth persevering on the clear path along the rugged ridge for some of the day's best views. Beyond **Carn na Con Dhu** the crest narrows briefly before the easy pull up to **Mullach na Dheiragain**, the sixth Munro of the day (in case you're counting) and, arguably, the least accessible 3000-er in the area. A narrow col links this with the final summit, Mullach Sithidh, from where the entire Gleann a' Choilich round is visible in an undulating arc.

Bear right from here to minor top 933m, then follow the line of least resistance downhill, heading roughly NNE and staying slightly further left than intuition suggests to avoid craggy ground lower down. The rough, sponge-like slopes lead quickly back to the shore of **Loch Mullardoch**.

Return 13–17km

It's back the way you came – either on foot or by boat.

The north Loch Mullardoch hills (Walk 15) from a camp near the head of the loch

On the east ridge of Sgurr nan Ceathreamhnan

Cluanie Horseshoe
from Glen Affric

*L*ike its northern neighbours Glen Strathfarrar and Glen Cannich, Glen Affric slices the mountain grain of Scotland, forming an idyllic through-route from the agricultural east to the wild west – forested, loch-filled and flanked by majestic high hills. Affric's extensive native pine woods are particularly notable, and ongoing reforestation should help secure their long-term future. South of the glen rises a great semicircle of peaks, including 1100-ers Mullach Fraoch-choire, A' Chràlaig and Sgurr nan Conbhairean.

A classic ridge walk with some optional scrambling, the so-called Cluanie Horseshoe is generally tackled from the more convenient south (Loch Cluanie) side, but while it's a shorter day this entails some messy backtracking and can hardly be described as a horseshoe at all. This northern variant is truer to the lay of the land, and the long approach up Glen Affric is more a treat than a chore.

↑ *Distant Cluanie Horseshoe from Mullach na Dheiragain (Walk 16); left to right –* 105
Sail Chaorainn, Sgurr nan Conbhairean and Mullach Fraoch-choire

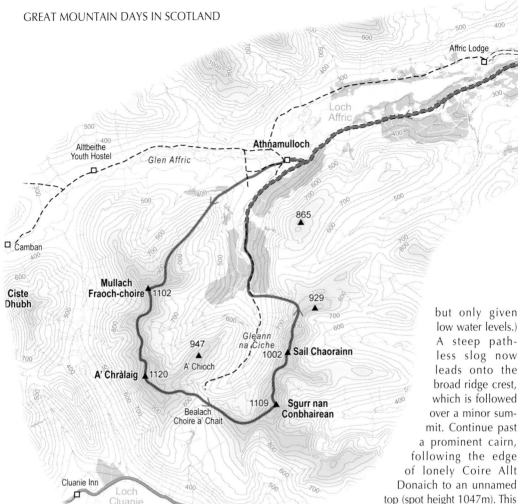

but only given low water levels.) A steep pathless slog now leads onto the broad ridge crest, which is followed over a minor summit. Continue past a prominent cairn, following the edge of lonely Coire Allt Donaich to an unnamed top (spot height 1047m). This is connected to the parent mountain by a narrow arête – fun but technically straightforward. A cairn marks the summit of **Mullach Fraoch-choire**, an airy perch with superb views over Glen Affric.

Descend the south ridge, where the sharp crest breaks into a row of little rocky towers. Climbed head on these provide brief but exciting scrambling; some might prefer the well-used path weaving between the towers. The ground soon eases as the ridge swings right, dropping to a low point before rising again to the minor top of Stob Coire na Cràlaig. A steady and largely grassy climb now leads up the long north ridge of **A' Chràlaig**, a bulky mountain with an unusually large summit cairn.

Follow the southeast ridge in descent, which soon levels off. Pass the top of a vague spur that leads to the satellite peak of **A' Chioch**, and continue for a few hundred metres to the point at which the hillside steepens and the main path drops S towards Loch Cluanie. Here cut east to follow a fainter path

Approach 7km

Just beyond the car park take the left branch of the track to cross a bridge over the river. The track now undulates gently through the woods on the south side of **Loch Affric** for several kilometres. By the River Affric, just beyond the head of the loch, the track forks. Take the right branch, passing the private house at **Athnamulloch**, then crossing a grassy meadow to go over a footbridge on the Allt na Ciche.

On the hill 15km

Pick your own line through boggy hummocks in the mouth of Gleann na Ciche, heading towards the foot of the northeast ridge of Mullach Fraoch-choire. Bear left to skirt left of a fenced forest enclosure that straddles the foot of the ridge. (This point could be reached more directly by staying longer on the Gleann na Ciche track before fording the burn,

ROUTE INFORMATION

Start/finish	Car park at the end of the Glen Affric road (NH 201 233)
Distance	32km (20 miles)
Ascent	1990m
Time	11hrs
Terrain	Forestry track in the glen and clear paths on the crests, but the initial ascent and final descent from the hills are steep and pathless. In summer the grade 1 scrambling on Mullach Fraoch-choire's south ridge can be avoided on an obvious path.
Summits	Mullach Fraoch-choire 1102m ('summit of the heathery corrie'); A' Chràlaig 1120m ('the basket/creel'); Sgurr nan Conbhairean 1109m ('peak of the keepers of hounds'); Sail Chaorainn 1002m ('heel of the rowan')
Maps	Inconveniently, OS Landrangers (1:50,000) 25, 33 & 34; OS Explorer (1:25,000) 414 & 415; Harvey British Mountain Map (1:40,000) Knoydart, Kintail and Glen Affric
Public transport	Bus to Cannich, then hitchhike
By boat	Put in near the car park, and Loch Affric would make a lovely waterborne approach
By bike	At least 2hrs of walking can be saved by cycling from the start to Athnamulloch; the stony track is best suited to bikes with front suspension

Accommodation	Bothy-like Alltbeithe YH (0845 293 7373) is an ideal base, although a long walk or cycle from the nearest road; alternatively, BCC 'Loch Ness' Hostel, Glen Urquhart (01456 476296) and Cannich Caravan and Camping Park (01456 415364)
Sleeping out	Camban bothy (NH 053 183) is a free alternative to Alltbeithe YH, although not perfectly placed for this walk. Camping at the head of Loch Affric is also worth considering.
Seasonal notes	Big but feasible in a single winter day, since the low-level sections are straightforward in darkness. Although technical difficulties are limited elsewhere on the circuit, Mullach Fraoch-choire needs some mountaineering competence in winter conditions – initially the northeast ridge and more so the pinnacled south ridge, which becomes a grade I winter climb. Note that the path flanking the pinnacles may be obscured by snow. In icy or iffy snow the steep final descent into Gleann na Ciche described here may be best avoided, in which case Glen Affric can be reached via Carn a' Choire Ghairbh.
Short cuts	Stalker's path from the Bealach Choire a' Chait is a useful mid-circuit escape route into Gleann na Ciche

↑ Looking towards Glen Affric from Carn na Coire Mheadhoin

down a defined spur. A tiny lochan is passed, then the ground becomes more complex and craggy on the final descent into the boulder-scattered **Bealach Choire a' Chait**.

Climb the steep, rocky ridge backing the hanging corrie of Toll Easach. Higher up this narrows into a sharp crest leading over the minor summit of Drochaid an Tuill Easaich – airy, but with no real scrambling. A final steady climb now gains the top of **Sgurr nan Conbhairean** and a strange cairn/windbreak that looks almost like a prehistoric burial mound. The outlook over the yawning eastern corrie is inspiring; it's a shame that this once isolated spot has seen recent track construction.

Descend roughly N along the corrie rim for the surprisingly gentle reascent onto the broad main summit of **Sail Chaorainn**. Of this Munro's two tops, the slightly lower northern summit, Carn na Coire Mheadhoin, is more dramatic, with better views. From this second top follow stony ground NNE and then N onto a saddle. Now descend roughly NW across an open slope to pick up a vague spur bounding the south side of a branched ravine. Initially rough and steep, the slope gradually relents, leading onto the soggy floor of **Gleann na Ciche**.

Return 10km

Pick up a track, in places boggy, following the river downstream through scattered woods into **Glen Affric** proper. Return the way you came.

Carn na Coire Mheadhoin and Sail Chaorainn from Gleann na Ciche

Beinn Fhada, The Brothers and the Five Sisters

With its charismatic summits and airy crests Kintail is the capital of West Highland ridge walking, and this is arguably its finest route. While the hill groups visited here can each be done separately, combining them in a single extended circuit gives ambitious walkers a logical and comprehensive tour through this grand area. The walk encompasses many varied peaks – sprawling Beinn Fhada; sharp, grassy Ciste Dhubh; the famously bonny Five Sisters; and their ruggedly handsome near neighbours The Brothers (aka North Glenshiel Ridge). Rough ground and daunting ascent/descent stats are compensated for by views that vary from tree-lined tidal Loch Duich to the empty acres at the remote head of Glen Affric. Light-and-fast fans might attempt a one-day challenge; the less fleet-footed have the choice of the mid-route Camban bothy or nearby rustic youth hostel (Alltbeithe).

Approach 1km

Take the road E past an outdoor centre, then cross a bridge over the River Croe. Follow a signed trail for the Falls of Glomach, go straight on past a house and then right towards the mouth of Gleann Chòinneachain.

On the hill 32.5km

On reaching a deer fence, instead of passing through the gate turn right, following the fence uphill to escape the enclosure via another gate in its top left corner. Now climb steeply onto the peaty shoulder of **Beinn Bhuidhe**. The knobbly ground ahead is the

↑ Sgurr nan Saighead from Sgurr Fhuaran

ROUTE INFORMATION

Start/finish	NTS centre in Morvich (NG 960 210)
Distance	35km (22 miles)
Ascent	3870m
Time	18hrs (2 days for most)
Terrain	Narrow ridges with occasional very easy scrambling (grade 1) and many steep inclines. Clear paths on The Brothers and Sisters, but fainter trails (at best) on Beinn Fhada's northwest ridge, in descent from Beinn Fhada to Camban, on the north slope of Ciste Dhubh and from the Bealach a' Chòinich to Sgurr an Fhuarail. Crossing the Allt Cam-bàn may need care in wet spells.
Summits	Beinn Fhada (aka Ben Attow) 1032m ('long hill'); Ciste Dhubh 979m ('black chest/coffin'); Aonach Meadhoin 1001m ('middle ridge'); Sgurr a' Bhealaich Dheirg 1036m ('peak of the red pass'); Sàileag 956m ('little heel'); Sgurr nan Spainteach 990m ('Spaniards' peak'); Sgurr na Ciste Duibhe 1027m ('peak of the black chest/coffin'); Sgurr na Carnach 1002m ('rocky peak'); Sgurr Fhuaran 1067m ('peak of springs'); Sgurr nan Saighead 929m ('arrows peak')
Maps	OS Landranger (1:50,000) 33; OS Explorer (1:25,000) 414; Harvey British Mountain Map (1:40,000) Knoydart, Kintail and Glen Affric

Public transport	Buses from Fort William to Portree stop at Shiel Bridge on request
Accommodation	Remote Alltbeithe YH (Glen Affric) (0845 293 7373) is an alternative mid-route stopover to Camban bothy, although not open year-round; Ratagan YH (01599 511243); Cluanie Inn (01320 340238); Kintail Lodge Hotel bunkhouse (01599 511275); Callaird B&B Inverinate (01599 511450); campsite in Shiel Bridge
Sleeping out	Recently refurbished, Camban bothy (NH 053 183) is well placed between Beinn Fhada and Ciste Dubh. The Bealach a' Chòinich provides camping at the halfway point of the walk, although boggy.
Seasonal notes	In full winter conditions this would require a minimum of 2 days. Under snow the ridges prove exciting, although any technicalities will be brief. The grassy slopes encountered either side of Fionngleann might sometimes pose an avalanche risk.
Short cuts	Avoid Ciste Dhubh and Aonach Meadhoin by ascending northeast ridge of Sgurr a' Bhealaich Dheirg direct from Camban. The path in Gleann Lichd allows Beinn Fhada and The Brothers/Sisters to be tackled on separate trips.

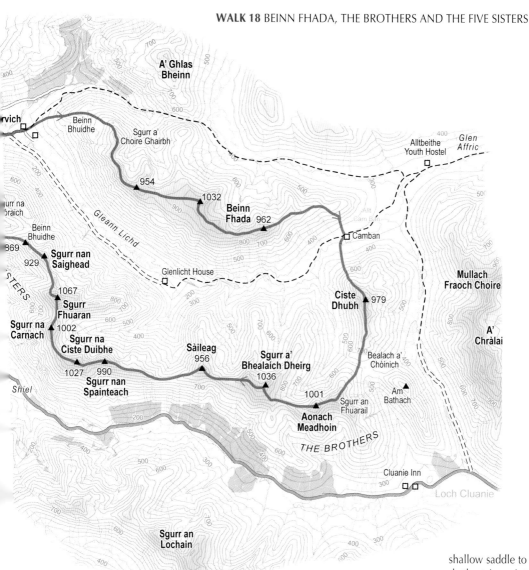

shallow saddle to
reach the trig point
on the mountain's high point;
although Beinn Fhada is of similar size and complexity to the nearby Five Sisters, it has been granted only this single Munro to their three. Continue S around the corrie edge, then follow the mountain's grassy east ridge, with an outlook along wild upper Glen Affric. Stay with the crest until the col just before point 647m (not marked on Landranger map), then cut S down a steep, pathless and tussocky slope. Gates give access to and escape from a fenced area of regenerating woodland, below which is the main path along Fionngleann and **Camban bothy** (Alltbeithe Youth Hostel is 30mins down-glen).

Continue S, crossing the Allt Cam-bàn at broad stony shallows. Now attack the northwest slope of **Ciste Dhubh** head on, a relentless slog up very steep

northwest ridge of
Beinn Fhada, the most atmospheric way up this grand mountain. Bear right to tackle the ridge in an ascending series of rocky steps – a path materialises as height is gained, weaving through the rocks. Follow the skyline over several lumps above impressive cliffs to **Sgurr a' Choire Ghairbh**, from where there's a short sharp downclimb on slabby rock (grade 1 scrambling) into a pronounced bealach. The ridge then continues in fine style over more minor peaks to terminate at Meall an Fhuarain Mhòir (cairn).

Here the hill suddenly broadens into **Fhada's** distinctive summit plateau, the grassy expanse of the Plaide Mhòr. A clear path leads E over a

111

On Beinn Fhada's long northwest ridge

grass – a prominent stream bed gives a good line. Beyond a level area is the summit, with its little cairn poised on the lip of sharp cliffs. The wedge-shaped character of the hill now becomes apparent; a clear path follows the narrow crest running S over the first minor summit before skirting right of the second and descending quite steeply onto the broad **Bealach a' Chòinich** ('pass of the bog' – appropriate).

The ascent of **Sgurr an Fhuarail** is initially steep, pathless and grassy; when rocks appear, so does a path, leading to the cairn at the apex of three ridges. Follow the west ridge over a little col to the flat summit of **Aonach Meadhoin**, easternmost Munro of The Brothers. Continuing W from here there is a short burst of scrambling on a rock arête (grade 1 – avoidable to the left), then a long, mainly grassy descent to a bealach before the plod up to **Sgurr a Bhealaich Dheirg**. The substantial summit cairn is set a little NE of the main ridge. An easy level stride now leads to spot height 1014m, topped by a cairn. This marks the start of a long rough descent over two minor summits, with some scrappy scrambling (mostly avoidable). Beyond a col at 872m the ridge rises to **Sàileag**, where an alluring view opens west to the Five Sisters.

Descend W to the Bealach an Làpain, low point of the entire ridge (with a handy escape option south to the Glen Shiel road). From here the continuation to **Sgurr nan Spainteach** is a long interesting climb over a rising series of false summits. Rocky ground then leads to a difficult step, a short steep descent of a buttress (grade 1). Once this is safely negotiated the path skirts an odd scree-filled trough to zigzag up stony slopes and heaped boulders onto the top of **Sgurr na Ciste Duibhe**, first of the famous 'Sisters'.

A rubbly descent and leg-sapping reascent gains **Sgurr na Carnach** ('peak of the stony place' – another fitting name). Now heading N, there's more of the same steep rocky ground dropping into Bealach na Carnach and on up the graceful peak of **Sgurr Fhuaran**, biggest of the Sisters and the highest

point on the walk. A direct descent N from here leads onto unpleasant scree, so it's best to start down the mountain's WNW ridge, from where an obvious path soon cuts right to gain the north ridge below the nasty stuff. The crest then curves left into the Bealach Buidhe. Above looms **Sgurr nan Saighead**; ignoring the flanking path on the left, follow the rim of the imposing cliffs onto the summit of the fourth Sister. By now less stoical walkers might be beginning to wish that the parents had been less prolific.

A pleasant ridge curves around cliff-walled Coire na h-Uaighe to **Beinn Bhuidhe**. This attractive minor top has been shunned, Cinderella-like, by the family, the title of fifth Sister going instead to the outlying and comparatively underwhelming lump of **Sgurr na Mòraich**; only the very keen will go all that way. For the rest, a path leads easily down Beinn Bhuidhe's west ridge, soon bearing slightly right to descend a muddy slope beside a little burn to meet the Allt a'Chruinn. Cross the stream to pick up a well-constructed trail along the right bank, passing a gorge to descend quite steeply to the roadside.

Return 1.5km

It's a short road walk back to the car park.

Sgurr nan Saighead (left), Sgurr Fhuaran and Sgurr na Carnach from Beinn Buidhe   113

South Glen Shiel Ridge to The Saddle

*T*he southern rim of Glen Shiel forms a single long rampart, scored with corries and crowned with a row of elegant peaks linked by curvy grass crests. Even in an area renowned for this sort of thing, the South Glen Shiel Ridge is an outstanding route – airy but never difficult, and with comparatively modest ups and downs between its seven adjacent Munros.

While many hillwalkers will quite legitimately be content with the seven, a more satisfying challenge incorporates their western neighbours too. This extended traverse leads over a neglected Corbett and the rugged Munro of Sgurr na Sgine to a grand climax on the rock peak of The Saddle, where an optional scramble keeps walkers on their toes till the end. Starting in the higher east saves some uphill struggle, but leaves the hardest ground for last. Bear in mind, too, that returning to the start point of this linear walk requires a bike, a bus, two cars or a thumb.

Approach 3km

Briefly walk east along the **A87**, then take a track on the right to cross a concrete bridge over the River Cluanie. Having passed a turnoff to **Cluanie Lodge**, this old tarmac road takes a circuitous course around the base of the hills, eventually leading to a path up Creag a' Mhàim's southeast spur.

But if you're impatient to get on to the hill, you can leave it sooner, at a bridge over the Allt Giubhais.

↑ *The Saddle, Glen Shiel and Loch Duich from Creag nan Damh*

Start	Car park by the Cluanie Inn (NH 075 117)	**By bike**	A pre-stashed bike can considerably aid post-ridge car-retrieval logistics
Finish	A87 between Cluanie Inn and Shiel Bridge (NG 968 143)	**Accommodation**	Ratagan YH (01599 511243); Cluanie Inn (01320 340238); Kintail Lodge Hotel bunkhouse (01599 511275); Callaird B&B Inverinate (01599 511450); campsite in Shiel Bridge
Distance	31km (19 miles)		
Ascent	2660m		
Time	15hrs	**Sleeping out**	Numerous grassy cols for a mid-route camp or bivvy
Terrain	The South Glen Shiel Ridge is characterised by clear paths on narrow grassy ridges, with occasional very light scrambling. Further west the ground tends to be rougher, with optional exciting scrambles on the Northeast Ridge of Sgurr na Sgine (grade 1) and the Forcan Ridge of The Saddle (grade 2).	**Seasonal notes**	In winter conditions this is likely to be a two-day trip or two separate day trips – see Short cuts, below. The west ridge of Aonach air Chrith has a mountaineering ambience under snow, but more notable are the Northeast Ridge of Sgurr na Sgine (grade I/II) and the Forcan Ridge of The Saddle (grade II), both serious climbs with an Alpine character. These are easily avoided, and non-climbers should definitely do so.
Summits	Creag a' Mhàim 947m ('rock of the large rounded hill'); Druim Shionnach 987m ('ridge of foxes'); Aonach air Chrith 1021m ('ridge of trembling'); Maol Chinn-dearg 981m ('bald red head'); Sgurr an Doire Leathain 1010m ('peak of the broad thicket'); Sgurr an Lochain 1004m ('peak of the little loch'); Creag nan Damh 918m ('rock of the stags'); Sgurr a' Bhac Chaolais 885m ('peak of the hollow of the narrows'); Sgurr na Sgine 946m ('peak of the knife'); The Saddle 1010m	**Short cuts**	The walk can be curtailed at several cols, in particular the popular get-out option of the Bealach Duibh Leac that divides the 'South Glenshiel seven' from the tough westward extension over Sgurr na Sgine and The Saddle. Subsidiary ridges also permit rapid descents to Glen Shiel from many summits, for instance Maol Chinn-dearg, Sgurr an Doire Leathain, Creag nan Damh and Sgurr na Sgine/Faochag
Maps	OS Landranger (1:50,000) 33; OS Explorer (1:25,000) 414; Harvey British Mountain Map (1:40,000) Knoydart, Kintail and Glen Affric		
Public transport	Feasible without a car; buses from Fort William to Portree pass through Glen Shiel and will stop at the Cluanie Inn on request		

On the hill 28km

Where the burn splits follow its left branch, passing around a fenced enclosure then continuing up into Coirean an Eich Bhric to climb the short north ridge of **Creag a' Mhàim**. The summit cairn marks the end of the day's biggest single ascent. Descend gently from Creag a' Mhàim, then climb the grassy ridge onto **Druim Shionnach**, Munro number two. The views of the Five Sisters and Gleouraich are superb; on a clear day Ben Nevis and the Cuillin are both visible. The ridge now broadens for a while, with easy walking over minor bumps before the pull onto

Aonach Air Chrith, the most rugged and interesting peak of this eastern group. From the summit a short scrambling detour can be made along the airy north ridge to a sharp mini-peak; for future reference, this ridge is the best way to climb the hill in isolation. Continuing W the main crest narrows airily, with some basic scrambling as it descends around the rim of craggy Coire nan Eirecheanach. After a low point of 855m the knobbly ridge leads onto the broad summit of **Maol Chinn-dearg**.

En route to the next little col a minor top is most commonly bypassed on the south flank. From

115

Gleouraich (right) and Spidean Mialach from Maol Chinn-dearg

the col, 1km of fairly gentle ascent leads to **Sgurr an Doire Leathain**, along a curving ridge marked by a line of sawn-off fence posts. The high point of Munro number five is a little way north of the main ridge line. An abrupt descent is then followed by a slog to the dramatic coned summit of **Sgurr an Lochain**, with a little very basic scrambling on the way. Descend W, then follow a contouring path on the south flank of Sgurr Beag to reach the Bealach Fraoch Choire. It's a fairly short climb now onto the broad top of **Creag nan Damh**, last of the South Glen Shiel Munros.

A path now descends into a little notch, then follows a ruined drystone wall down the knobbly west ridge to the **Bealach Duibh Leac** (see Short cuts, above). The wall continues up the rough east ridge of **Sgurr a' Bhac Chaolais** and on down the far side; in descent a short steep crag and scree slope are negotiated before the easy ground of the Bealach an Toiteil. The rock-ribbed gable end of **Sgurr na Sgine** rears dead ahead. Direct assault is unlikely, so either cut W, as indicated by another stretch of wall, to gain the straightforward ascent route of the south-west spur, or climb diagonally right up rough slopes below the crags onto the narrow northeast ridge, an enjoyable and little used scramble (grade 1 by the easiest variations).

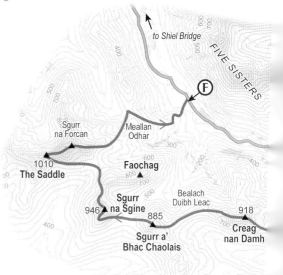

From the main summit head to the lower northwest top, then descend N onto a saddle. Continue along the ridge, climbing slightly onto a minor rise (spot height 880m on some maps). Here look out for a cairn on the left, marking the eroded descent path to the Bealach Coire Mhàlagain. Ahead is **The Saddle**, with the spined dragon's back of the Forcan Ridge seen in profile. Start towards the distinctive rock peak of **Sgurr na Forcan** to pick up a well-trodden path that slants left on a rising traverse below the crags. An old drystone wall shows the best way across a scree patch for the final steep zigzags onto the mountain's grassy summit area; the trig point is just to the N.

There are now three choices. First, as a final flourish those with spare energy can make a direct descent of the famous Forcan Ridge. Sticking to the airy crest gives an excellent grade 2 scramble on sound blocky rock, most problems being open to variation. In this direction the renowned bad step onto the sharp summit of Sgurr na Forcan is actually done in ascent and proves reasonably easy, although eroded gullies on either side of it are easier still. Secondly, as an alternative, less confident scramblers can follow an obvious lower path that avoids the chief difficulties of the crest. Thirdly, to miss out all scrambling reverse

Sgurr a' Bhac Chaolais (left) and Sgurr na Sgine from the Bealach Duibh Leac

your route of ascent to the Bealach Coire Mhàlagain and follow a contouring path under the crags of the ridge.

All variations rejoin at a grassy shoulder at the eastern foot of the ridge. From here a clear path descends NNE across the flank of **Meallan Odhar** onto the Bealach na Craoibhe, then cuts back right to drop in a series of zigzags to the **A87** in the floor of Glen Shiel.

Ladhar Bheinn and Loch Hourn

Spearing a kilometre high from a pristine shore, the mainland's most westerly Munro is a real show-stopper. Its graceful lines, its ruggedly inaccessible location in the fabled Knoydart peninsula, and the expansive summit views over jostling ranges and fjord-like sea lochs all combine to give Ladhar Bheinn a rare charisma. With several radiating ridges this complex mountain can be approached from a variety of angles, and arguably the conventional route described here from Kinloch Hourn is the best of the bunch.

This is one of the great wild walks of the British Isles, stride-stoppingly beautiful every step of the way. Snaking along glass-clear Loch Hourn through groves of native Scots pine, the approach route is a hard act to follow. But the hill stage tops even this – a strenuous scrambly circuit over the rocky ridges and chiselled peaks that encircle cavernous Coire Dhorrcail. While it's possible to pull off in a single hurried day, Knoydart deserves better. Staying a night at Barrisdale permits a more leisurely pace.

Approach 10km

Even reaching Kinloch Hourn is an adventure, 35km of wiggly single-track road from the A87, passing through big country. Park on the left (small fee), then continue along the road on foot. This soon dwindles into a footpath, solidly built above the rocky shore of Loch Hourn. It is level going as far as the isolated cottage at **Skiary**, beyond which is the first of

↑ *Ladhar Bheinn from Barrisdale Bay, early morning*

ROUTE INFORMATION

Start/finish	Car park at Kinloch Hourn (NG 950 066)
Distance	33km (20½ miles)
Ascent	2030m
Time	13hrs
Terrain	The Loch Hourn path is rough and wet in places. The circuit of Coire Dhorrcail is well-trodden ground, although steep and very rocky at times. A short but fairly serious grade 1 scramble leads up the prow of Stob a' Chearcaill (optional), and other brief scrambly moments crop up elsewhere.
Summits	Ladhar Bheinn 1020m ('hoof mountain')
Maps	OS Landranger (1:50,000) 33; OS Explorer (1:25,000) 413; Harvey British Mountain Map (1:40,000) Knoydart, Kintail and Affric
Public transport	No public transport anywhere near Kinloch Hourn. Although it would be a shame to miss the shoreline path, a private boat service can be booked, picking up at Kinloch Hourn or Arnisdale and dropping off at Barrisdale (see www.arnisdaleferry. com). Rail travellers can reach Knoydart via a train to Mallaig, from where regular boats run to Inverie, the peninsula's only village – about 12km on foot from Barrisdale.
By boat	The kayak trip from Kinloch Hourn to Barrisdale is as beautiful as the famous shoreline path. The narrow upper loch is often sheltered from the worst of the weather, but there's a powerful tidal flow at the narrows of Caolas Mor. It's easiest to paddle W on an outgoing tide, but aim to reach Barrisdale Bay when the water is still relatively high to avoid a long portage over low tide sands. Time the eastwards return journey to coincide with rising water.
By bike	Bikes are useless on the Loch Hourn path; cyclists would have more joy approaching Ladhar Bheinn from Inverie
Accommodation	At Barrisdale the budget choice is either a bothy or the adjacent campsite; both are paying facilities, but very cheap. Alternatively, groups can book a self-catering bunkhouse (see www.barrisdale.com).
Sleeping out	Given the paying facilities at Barrisdale it might not be tactful to wild camp near here. The floor of Coire Dhorrcail is suitable though.
Seasonal notes	The round of Coire Dhorrcail is a classic grade I winter mountaineering route with an expeditionary feel. The crux sections are the northeast prow of Stob a' Chearcaill and the traverse of the Stob a' Choire Odhair ridge.
Short cuts	Few options

three big climbs, a steep eroded 100m ascent onto a heathery headland overlooking the water. A winding descent now leads back to the shore (good camping); then it's the second 100m climb, over a little pass and back down again, passing behind **Runival** cottage to rejoin the loch.

The next section is uniquely beautiful, the ancient path hugging a craggy shoreline overhung by venerable Scots pines. The woods gradually thin as you pass the narrows at Caolas Mor, where the far shore seems almost close enough to touch. A final, rather less brutal up-and-over now leads to a junction with a 4WD track near the mouth of **Barrisdale Bay**, from where the view of Ladhar Bheinn is inspiring. Follow this S for nearly 2km, passing **Barrisdale** house to reach the bothy, bunkhouse and campsite

next door to the stalker's cottage. Expect company on summer weekends, but out of season Barrisdale can feel like the end of the earth.

On the hill 13km

The circuit is best done clockwise so that scrambles are met in ascent. Non-scramblers could avoid the prow of Stob a' Chearcaill by instead starting the round from Mam Barrisdale via the Barrisdale–Inverie path.

Cross the River Barrisdale on a wooden bridge near the bothy, then branch right onto a grassy path that heads downstream across the salt marsh. Bearing roughly W, this old stalker's path then zigzags up the steep hillside to gain a shoulder overlooking Loch Hourn. From about the 230m contour the path descends slightly to loop into the mouth of **Coire Dhorrcail** – you'll be coming back this way later, but for now quit it at its high point and head SW up rough slopes to gain the crest of Creag Bheithe.

An ascending series of rocky bluffs leads up the ridge, with a clear path underfoot. The improbable northeast prow of **Stob a' Chearcaill** soon sprouts into view ahead. An eroded path skirts just left of the initial nose before climbing an obvious depression; vegetation and loosely embedded rocks make this fairly serious. Safer (although it's counter-intuitive) is to take the nose head on, following the best-trodden line as it weaves up short mossy rock tiers and inter-vening grass ledges. Either option demands caution, especially in the wet. The exposure relents towards the top of the buttress.

A superb stretch of ridge walking now leads onto the flat summit of **point 849m**; from here descend NW into the Bealach Coire Dhorrcail. Next comes another unnamed summit (point 858m), which crowns the huge corrie headwall. It's a rough climb, and scrambly steps add interest. A final steep slog of

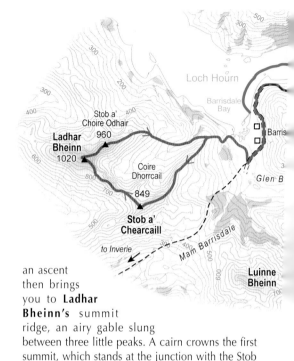

an ascent then brings you to **Ladhar Bheinn's** summit ridge, an airy gable slung between three little peaks. A cairn crowns the first summit, which stands at the junction with the Stob

Loch Hourn, evening

a' Choire Odhair ridge; but the highest point is actually the middle peak, a short walk W and also cairned. Return to the first summit and follow a path ENE down the rock-and-grass crest, easy but exposed. Beyond a dip is a short climb onto **Stob a' Choire Odhair**, a sharp pike with an unrivalled perspective of Coire Dhorrcail's cliffs and gullies.

The ridge to **Druim a' Choire Odhair** drops off steeply at first, but soon broadens and becomes easier. Stay with the high ground for about 1km until a descent rightwards into the corrie can be made,

threading between bogs and outcrops. Once on the corrie floor cross the burn to pick up the stalker's path used earlier in the day. This traverses spectacularly above a wooded gorge before climbing around the foot of Creag Bheithe to return to **Barrisdale**.

Return 10km

Luckily the tiring walk-out to Kinloch Hourn is just as attractive in reverse.

The Coire Dhorrcail crags from Stob a' Chearcaill summit ridge

The Sgurr na Ciche range –
a Rough Bounds round

*K*noydart may be known for its rugged isolation, but the well-named Rough Bounds just to its east are wilder and more challenging still. These are some of the least convenient peaks in the country – hard to reach and harder still to climb. While day raids are possible, most will prefer to spend a night in the area, camping or bothying. It's worth all the effort.

Even by local standards these hills are uncompromising – Ben Aden, one of the roughest (and best) of all Corbetts; the majestic steep-pitched cone of Sgurr na Ciche at the head of fjord-like Loch Nevis; and the superb scrambly ridge walking on Garbh Chioch Mhór. It's customary (hackneyed even) to come at the Munros from Glen Dessarry in the southeast, but this makes it hard to include Ben Aden – a major omission. This longer way via Loch Quoich makes good on this, and offers an aesthetic advantage, too, as the skyline to be traversed is visible for most of the approach.

Approach 12km

Take the road W, then hop the burn at the head of Loch Quoich's NW arm and follow the boggy shore SE (vague path) towards a headland, where a short stretch of old dam access road is met. When this disappears into the loch a muddy path continues WSW along the shore. Ben Aden and Sgurr na Ciche are prominent ahead, although still distant. After about 2.5km on this path bear a little right to cross the neck of a headland, passing through an old deer

↑ *Garbh Chioch Mhór (left), Sgurr na Ciche and Ben Aden from Sgurr nan Coireachan*

Start/finish	Layby on the Kinloch Hourn road (NG 993 035)	
Distance	37km (23 miles)	
Ascent	2740m	
Time	14hrs	
Terrain	The name Rough Bounds gives a clue – numerous bogs on the low ground and countless rock outcrops scattered across the hills. Brief moments of grade 1 scrambling on the northeast ridge of Ben Aden and the traverse of Garbh Chioch Mhór. The complex ground needs close navigation, and in parts trails are vague.	
Summits	Ben Aden 887m ('hill of the face'); Sgurr na Ciche 1040m ('peak of the breast'); Garbh Chioch Mhór 1013m ('big rough place of the breast'); Sgurr nan Coireachan 953m ('peak of the corries')	
Maps	OS Landranger (1:50,000) 33; OS Explorer (1:25,000) 398 & 414; Harvey British Mountain Map (1:40,000) Knoydart, Kintail and Affric	
Public transport	None	
By boat	Loch Quoich gives one of Scotland's best fresh water hill approaches.	

Put in at the start point of the walk and allow 2–3hrs. Bear in mind that strong easterly or westerly winds blowing the full length of the loch will build up considerable waves, and that in the event of a mishap help is distant.

Accommodation Invergarry Lodge YH (0845 293 7373)

Sleeping out Excellent campsites at the head of Loch Quoich, the foot of Ben Aden and on the cols between the hills. The nearest bothies are Sourlies (NM 869 950) and A'Chuil (NM 944 924)

Seasonal notes Although falling short of graded climbing, several sections are entertaining in winter conditions – the northeast ridge of Ben Aden, the ascent and descent of Sgurr na Ciche, and the traverse of Garbh Chioch Mhór. In wet weather the Abhainn Chosaidh can be hard to cross (see Approach, below).

Short cuts Although it would be a shame to do so, Ben Aden can be missed out by climbing Sgurr na Ciche direct from Loch Quoich via Coire nan Gall

fence to reach the **Abhainn Chosaidh** where it empties into a bay in Loch Quoich. This burn is easily crossed in low water, but in spate it might take a long detour upstream or a swim/wade across the bay.

Beyond the burn continue along the shore to pick up a continuation of the old access road (shown as a path on some maps). Spongy and moss-covered in places, this leads in about 3km to the twin dams at the far western head of Loch Quoich. Cross both dams, then head briefly S to join a path heading W onto a little col above idyllic **Lochan nam Breac**.

On the hill 14km

At the high point of the col leave the path to follow the cascading Allt Coire na Cruaiche upstream into the rugged corrie east of **Ben Aden** (no real path). After about 1km beside the burn bear right onto the mountain's broad northeast ridge, a classic but little-used scramble. Weave uphill through a chaos of rocky knobbles, with occasional bits of light scrambling on clean rough slabs and unfolding views back

down Loch Quoich. As height is gained a large flat rock pavement is crossed, then the ridge narrows and two quite spectacular minor tops are traversed (easily) en route to the complex knolls of the summit, which must rate as one of the least accessible in Scotland.

All the ground between here and Sgurr na Ciche needs care in mist. First retrace your steps to the top of the northeast ridge, and before reaching the first of the minor tops cut right, descending steeply to a pronounced grassy terrace heading E. This ends in a crag, so at this point trend left to descend rough ground onto a bealach at the head of Coire na Cruaiche. Rough going among complex outcrops and bogs leads over a minor top (spot height 717m). Pass a series of pools on the saddle beyond. Start climbing towards **Meall a' Choire Dhuibhe**, but before reaching the top turn S to traverse an obvious grassy line among the crags of its western flank to reach a pronounced col separating it from Sgurr na Ciche.

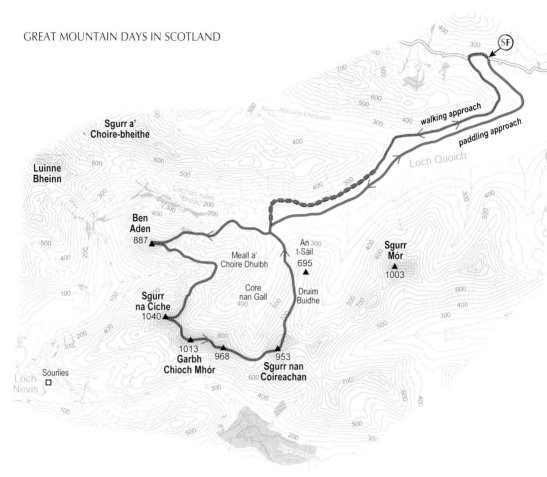

Sgurr Mór (right), the Gleouraich hills (left) and Loch Quoich from the rough ground east of Ben Aden

Sgurr Mór and Loch Quoich from Ben Aden's northeast ridge

*The Rough Bounds from Loch Quoich; left to right –
Garbh Chioch Mhór, Sgurr na Ciche and Ben Aden*

Sgurr na Ciche is reached by a long rough ascent weaving between outcrops. Beyond a minor top is the summit cone and a stretch of old drystone wall. When the wall trends left of the crest continue straight up to reach the east end of the final summit ridge. The summit offers a superb view of the Knoydart peaks (Walk 20) and along Loch Nevis to Eigg and Rum (Walk 46); the sense of remoteness is palpable. Now that you are on the standard Munro round, the way is well trodden and more easily followed. Briefly backtrack E then pick up an eroded path down Sgurr na Ciche's steep southeast flank to the high col below Garbh Chioch Mhór.

The wall is rejoined in the ascent of this hill, passing a tiny lochan and with occasional moments of easy scrambling. Beyond a minor top is **Garbh**

Chioch Mhór's main summit, with an airy outlook over steep crags. Stay with the ridge (and wall) which now undulates E over several rocky tops, giving spectacular walking for about 2km, and trending gradually down to a boggy col. A strenuous ascent, initially just right of the crest, then wins the summit of **Sgurr nan Coireachan** at the apex of three ridges.

Follow the obvious corrie edge NE for a few hundred metres before peeling left to descend onto the knobbly **Druim Buidhe** ridge. On about the 700m contour – and still some way short of the final summit – trend left to pick up a fantastic old stalker's path (easily missed in mist) that makes a descending traverse across the steep grassy slopes above **Coire nan Gall**. Once the path starts contouring (at about 350m altitude) abandon it and make straight towards the Loch Quoich dams. Hop over the **Allt Coire nan Gall** upstream of the loch to regain the approach path.

Return 11km
Reverse the approach route to the Kinloch Hourn road.

Glen Finnan circuit

S *gurr nan Coireachan and Sgurr Thuilm rise in a remote setting, yet the private road that runs to their feet makes them easily accessible. These two bulky domes contrast with the sharp peaks and crests of nearby Streap, an intriguing hill that has escaped the doubtful accolade of Munro status by mere metres, and in all the more important respects far overshadows its 3000ft neigh-bours. But there's no need to choose between these peaks – they can all be done together. The most obvious route on the Munros is an excellent*

Stob Coire nan Cearc (left), Glen Finnan and the distant Moidart hills (Walk 23) from Streap's southwest ridge

horseshoe of the knobbly ridges enclosing Coire Thollaidh; throw in Streap, too, and you've got some-thing more substantial still – a circuit both diverse and challenging.

↑ *Streap (left) and Sgurr Thuilm from Strathan near the head of Loch Arkaig*

Start/finish	Car park at the turnoff for the private road up Glen Finnan (NM 905 809)
Distance	25km (15½ miles)
Ascent	2150m
Time	9½hrs
Terrain	Surfaced road to Corryhully, then clear paths on the ridge crests with only a few mildly scrambly moments. However, three significant pathless sections require careful route finding and a sure footing on very steep grass – the descent from Sgurr Thuilm, the ascent of Streap and the final descent to Corryhully.
Summits	Sgurr nan Coireachan 956m ('peak of the corries'); Sgurr Thuilm 963m ('peak of the knoll'); Streap 909m ('to climb')
Maps	OS Landranger (1:50,000) 40; OS Explorer (1:25,000) 398
Public transport	Train to Glenfinnan on the Fort William – Mallaig line
By bike	Nearly 8km of tarmac walking can be saved by cycling from the start to Corryhully and back
Accommodation	Glenfinnan Sleeping Car – an unusual bunkhouse at the station (01397 722295)
Sleeping out	Corryhully bothy is the most convenient (if not particularly salubrious) overnight option, and the walk has been tailored with this in mind. Firewood is plentiful here, and there's even electric lighting.
Seasonal notes	With the long low-level approach and only short steep sections Sgurr nan Coireachan and Sgurr Thuilm are amenable winter Munros. Streap is a different proposition. Its narrow crest is a brilliant introduction to winter mountaineering ridges and may (briefly) merit grade I in hard conditions. Both sides of the col between Sgurr Thuilm and Streap need respect in snow or ice, and are not ideal for winter novices; likewise the descent to Corryhully.
Short cuts	Glen Finnan forms a natural break, allowing the walk to be split into two. Sgurr nan Coireachan and Sgurr Thuilm are a popular combination, while Streap may be done on its own either from Corryhully or Glen Dubh Lighe.

Approach 5km

From the car park the private tarmac road running up Glen Finnan is obvious. Soon pass under the Victorian railway viaduct, a mould-breaking early concrete construction latterly made famous by the Harry Potter films, then follow the River Finnan meandering between pines. After nearly 4km the road crosses a bridge and splits. The left branch goes to Glenfinnan Lodge; take the right branch along an unsurfaced track, which passes **Corryhully bothy** then continues up-glen between crags and the cascading river. About 1km beyond the bothy take a turnoff on the left (cairn, and signpost for Sgurr nan Coireachan).

On the hill 16km

Occasional scrambly bits can be enjoyed on the long ascent of Sgurr nan Coireachan's southeast ridge. An excellent stalker's path climbs the east side of the obvious spur, then moves onto the crest to weave up between knobbly outcrops and boggy hollows.

Beyond a level section the ground steepens; here the path traverses briefly across the left flank before cutting directly uphill (steep and eroded) onto the minor top of Sgurr a' Choire Riabhaich. The path now follows Coire Thollaidh's craggy rim, where the lumpy terrain can be confusing in poor visibility, before making a final steady climb onto **Sgurr nan Coireachan**.

Descend the mountain's defined east ridge, with a couple of easy rocky steps. Now stay with the high ground ringing the head of Coire Thollaidh, over the knobbly minor summits of Meall an Tàrmachain and **Beinn Garbh** (and others). The path is generally clear underfoot, its course occasionally confirmed by an intermittent line of rusty old fence posts – anywhere except remote hilltops such detritus would rightly be classed as litter. Eventually a stiff ascent of about 100m leads onto the level top of point 858m (unnamed on OS maps) before the pull onto **Sgurr Thuilm's** rounded summit.

Head S to pick up a path running down the grassy ridge of **Druim Coire a' Bheithe**. This path

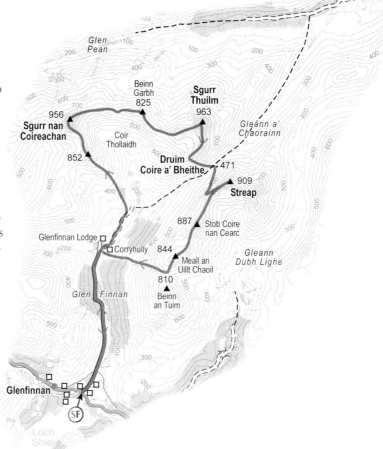

is the quickest return route to Glen Finnan, while the continuation to Streap is rather more taxing; its forbidding flank taunts you from across a too-deep, too-steep trench. Between the 800m and 750m contours quit the path with regret and ad-lib carefully down the breakneck slope, linking strips of grass between outcrops and scree, bearing slightly left towards the bealach that separates Glen Finnan from Gleann a' Chaorainn (**spot height 471m** on the maps).

Reach the glen floor just downhill of the bealach, then get stuck into a similarly relentless ascent. At first glance an attempt on Streap's rocky northwest flank appears ill-advised, but

Sgurr nan Coireachan from Glen Finnan

The summit of Streap from the northwest ridge

there is a breach in the defences; bear gradually right as you climb to pick up a rightwards-slanting diagonal grassy line that cuts through the dank cliffs; this may not be scrambling per se, but it does need a sure footing, and would be worrying in the wet. Above the steep ground an unmistakeable grassy terrace is soon met; go left up this to gain the ridge crest.

Turn left to follow the narrow arête towards **Streap**, a classic wedge shaped summit rising over a boulder-strewn corrie. Although it may look daunting from a distance the final ascent is airy rather than difficult, with only minimal scrambling. Having reached the summit cairn retrace your steps back down the ridge, then continue strenuously on to rugged **Stob Coire nan Cearc**. The ridge-top path now begins to grow faint in places, so pick your own line down through outcrops to the Bealach Coire nan Cearc and on up to flat-topped **Meall an Uillt Chaoil**.

By now it will have dawned on you that Streap is more a range in miniature than a single hill, and the distinctness of each of its summits means a lot of upping and downing. Bear just a little right for the easiest descent onto the next bealach. Ahead rises **Beinn an Tuim**; although it promises a great outlook along Loch Shiel the substantial reascent may put you off, coming this late in a tiring day. Faced with waning light or enthusiasm the quickest way home is to ignore this final top for a direct descent to Corryhully. From the bealach follow the burn initially, then as it begins to carve a gorge bear slightly right to carefully descend the adjacent steep grass slopes. As the angle eases stay on the north bank of the burn to pass a plantation.

Return 4km

A bridge is soon met and a forest track along Glen Finnan; easier still is to continue downhill to **Corryhully bothy**, then retread the tarmac.

Beinn Odhar Bheag
and the Rois-Bheinn group

*W*ith their rock-studded flanks and bog-riddled glens the gnarled hills of Moidart demand a lot from the walker, but this wild area more than justifies the effort, benefiting as it does from a lack of crowd-pulling Munros. In the east the Beinn Odhar twins rise abruptly out of the long ribbon of Loch Shiel – secluded, little-trodden and uncompromisingly rough. Busier, although only relatively, is the famous Rois-Bheinn massif further west – shapely peaks offering spectacular island-scattered sea views. By making use of the railway both groups can be strung together into this long linear walk, a challenging trip over five Corbetts and a couple of equally worthwhile non-listed peaks. Go east to west to catch the sunset behind Rum.

Approach 1km

From **Glenfinnan** station cross the A830 and go down a minor road. At the bottom of the hill branch right, cross a bridge over the Abhainn Shlatach and continue past a smart modern house to a boat house on **Loch Shiel**.

On the hill 22km

Follow the boggy shore, then climb over a little headland to a bay and small fish farm. Now leave the loch and climb roughly W through knee-deep tussocks and rock outcrops, painfully gaining height up a seemingly endless series of knobbles. A rough and readily disappearing trail approximately follows

130   ↑ *Loch Shiel, Beinn Odhar Bheag (right) and Sgurr Ghiubhsachain from Glenfinnan*

ROUTE INFORMATION

Start	Glenfinnan train station (NM 898 809)
Finish	Lochailort train station (NM 769 826)
Distance	25km (15½ miles)
Ascent	2600m
Time	12hrs
Terrain	Variations on the theme of bog, rocks and tussocks. The ascent of Beinn Odhar Mhor described here covers incredibly uncompromising ground, although an easier route exists – see Short cuts, below. From here paths are sketchy and intermittent, and the terrain remains challenging all the way to the Rois-Bheinn group, where grassier ground and clear paths predominate. Some easy scrambling (grade 1) on the east-southeast ridge of Druim Fiaclach.
Summits	Beinn Odhar Mhor 870m ('big dun-coloured hill'); Beinn Odhar Bheag 882m ('little dun-coloured hill'); Beinn Mhic Cèdidh 783m ('MacCedidh's hill'); Druim Fiaclach 869m ('toothed ridge'); Sgurr na Ba Glaise 874m ('peak of the grey cow'); Rois-Bheinn 882m (possibly 'mountain of horses', Norse); An Stac 814m ('the stack')
Maps	OS Landranger (1:50,000) 40; OS Explorer (1:25,000) 390, 391 & 398
Public transport	This linear walk is predicated on the use of the Fort William – Mallaig railway; note the limited timetable (it's a long road walk from Lochailort to Glenfinnan)
By bike	Cycle between Lochailort and Glenfinnan and you're not tied to the train timetable
Accommodation	Glenfinnan Sleeping Car – an unusual bunkhouse at the station (01397 722295)
Sleeping out	Many potential camp sites among the knolls and hollows. With variations on the walk as described it would be possible to use Essan bothy (NM 817 817) just to the north of the hills.
Seasonal notes	A long rough walk for winter, but feasible if the easier variation up Beinn Odhar Mhor is used. Technical difficulties are confined to the east-southeast ridge of Druim Fiaclach, which promises exciting mountaineering – grade 1 seems a fair guesstimate. This might be avoided by contouring below the mountain to approach from the north.
Short cuts	Those doing without the train can indulge in a rather quicker ascent of Beinn Odhar Mhor starting from the A830 at NM 857 813 – cross a burn on a bridge, then the railway where it passes through a short tunnel, before bearing right to gain the hill's broad north-northwest ridge. At the far end of the walk An Stac might be missed out via a muddy argocat track in Coire a' Bhùiridh.

Eigg and Rum (Walk 46) from Rois-Bheinn

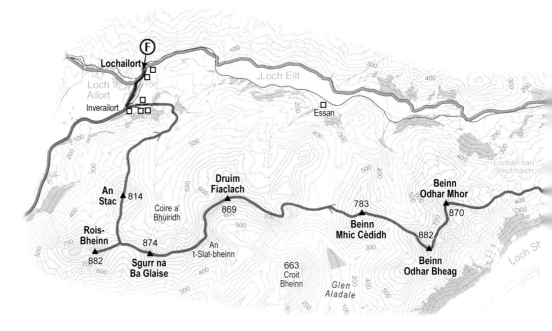

a burn, taking the left branch where it forks to climb into a pronounced notch. From here climb right, then back left, to eventually reach a minor top overlooking **Lochan nan Sleubhaich**. Continue W onto spot height 529m, then stay with the high ground to gain a more pronounced ridge that leads at long last to **Beinn Odhar Mhor's** summit cairn.

With bird's-eye perspectives on Loch Shiel descend S along the edge of the impressive Coire na Lotha and Coire nan Clach, then ascend an expanse of rough rock slabs en route to **Beinn Odhar Bheag's** airy summit. Drop down the grassy NW ridge to the low saddle of the Bealach a' Choire Bhuidhe. Continuing W it's a tough uphill slog onto **Beinn Mhic Cèdidh**; a little cairn marks the high point overlooking the craggy west face. Although an undistinguished Corbett in itself, this is a great viewpoint looking out to the Rois-Bheinn group. Descend quite steeply W, threading through the outcrops to reach a dispiritingly low, boggy bealach above lonely **Glen Aladale**.

The route onto Druim Fiaclach could be confusing in mist. Just W of the bealach is a deep burn-cutting, bounded on its left side by a steep tiered ridge, and with a prominent waterfall high up. The burn's right-hand ridge is a much gentler proposition, so follow this to reach a rugged hollow above the waterfall. Head S across its floor to meet **Druim Fiaclach's** east-southeast ridge, the ascent of which demands some easy scrambling. Continue along the airy upper crest

over a series of little rocky pinnacles. The hands-on technicality is modest, but the positions are superb. Beyond the high point, roughly midway along the ridge, the going becomes easier, and because you're now on a popular hillwalking circuit there's a clear path underfoot for the first time all day.

Beyond a pronounced bealach there's a gentle climb over the multiple tops of **An t-Slat bheinn** before the ascent onto the domed Corbett summit of **Sgurr na Ba Glaise**. Descend to the grassy Bealach an Fhiona, then make what feels by this stage to be a fairly taxing climb beside an old drystone wall onto the top of **Rois-Bheinn** itself. Having 'oohed' and 'ahhed' over some of the most inspiring sea views in Scotland, return to the bealach and take a rough path down to the lower bealach under **An Stac**. The steep ascent of this rugged outlying summit calls for some willpower, but again the views are worth it. From the summit a path heads N down rocky ground onto the minor top of Seann Chruach. Continue NE into the marshy mouth of **Coire a' Bhùiridh**, where there's a mucky argocat track and a pleasant footpath. The latter weaves deviously through scattered woods to reach level ground.

Return 2km
Follow a track W through sheep pastures to the main road at **Inverailort**; turn right for the junction with the A830, and right again for **Lochailort** station.

Heading west on Druim Fiaclach

The Beinn Odhar hills from Druim Fiaclach

Creag Meagaidh

*C*reag Meagaidh sprawls across Scotland's east–west watershed, combining a Cairngorm-like tendency to flat-topped mass with craggy hidden corners that speak more of nearby Lochaber. To the south are the forested shores of Loch Laggan and the wilds of Ardverikie / Ben Alder (Walk 25); northward and east the ground rolls out into the peaty heart of the Monadhliath. Meagaidh (or 'Meggy') is more a range than a single entity, a high central plateau radiating whalebacked ridges, with grassy satellites and several impressive cirques. Foremost among these is Coire Ardair, one of the great corries of the Highlands and showpiece of a thriving National Nature Reserve. From the lower birch woods to the huge verdant crags at its head, the corrie gives a superb approach to the hill and makes an obvious focus for this circular walk, with a return leg over the Munros of Stob Poite Coire Ardair and Carn Liath.

ROUTE INFORMATION

Start/finish	Creag Meagaidh National Nature Reserve car park (NN 483 873)
Distance	20km (12½ miles)
Ascent	1280m
Time	7hrs
Terrain	Largely grassy, with clear paths throughout
Summits	Creag Meagaidh 1130m ('bogland rock', possibly); Stob Poite Coire Ardair 1053m ('peak of the pot of the high corrie'); Carn Liath 1006m ('grey hill')
Maps	OS Landranger (1:50,000) 34; OS Explorer (1:25,000) 401
Public transport	Tulloch station is the nearest rail link; there are no public buses on the A86
Accommodation	Newtonmore Hostel (01540 673360)

Sleeping out	The best camping in Coire Ardair is by Lochan a' Choire
Seasonal notes	Being inland and high the snow-holding potential of Creag Meagaidh is well known, the dankness of its cliffs translating into great ice climbing. Walkers should note that the summit plateau is a serious place in a white-out, and that the edges can carry big cornices. The mountain is renowned for avalanches; the slopes around The Window are a particular concern, but even in the lower corrie large slides have been known to sweep the path.
Short cuts	The quickest descent from the main summit is to return along Coire Ardair; alternatively, the ridge bounding the south side of the corrie is shorter than that to the north

Approach 5.5km

From the car park the well-engineered Coire Ardair path runs along a fringe of woodland, passes the National Nature Reserve field centre at **Aberarder**, then climbs into the mouth of the corrie. Pass through the scattered (but gradually regenerating) woods of Coille a' Choire, then cross open ground, with the Coire Ardair cliffs growing ever more massive ahead, to reach the north shore of Lochan a' Choire. Across the water rise the pyramidal Pinnacle Buttress and the vegetated mass of the Post Face, seamed with gloomy gullies ('posts') and home to classic winter climbs. Beside the lochan the groomed glen trail becomes an unkempt hill path.

On the hill 13km

Climb a steepening slope below the cliffs of the Inner Corrie. Eroded scree leads into **The Window**, the rock-choked notch that cuts through the massif between Creag Meagaidh and Stob Poite Coire Ardair. At the west end of The Window turn left, where more steep stony slopes lead onto Creag Meagaidh's plateau.

135

Coire Ardair from Carn Liath

Before heading to the summit it's worth following the edge of Coire Ardair to the minor top of **Puist Coire Ardair** for a different outlook on the cliffs below. The height-hardened might also like to scramble out onto the exposed promontory at the top of Pinnacle Buttress, which almost seems to over-hang Lochan a' Choire. Poor visibility and/or big cornices might render these detours inadvisable.

Now bounce pinball-like back W across the swelling plateau to reach a huge double cairn on a shoulder over-looking the mountain's northern cliffs. Local folklore has it that Mad Meg's Cairn marks the grave of an 18th-century suicide victim, but its main role now is to mislead fogbound walkers – the true summit of

Aberarder farm, Loch Laggan and the Ardverikie Forest from Carn Liath

Creag Meagaidh is actually a rise several hundred metres further west, crowned with a less monu-mental cairn.

Return directly to The Window and take a clear path up onto **Stob Poite Coire Ardair**, the day's second Munro. Now simply follow the rounded ridge crest along the corrie rim, pausing occasionally to admire its ice-gouged architecture. Largely grassy ground leads over a series of minor tops before a final gentle climb to the stone-strewn top of **Carn Liath**. Although of no great merit of its own, this final Munro of the round offers expansive views over Loch Laggan and along the trench of Coire Ardair.

From the summit head back briefly towards Creag Meagaidh to pick up a well-used path that descends the mountain's southern shoulder to reach the little top of **Na Cnapanan**, where the trail is easily misplaced. Keep heading more or less S for a final rough descent through scrubby new-growth woodland to regain the Coire Ardair path.

Return 1.5km
Head back down past **Aberarder** to the car park.

Lochan a' Choire from the top of Pinnacle Buttress

Ben Alder
and the Geal-chàrn group

*A*t the heart of the Central Highlands is a great tract of wild land, its long lochs and big burly
peaks sliced by glens into distinct massifs. With estate tracks and stalker's paths giving easy
access to the interior, this is ideal backpacking country. A day's walk in any direction from the nearest
public road, journeys here have the feel of expeditions. Ben Alder is the grandest of the mountains,
its high summit plateau buttressed by rocky ridges and snow-holding corries.

Ben Alder is perhaps most frequently tackled in isolation, generally from Dalwhinnie in the
northeast, where the huge approach is rendered convenient by bike. However, this walk starts at
Corrour station instead, allowing a more satisfying circuit to be made and incorporating the neighbouring Geal-chàrn group too. These are fine hills in their own right, matching Ben Alder for scale
and remoteness. With a descent of the scrambly Long Leachas ridge, a night in the justifiably popular
Culra bothy and an exciting climb next day up the Lancet Edge, this route is a memorable classic. It
is the only walk in this book for which rail is the sole means of access.

↑ *The Geal-chàrn range from Loch Laggan; left to right – Geal-chàrn, Aonach Beag and Beinn Eibhinn*

On the Lancet Edge

ROUTE INFORMATION

Start/finish	Corrour station (NN 356 664)
Distance	40km (25 miles)
Ascent	1880m
Time	16hrs (best done over 2 days)
Terrain	The glens are threaded with estate tracks and well-trodden paths, but away from the best-drained trails low-lying ground has a tendency to bogginess. The hill stages follow clear paths for the most part, although a DIY approach is needed on the ascent of Ben Alder and the descent from Beinn Eibhinn. Ben Alder's Long Leachas and the Lancet Edge of Sgòr Iutharn are exposed rocky ridges with some basic scrambling (low grade 1).
Summits	Ben Alder 1148m ('rock and water mountain', possibly); Sgòr Iutharn 1028m 'hell peak', possibly); Geal-chàrn 1132m ('white cairn'); Aonach Beag 1116m ('little ridge'); Beinn Eibhinn 1102m ('delightful mountain')
Maps	OS Landranger (1:50,000) 41 and 42; OS Explorer (1:25,000) 393 & 385
Public transport	This is the only walk in the book to be accessible solely by public transport, via the Glasgow to Fort William railway. Even the starting point of the walk is remote; Corrour station is an isolated building on the edge of Rannoch Moor's bleak vastness, far from the nearest public road.
By boat	With an alternative start in Dalwhinnie the hills can be accessed along the fjord-like ribbon of Loch Ericht, the longest and arguably the best amphibious approach in the area

By bike	The tracks ringing Loch Ossian can easily be cycled as far as Corrour Lodge, saving about 11km of walking in total. Bike space on the train may have to be booked in advance.
Accommodation	Loch Ossian YH for superb remote bunkhouse-type accommodation (01397 732207); nearby Corrour YH offers more luxury (01397 732236)
Sleeping out	Grassy plots can be found beside Uisge Labhair and near Culra. The bothy at Culra (NN 522 762) is excellent, and ideally situated at the middle point of the walk; it is often packed at weekends. A three-day walk could be made by adding the Sgòr Gaibhre Munros and a night at Benalder Cottage bothy (NN 498 680) – though beware the resident ghost.
Seasonal notes	Because long sections are at glen level this walk is suited to brief winter days, although even the glens are high and exposed in poor weather. These are the highest mountains between Lochaber and the Cairngorms, with great snow-attracting potential. Ringed by steep ground and substantial cornices, the extensive summit plateaux of Ben Alder and Geal-chàrn can be dicey in a white-out. In full winter condition the Long Leachas and the Lancet Edge become grade I mountaineering ridges.
Short cuts	Climb just one of the hill groups flanking the Bealach Dubh instead of both; a good trail then allows a less strenuous return to Corrour through the glens

Approach 10km

From Corrour station (which featured in the film 'Trainspotting') take the track to **Loch Ossian**, passing the waterside rustic youth hostel to follow the south shore through attractive mixed woodland. At the far end of the loch bear left past estate buildings to cross a bridge over the River Ossian, then just before reaching **Corrour Lodge** turn right onto a path. This runs beside a patch of recently felled timber to cross a bridge over the **Uisge Labhair**. Ignore a prominent argocat track and instead cut right immediately after the bridge, where a path follows the burn upstream into the hills for about 4km (boggy in places).

On the hill 23km

Once the burn becomes tortuously wiggly ford it and strike E(ish) up a rough boggy slope

(no trail) to meet a path bound for the Bealach Cumhann. Cross this and continue climbing roughly E to reach a vague spur, which leads quickly onto **Ben Alder's** gently sloping grassy plateau. The summit trig point sits on the far side of this, near the cliffs of east-facing Garbh Choire. From the top walk 500m NE to the plateau edge, then N for 1km. Above Coire na Lethchois the plateau narrows into a level promontory running out to the top of the **Long Leachas ridge**. This may be hard to locate in poor visibility; look out for a cairn.

The narrow rocky arête of the Long Leachas is a superb route off

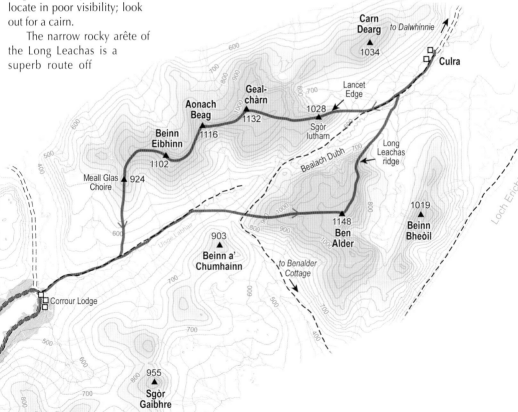

Dawn at Culra – Ben Alder (left) and Sgòr Iutharn

the hill, offering airy situations but minimal scrambling difficulty. A well-trodden path shows the best way; the only spot that might give pause for thought is a short rubbly chimney, and even this proves easier than it looks. Once the scrambling is over continue on the ridge until it terminates in two mini rocky tops.

Most people will be happy to head for the Culra bothy and call it a night there; otherwise aim straight for **Sgòr Iutharn**. For the bothy, descend NNE across the boggy lower slopes to reach the Allt a' Bhealaich Dhuibh just upstream of its junction with the Allt a' Bhealaich Bheithe. If the former can be safely crossed then do so; on the far side is an excellent path leading quickly to **Culra bothy**. If the crossing looks doubtful then stay on the east bank, walking downstream to a bridge a little beyond Culra.

From the bothy walk back SW along the burnside path, heading towards the Bealach Dubh, the rift between Ben Alder and the Geal-chàrn group. Overhead towers Sgòr Iutharn; on meeting the stream that drains Loch an Sgòir leave the bealach path and head direct for its northeast prow. As it rises the hill narrows into the magnificent **Lancet Edge**.

This rocky ridge may not be quite as scalpel-sharp as the name promises, but does offer some light scrambling in a magnificently exposed position (slippery when wet).

From the top of **Sgòr Iutharn** cross a broad saddle and climb quite steeply onto **Geal-chàrn's** summit plateau, almost as extensive as Ben Alder's and similarly confusing in mist. The top is about 1km to the west, close to the edge of Coire na Coichille. From here follow a pleasant slender crest down into a gap and on up to the flat little summit of **Aonach Beag**. More of the same then leads around to **Beinn Eibhinn**, last of the walk's Munros; the main top is a short distance along the curving summit ridge. From here go W for about 1km before dropping S, crossing a little gap onto the rounded minor peak of **Meall Glas Choire**. Continuing to descend S gives easy ground at first, but the boggy lower slopes are hard going. Eventually meet the Uisge Labhair path.

Return 7km
Once back at **Corrour Lodge** it's worth following the forest track along the north bank of Loch Ossian for the sake of variation – a long gentle wind-down.

Sgòr Iutharn (left) and Ben Alder from Geal-chàrn

Lochaber Traverse

*D*isproving all that rot about less being more, the Lochaber Traverse links three distinct hill groups to create something greater than the sum of its parts, a must-do epic with a mountaineering character. The scale and drama steadily build, from the sinuous stony ridges of the Grey Corries, over the hulking Aonachs to a grand scrambling finale along the famous Carn Mòr Dearg (CMD) Arête to end on the highest high in the British Isles, the cliff-girt plateau of Ben Nevis. Ambitious runners might like to combine the Lochaber Traverse with the Mamores ridge (Walk 27) in a sub-24hr dash known as Tranter's Round, while the inhumanly sprightly can try adding the five Loch Treig Munros too on the truly astounding Ramsey's Round. The rest of us will be more than happy with the route described here, and it's no disgrace to stretch it over two pretty full days.

↑ *Looking along the Grey Corries ridge to Ben Nevis and the Aonachs, from Stob a' Choire Leith* 143

ROUTE INFORMATION

Start	Car park on the forestry track above Coire Choille farm (NN 255 788)
Finish	'North Face' car park near Torlundy (NN 145 764)
Distance	32km (20 miles)
Ascent	2800m
Time	15hrs (perhaps best over 2 days)
Terrain	Rough and remote, with some narrow ridges and occasional easy scrambling. Paths are generally easily followed, although less so on the ascent of Aonach Beag and the descent from Aonach Mòr.
Summits	Stob Choire Claurigh 1177m (obscure); Stob Coire an Laoigh 1116m ('peak of the corrie of the calf'); Stob Coire Easain 1080m ('peak of the corrie of the waterfalls'); Sgùrr Choinnich Mor 1094m ('big mossy peak'); Aonach Beag 1234m ('little ridge'); Aonach Mòr 1221m ('big ridge'); Carn Mòr Dearg 1220m ('big red cairn'); Ben Nevis 1344m (obscure)
Maps	OS Landranger (1:50,000) 41; OS Explorer (1:25,000) 392; Harvey British Mountain Map (1:40,000) Ben Nevis and Glen Coe
Public transport	Access by train, starting at either Spean Bridge station or Corrour station and finishing at Fort William. Both starting points add considerable distance and would make a one-day traverse difficult.
By bike	Teams with only one car could pre-stash bikes at the walk's end, then cycle tracks through Leanachan Forest back to the start
Accommodation	Bunkhouse at Roy Bridge Hotel (01397 712236); or Glen Nevis YH (01397 702336); Ben Nevis Inn (01397 701227); Calluna, Fort William (01397 700451)
Sleeping out	The small Lairig Leacach bothy (NN 282 736) is a detour from the route described. Several of the Grey Corries' corries provide good wild camping, and the Aonach Beag – Grey Corries col is ideally placed for a midway stay. The Ben Nevis summit shelter is another option, although it's sometimes used by the socially challenged as the highest toilet in Britain.
Seasonal notes	On these high mountains winter conditions might last into summer. Cornices pose a considerable hazard, and because of the varied slope aspects encountered the possible avalanche risk must be cautiously weighed. The east ridge of Carn Mòr Dearg and the CMD Arête become grade I winter climbs and may develop knife-edged snow crests. In white-out conditions Ben Nevis and Aonach Beag both demand precise navigation, with featureless summit areas ringed by hazardous ground. The steep descent from Aonach Mòr also needs care.
Short cuts	The two low-level bealachs separating the three hill groups provide bad-weather escape routes

Approach 2km

From the car park continue on the track, which passes through a gate into felled forestry then zig-zags uphill past the carved wooden statue of a black-robed preacher. At a gate on the far boundary of the woods turn right off the track onto boggy ground.

On the hill 30km

Initially shadow the forest, then peel S on a path up a long grassy incline to the corrie rim at **Stob Coire Gaibhre**. Follow the edge on stonier ground to reach a curious hollow where the ridge to the sharp out-lying summit of Stob Coire na Ceannain meets the main mountainside (worthwhile diversion). Climb onto **Stob Choire Claurigh's** narrow northeast ridge,

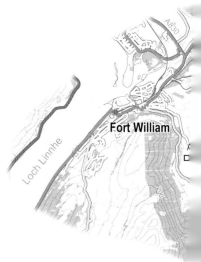

Fort William

Loch Linnhe

a rocky arête that provides some light hands-on entertainment en route to the summit. As the 15th highest in Scotland this graceful peak affords stunning views, most notably westwards along the twisting spine of the Grey Corries to the Aonachs and, rising above even them, Ben Nevis; there's clearly some hard work in store.

First things first – the Grey Corries ridge, a slender crest liberally scattered with the pale quartzite screes that give the range its name. After the initial descent from Stob Choire Claurigh the ridge snakes over several imperceptible tops to reach **Caisteal**, from where there's a more marked descent and reascent around the edge of cliffs onto the big summit of **Stob Coire an Laoigh**. Here the ridge swings right to **Stob Coire Easain** for a view over the immensity of An Cul Choire, the isolated corrie system shared by Aonach Beag and Aonach Mòr. The scale of these 1200-ers is now striking – Beag ('small') is actually the taller of the two, a majestically rugged dome,

while its companion was presumably dubbed Mor ('big') in honour of its bulk.

With a little easy scrambling, a narrow rocky crest drops steeply SW to the Bealach Coire Easain, which cleanly divides the Munro **Sgùrr Choinnich Mor** from the rest of the Grey Corries. Although green rather than grey, this striking pyramid is arguably the best of the lot; a steep initial climb gains the ridge to the airy summit. Beyond is the quirky little top of **Sgùrr Choinnich Beag** – better climbed than outflanked – then a knee-jarring descent to the bealach below the formidable ramparts of Aonach Beag (curiously nameless on the maps for such a major col).

The onward route is menaced by dank cliffs, and although a direct ascent can be made up a rough prow between Coire Bhealaich and Coire a' Bhuic, its start is not obvious. If in doubt (or poor

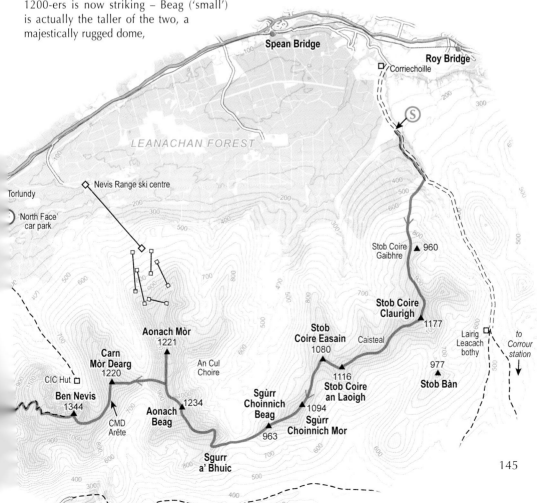

*Misty Loch Eil from the summit plateau of Ben Nevis – on the horizon behind the figure are
the Rum Cuillin (Walk 46) and, to the right, the Skye Cuillin (Walk 47)*

weather) traverse W from the col towards **Sgurr a' Bhuic** until a line of ascent can be seen overhead, breaching the crags; a stiff climb gains easier ground above. Turn right onto a path that follows the cliff edge to a point overlooking the col (the top of the direct route), then cut hard left where a well-defined ridge leads W above the huge face of An Aghaidh Gharbh. Stay close to the edge (beware cornices) for the long final climb onto the spacious top of **Aonach Beag**. With cliffs all around, descent in poor visibility needs an accurate bearing; on approach to the Aonach Mòr/Aonach Beag col beware a deep gouge in the right-hand cliff edge.

From the col an easy ascent N leads along the elongated summit plateau of **Aonach Mòr** to the cairn on its high point. Return to a point about 20m (altitude) above the Mor/Beag col, then traverse WNW along the 1100m contour until a steep,

eroded line of descent can be picked up, leading to the major pass between the Aonachs and Carn Mòr Dearg. Above the pass the East Ridge of **Carn Mòr Dearg** is seen end-on; the ascent path starts at a short length of stone wall. The crest soon becomes well defined, with occasional scrambly moments. The summit is a graceful perch at the start of the **CMD Arête**.

This scything line is one of the most aesthetic easy ridge scrambles in Britain. The ground barely merits grade 1, but the surroundings more than compensate, with superb angles on the huge crags of Ben Nevis. Follow the blocky arête as it curves down and then back up to a junction with The Ben (here is a possible escape on scree and outcrops into Coire Leis, marked by intermittent metal abseil posts; beware if icy). Clamber up a horrid boulder slope, keeping safely left of the corrie rim, to arrive on the

← *Stob Coire Easain from Sgùrr Choinnich Mor*

stony summit plateau of **Ben Nevis**, littered with the remains of a Victorian weather observatory and the detritus of modern visitors.

It's all downhill from here. Ben Nevis is ringed with steep ground, and in poor visibility the corniced edges and gullies are a hazard. A new rank of cairns marks the safe way off, their size indicative of the depth of winter snows. If even they are obscured, walk 150m from the trig point on a bearing of 231° grid to safely skirt Gardyloo Gully, then 282° grid for nearly 1km, bearing in mind the invisible man-eating Five Finger Gully on your left, to reach the infamous zigzags. At the time of writing this stretch of trail was enjoying a partial resurface, and in future years will hopefully be less unpleasantly stony.

Follow the path to a junction just above Lochan Meall an t-Suidhe. Branch right here on a new path that terminates incongruously at the outflow of **Lochan Meall an t-Suidhe**. Just before reaching this dead-end cut off right, where any of several vaguely trodden trails lead N across the bogs, descending past a rusting fence line to reach the **Allt a'Mhuilinn**. Ford the river, or cross it using a deer fence, then climb a stile into a car park used by local climbing guides. Follow the forest track briefly downstream; ignore the first right-hand turnoff and take the second, where a newly built path leads downhill through the woods to the 'North Face' car park near **Torlundy**.

Aonach Beag and the Grey Corries from Ben Nevis

The Mamores

*T*he Mamores are a west-coast treasure, their many fine summits strung together by elegant crests like pearls on a necklace. Treading a high spine above the depths of Glen Nevis, with the grandeur of Ben Nevis to the north and Glen Coe's rumpled ruggedness to the south, a traverse of the range is one of the ridge-walking treasures of Europe.

The group encompasses ten Munros and several unlisted tops. Although all could be visited by the fittest and most determined, the to-ing and fro-ing that results makes for a breathless, illogical route. This more coherent – and less taxing – alternative ignores three or four outlying Munros, concentrating on the main ridge from Binnein Mòr to Mullach nan Coirean. From its start among the incomparable confines of Glen Nevis to the occasional bursts of easy scrambling that enliven the traverse, this is a walk worthy of superlatives.

↑ *Sgurr a' Mhaim (left) and Stob Bàn from Ben Nevis, with the Glen Coe peaks (Walk 28) and Ben Cruachan (Walk 31) in the distance*

ROUTE INFORMATION

Start/finish	Car park at the end of the Glen Nevis road (NN 168 691); or lower down the glen (NN 145 683)
Distance	29.5km (18½ miles) (including optional leg to Sgurr a' Mhaim)
Ascent	2615m
Time	13hrs
Terrain	Narrow ridges, some stony, with a clear path once the main crest has been gained. A little light scrambling, most notably on the northeast ridge of Binnein Mòr (grade 1), which can be avoided by using the north ridge instead.
Summits	Binnein Mòr 1130m ('big peak'); Na Gruagaichean 1055m ('the maidens'); Stob Coire a' Chairn 981m ('peak of the corrie of the cairn'); Am Bodach 1032m ('the old man'); Sgurr a' Mhaim 1099m ('peak of the breast'); Stob Bàn 999m ('white peak'); Mullach nan Coirean 939m ('summit of the corries')
Maps	OS Landranger (1:50,000) 41; OS Explorer (1:25,000) 392; Harvey British Mountain Map (1:40,000) Ben Nevis and Glen Coe
Public transport	Coach or train to Fort William; local bus down Glen Nevis in summertime

By bike	Leaving a bike at Polldubh would ease the end-of-day tarmac slog
Accommodation	Glen Nevis YH (01397 702 336); Ben Nevis Inn (01397 701227); Calluna, Fort William (01397 700451)
Sleeping out	Away from the road there's potential at the Steall meadow and further up-glen. For higher-level camps the Binnein Beag – Binnein Mòr col is an obvious choice. On the traverse itself some excellent sites can be found by dropping slightly from the ridge crest.
Seasonal notes	With a dark start and finish and optimum conditions this walk is feasible as an epic winter day. Several sections take on a mountaineering character – the northeast ridge of Binnein Mòr (grade I); linking the two summits of Na Gruagaichean; the steep northeast spur of Am Bodach; the Devil's Ridge (grade I, optional); the east ridge of Stob Bàn.
Short cuts	Various options – omit Binnein Mòr and Na Gruagaichean by ascending the An Gearanach ridge (grade 1 scramble); ignore the Devil's Ridge to Sgurr a' Mhaim; cut out Stob Bàn and Mullach nan Coirean by descending Coire a' Mhusgain

Approach 6km

Glen Nevis is one of the grandest of Scottish glens. From the car park follow the well-trodden path through the dramatic wooded gorge to emerge at the hidden meadow of **Steall**; high peaks loom in the background and a 100m waterfall foams down the craggy glen wall. Stay with the path on the boggy north side of the Water of Nevis for a further 3km. At a broad shoulder scored with peat hags turn off right, crossing the river (dodgy in spate) then making a steep pull beside a burn-cutting to reach the

Steall Falls

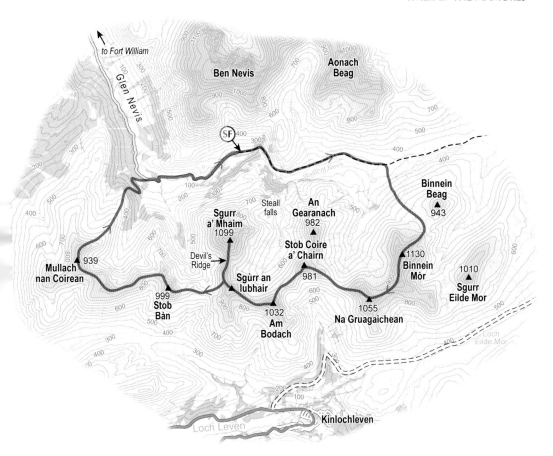

saddle between **Binnein Beag** and Binnein Mòr. The former could be bagged from here, although it is a fairly uninteresting scree cone.

On the hill 20km

Above a lochan rises the steep terminal spur of Binnein Mòr's northeast ridge, Sron a' Garbh-Choire. Attack this head on – there are signs of previous walkers, but no real path. At the top of the spur an unusual level crest leads to the steeper, rockier upper ridge. This is a short fun scramble (grade 1); harder steps can be found, although all are avoidable. Having gained the summit crest clamber airily over the rocks to **Binnein Mòr's** main top, high point of the day.

A clear path treads the well-defined south ridge to an unnamed summit. Turn right here, following the spine of the range up to the higher of **Na Gruagaichean's** twin tops. From this stony summit descend into a steep notch between the peaks before continuing up the narrow ridge onto the level grassy top of the lower summit. Gentler slopes descend W to a low col, from where escape is possible south to Kinlochleven or north to Glen Nevis. An easy ascent now leads up **Stob Coire a' Chairn**, one of the peaks on the famous Ring of Steall. Energetic baggers could take an optional detour from here, scrambling over the rugged fang of **An Garbhanach** to outlying Munro An Gearanach.

Continuing with the main Mamores ridge, an unnamed minor top is crossed en route to another well-defined col. As for the previous bealach, this too provides escape options to either side, although note that a direct descent out of Coire a' Mhàil into Glen Nevis would hit dangerous ground alongside the Steall Falls. Ahead rises **Am Bodach**, ascended by an unpleasant eroded path weaving among outcrops and scree. From the stony summit overlooking fjord-like Loch Leven drop W along the crest to the next saddle. A contouring path could now be picked up skirting S of **Sgùrr an Iubhair**, although it's better climbed. The far side of the hill is gouged into a line of crags, barring direct descent W.

From the summit there are two paths – one loops left to avoid the cliffs; the other cuts hard right and is described here. First gain the col between Sgùrr

151

an Iubhair and Stob Choire a' Mhail. A dead-end leg from here over Stob Choire a' Mhail and along the Devil's Ridge to outlying Munro **Sgurr a' Mhaim** comes highly recommended; the way is obvious and very dramatic, with some basic scrambling. Having returned from Sgurr a' Mhaim to the col below Sgùrr an Iubhair, follow an old stalker's path as it zigzags W down to tiny Lochan Coire nam Miseach, cupped beneath slabby cliffs. Cross the lochan outflow to regain the main Mamores ridge.

The east ridge of Stob Bàn gives a steep ascent on an eroded path. Just shy of the summit the path kinks slightly left to skirt the head of a gully (care in winter conditions). With its complex east face and a summit of pale quartzite chunks **Stob Bàn** is the most distinctive peak in the Mamores. To descend follow the broad north ridge over a jutting shoulder. Stony ground is soon replaced by grass; here a contouring path cuts left onto the bealach above Coire

an Lochain. The grassy spine of the range now leads over three minor summits, with a short easy scramble where the rim of Coire Dearg briefly narrows, to reach **Mullach nan Coirean**.

From the summit a path heads N, hugging the corrie edge as it curves right to descend the northeast ridge. Lower down the crest broadens, and a deer fence is followed down steep boggy slopes to cross a ladder stile at the edge of a forestry plantation. In the trees the ground is wet, and the path may be masked beneath pine needles. A vehicle track is soon met; turn right onto this, forking left at the first junction before zigzagging down to a lower junction. Turn right here to regain the **Glen Nevis Road**.

Return 3.5km

Follow the road E to cross the impressive waterfall at Polldubh and continue up-glen through wooded craggy terrain to reach the road-end car park.

← *Binnein Beag and the Grey Corries (Walk 26) from Binnein Mòr's northeast ridge*

↑ *Loch Leven and the Glen Coe peaks (Walk 28) from Am Bodach*

Glen Coe circuit

*O*n the approach to Glen Coe from the east a monumental rock pyramid sprouts improbably out of the tundra of Rannoch Moor. This is Stob Dearg, a forbidding façade beyond which hides the multi-summited spine of Buachaille Etive Mòr. Beside it stands the prow at the leading edge of Buachaille Etive Beag – cut from a similar cloth to its neighbour, if less extravagantly. The glen then drops into a canyon-like trench, its north wall a confusion of deep-scored gullies and tottering rocks rearing to a climax on the serrated crest of Aonach Eagach, most infamous of mainland scrambles. To the south loom the bluffs of the Three Sisters, terminal ends of ridges thrown down from the heights of the Bidean nam Bian massif, a clutch of graceful peaks and secretive corries. Among the best routes in an area not short on quality is this epic lap of the entire glen, taking in every Munro and major ridge. For most it's a two-day proposition; as a clockwise circuit starting in the east it allows a choice of mid-route accommodation at Glencoe village.

↑ *Looking over Buachaille Etive Beag to the Bidean range from Buachaille Etive Mòr*

ROUTE INFORMATION

Start/finish	Car park at Altnafeadh (NN 220 563)
Distance	41km (25½ miles)
Ascent	4200m
Time	20hrs (best over 2 days)
Terrain	Steep and stony throughout. Paths are generally clear, although not east of Sron Garbh or between Stob Dubh and Stob Coire Sgreamhach. Most challenging is the traverse of Aonach Eagach, a long, thrilling grade 2 scramble. The rock is polished, the drops considerable and in slimy conditions beginners should steer clear. If escaping Aonach Eagach note that the Clachaig Gully path is very steep and unpleasant, and has seen accidents: indeed east of Sgorr nam Fiannaidh there is no safe way into Glen Coe until Am Bodach.
Summits	Buachaille Etive Mòr (Beag) ('big (little) herdsman of Etive'); Stob Dearg 1022m ('red peak'); Stob na Bròige 956m ('peak of the shoe'); Stob Coire Raineach 925m ('peak of the bracken-filled corrie'); Stob Dubh 958m ('black peak'); Stob Coire Sgreamhach 1072m ('peak of the horrible corrie'); Bidean nam Bian 1150m ('peak of the mountains', possibly); Aonach Eagach ('notched ridge'); Sgorr nam Fiannaidh

	967m ('peak of the Fingalians' [warriors]); Stob Coire Leith 940m ('peak of the grey corrie'); Meall Dearg 953m ('red hill'); Am Bodach 943m ('the old man')
Maps	OS Landranger (1:50,000) 41; OS Explorer (1:25,000) 384; Harvey British Mountain Map (1:40,000) Ben Nevis and Glen Coe
Public transport	Glasgow to Fort William buses stop in Glencoe village
Accommodation	Glencoe YH (01855 811219); Clachaig Inn (01855 811252); Kings House Hotel (01855 851259)
Seasonal notes	In full winter conditions Aonach Eagach is a grade II mountaineering adventure of great scale and seriousness. The hills south of the glen are winter walker friendly, but still challenging; Coire na Tulaich of Buachaille Etive Mòr has been the scene of multiple avalanche fatalities, and Bidean nam Bian needs respect.
Short cuts	Aonach Eagach can be shortened by omitting the Pap of Glencoe and/or the extension to the Devil's Staircase (instead descending SE from Am Bodach to the road). The Buachailles and the Bidean nam Bian massif can all be done individually.

On the hill 41km

From the A82 head S towards Buachaille Etive Mòr. Cross a footbridge over the River Coupall, pass the private hut of **Lagangarbh**, and when the path splits stay right. Soon cross a burn, then ascend the steepening floor of Coire na Tulaich, the only pedestrian-friendly breach in the mountain's formidable northern defences. The engineered path eventually runs out, and the final climb up the corrie headwall is on loose scree (see Seasonal notes, above). From a cairn on the saddle above, head E on a stony path to **Stob Dearg**, the apex of The Buachaille's precipitous pyramid.

Return to the saddle, and continue W to a minor summit, then follow the ridge SW to climb onto the conical top of **Stob na Doire**. Staying with the crest the path now descends quite steeply to a grassy bealach, then continues more gently over Stob Coire Altruim to **Stob na Bròige**, the Munro that bookends Buachaille Etive Mòr. Head back to the grassy bealach to pick up a well-scuffed path descending into the Lairig Gartain.

Having crossed the River Coupall turn left onto the main Lairig path briefly. On the right is a cascading burn, and a sketchy path climbs beside this to meet a pronounced saddle on the crest of Buachaille Etive Beag. From here first turn right for a short, stony ascent onto the Munro **Stob Coire Raineach** before returning to the saddle and continuing SW along the ridge, passing over an unnamed top to reach **Stob Dubh**, the airy Munro summit at the opposite end of the Buachaille Etive Beag crest.

Descent to the Lairig Eilde is problematic, and there are two obvious choices. For the first option (shown on the accompanying map), continue briefly SW along the crest, then head roughly W as if making directly for Stob Coire Sgreamhach, picking carefully down a vague spur between rotten little crags and steep scree. For the alternative option, continue briefly SW along the crest, then bear SSW down a better defined spur on easier angled scree; soon after the scree turns to grass, cut hard right to make a descending traverse across a steep broken slope. Both options meet up at a cairn marking the high point of the Lairig Eilde.

Continue WSW over soggy ground, veering left to climb into a shallow grassy corrie that leads steeply to a col between Stob Coire Sgreamhach and an unnamed minor blip (**spot height 778m**). A long, fairly gradual climb NW gains **Sgreamhach**, a dramatic sharp top hanging high over the 'Lost Valley' of Coire Gabhail. Follow rough rocky ground down the sharp crest to the Bealach Dearg (unnamed on small scale maps), then take the ridge above the craggy Lost Valley Buttresses before a final uphill pull to the twin tops of **Bidean nam Bian**; the first is higher. North-facing crags drop away below, giving Bidean a tremendous spaciousness. The conical satellite peak of Stob Coire nan Lochan looks attractive, but maybe not today.

Continue W over the lower West Top of Bidean, then descend the ridge around the cliff edge to **Stob Coire nam Beith**, a minor summit with a huge north face of its own. A gravelly path descends W, staying well away from the cliff and following the ridge as it curves N to a vague col. From here the path drops into Coire nam Beitheach, steadily descending the sloping corrie floor. Once below the rambling west face of Aonach Dubh, the path briefly enters the bed of the Allt coire nam Beitheach, with some mildly scrambly moments, before ascending slightly to follow the left bank. Descend past waterfalls to reach the **A82** near Loch Achtriochtan. Turn off onto the minor road that runs past the **Clachaig Inn** towards Glencoe village.

A full traverse from the Pap of Glencoe to the Devil's Staircase on the West Highland Way is one of the best ways to do Aonach Eagach, heading east as opposed to the more common westerly crossing. Roughly 1km before Glencoe village take a gated track on the right, which runs straight uphill to a stream-side water-treatment works. Crossing the burn, the route now dwindles to a narrow path climbing through bracken, then contours right a short distance before a final ascent close to a burn to the col between Sgorr nam Fiannaidh and the **Pap of Glencoe**. It's

Climbing the ridge above the Lost Valley to Bidean nan Bian

Buachaille Etive Mòr from Blackrock Cottage, a hangout of the Ladies Scottish Climbing Club

worth climbing the latter for the bird's-eye views of Loch Leven; ascend via a rocky path that cuts up rightwards to breach the summit crags. Returning to the col, continue SE up rough slopes (occasional traces of path) to the western spur of **Sgorr nam Fiannaidh**, then over easier angled stony ground to the summit.

A pleasant ridge leads E to **Stob Coire Leith**, where the scrambling starts. Beyond a steep descent

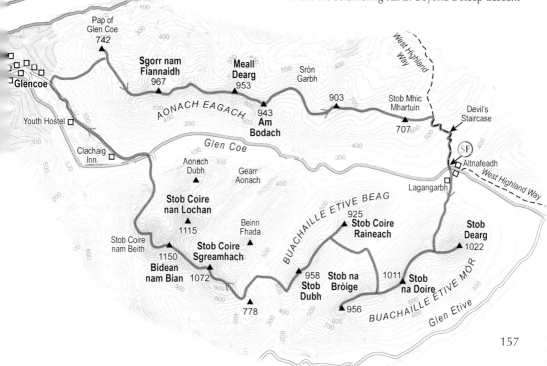

are the famous pinnacles, a serrated rank of towers hanging high over the glen; this is the true Aonach Eagach ('notched ridge'). Route finding is intuitive – simply follow signs of wear, with the best line climbing directly over some towers and dodging around the side of others. Scrambling comes in bursts, with short tricky ascents and descents on smooth-polished rock. The main difficulties of the pinnacles end with the descent of a steep gully to a little gap in the ridge.

Easier ground then leads onto the broad top of **Meall Dearg**. Continuing E, occasional pockets of scrambling maintain the interest on the ridge approaching the rocky west buttress of **Am Bodach**, where a sting in the tail awaits. From a rusty fence post first go up a smooth slabby ramp on the right side of the crest, then shortly afterwards climb steep blocky rock to a big boulder. Airy ledges now cut up the left flank of the ridge to safe ground on top of the buttress, with the summit of Am Bodach now just a short stroll away.

A path continues NE around the craggy corrie rim, a soothing grassy contrast to all that rocky clambering. **Sròn Garbh** can be skirted on the right, but summit 903m (unnamed) has to be climbed. From here keep heading E along the broad crest, meeting boggy ground on the way to **Stob Mhic Mhartuin**. Here a better trodden (frankly, muddy) path appears, leading quickly to a cairned junction with the West Highland Way. Descend the **Devil's Staircase** zigzags to **Altnafeadh** on the A82.

Heading east along Aonach Eagach from Sgorr nam Fiannaidh,
with Buachaille Etive Beag and Mor across the glen

Black Mount Traverse

*M*uch photographed from the A82, the Black Mount's distinctive squat skyline combines the rocky west with the sweeping horizons of the east, serving as a watershed between the two. Below the range stretches the dun desolation of Rannoch Moor, a peaty blanket bog pitted with strings of lochs. This expanse was once home to Britain's largest ice sheet, from where glaciers ploughed down radiating glens. There's more than a whiff of the arctic tundra about it even today. The Black Mount offers arguably the best views over the moor.

   A famous walk, sometimes called the Clachlet Traverse, links the Inveroran Hotel in the south with Kings House Hotel in the north via every summit in the Black Mount range. Although tradition-ally linear, the walk is logistically more straightforward as the circuit described here, making use of a stretch of the West Highland Way.

↑ *The Black Mount from Beinn Udlaidh*

ROUTE INFORMATION

Start/finish	Car park west of Loch Tulla, near Victoria Bridge (NN 270 419)
Distance	27km (17 miles)
Ascent	1700m
Time	10hrs
Terrain	Plenty of rough ground and bogs, with sketchy paths in places. Short bursts of very easy scrambling on Aonach Eagach and the Creise – Meall a' Bhùiridh ridge.
Summits	Stob Ghabhar 1090m ('peak of goats'); Clach Leathad (aka Clachlet) 1099m ('the stone of the slope'); Creise 1100m (obscure); Meall a' Bhùiridh 1108m ('hill of the roaring')
Maps	OS Landranger (1:50,000) 50 and 41; OS Explorer (1:25,000) 377 and 384; Harvey British Mountain Map (1:40,000) Ben Nevis and Glen Coe
Public transport	Buses and trains from Glasgow to Fort William both stop at Bridge of Orchy, from where it is about 4km to Victoria Bridge either by road or the West Highland Way
By bike	Stash a bike near Blackrock Cottage and the Glen Coe ski centre to do the route as a linear south–north walk, with a cycle back along the West Highland Way (stony) or the A82 (longer)
Accommodation	Bridge of Orchy Hotel (and bunkhouse) (01838 400208); Crianlarich YH (01838 300260); Inveroran Hotel (01838 400220)
Sleeping out	Roadside camping quite popular by a bridge close to the car park. Many wild camp possibilities in the hills – Coirein Lochain and Coireach a' Bà, for instance.
Seasonal notes	A superb winter trip with short sections of very easy mountaineering (arguably grade I) on Aonach Eagach and the ridge scramble between Creise and Meall a' Bhùiridh. Given favourable snow conditions the walk is feasible in one long day, the finish along the West Highland Way being fine in the dark. Note that the descent E from Creise can be heavily corniced into spring.
Short cuts	Bogs around the River Bà make an early descent to the West Highland Way unattractive

Clach Leathad, Creise and Meall a' Bhùiridh from Beinn an Dòthaidh (Walk 32)

Approach 4km

Follow the road N over a bridge to **Forest Lodge**. Go left here on a track running through trees and then alongside the broad **Abhainn Shira** to reach a private club hut. Turn right here onto a muddy path beside the Allt Toaig. This ascends steadily to a parting of ways beside a burn junction.

Rannoch Moor from Meall a' Bhùiridh

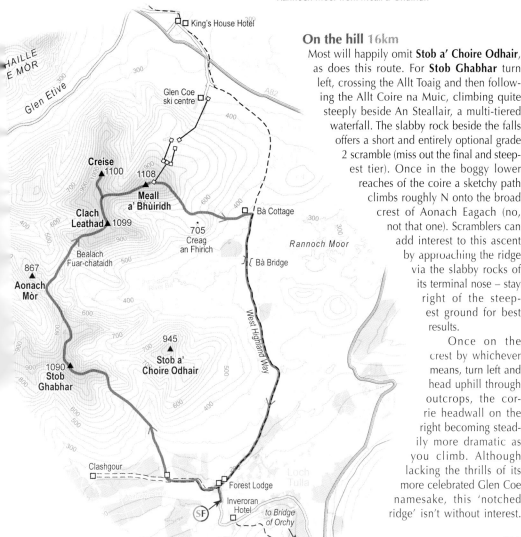

On the hill 16km

Most will happily omit **Stob a' Choire Odhair**, as does this route. For **Stob Ghabhar** turn left, crossing the Allt Toaig and then following the Allt Coire na Muic, climbing quite steeply beside An Steallair, a multi-tiered waterfall. The slabby rock beside the falls offers a short and entirely optional grade 2 scramble (miss out the final and steepest tier). Once in the boggy lower reaches of the coire a sketchy path climbs roughly N onto the broad crest of Aonach Eagach (no, not that one). Scramblers can add interest to this ascent by approaching the ridge via the slabby rocks of its terminal nose – stay right of the steepest ground for best results.

Once on the crest by whichever means, turn left and head uphill through outcrops, the corrie headwall on the right becoming steadily more dramatic as you climb. Although lacking the thrills of its more celebrated Glen Coe namesake, this 'notched ridge' isn't without interest.

Just beyond a sharp minor summit (point 991m) the ridge narrows into a short stretch of exposed arête with some very basic scrambling. Unfortunately it broadens again rather too soon. A short pull then gains the summit of **Stob Ghabhar**.

The section from here to Clach Leathad is tricky to navigate in poor visibility. Descending NW, continue briefly around the almost-level corrie rim. Turn left at the top of Sròn nan Giubhas, following a sometimes disappearing path downhill onto the **Aonach Mòr** ridge. Stay with the high ground over several knobbly mini-summits. After about 1km of complex ground cross a dip and ascend onto an 850m top; here turn NE, descending steeply onto a grassy saddle. Continue over a minor summit to reach the low point of the Bealach Fuar-chataidh. A sketchy path now attacks the steep flank of **Clach Leathad**. The angle eventually relents, the path veering rightwards over the stony upper slopes to reach the summit cairn on the edge of craggy Coire an Easain.

Head N along the corrie rim (often corniced), passing a cairn at the turn-off for Meall a' Bhùiridh (NN 238 500) and continuing gently uphill to the top of **Creise**. Retrace your steps to the cairn, then descend E down a rocky spur with some very basic scrambling. The continuation up **Meall a' Bhùiridh's**

rocky west ridge includes further scrambly steps, although nothing unavoidable. A cairn marks the day's high point. Continue E along the rocky summit ridge, passing the top tow of Glencoe Mountain ski centre and following a walled track to the easternmost top.

A rough, easily lost path now descends the mountain's blunt eastern spur, where steep stony slopes soon ease into bogs. Bear slightly right to reach a saddle between the parent mountain and the grassy dome of a mini-summit, **Creag an Fhirich**. Instead of climbing the peak bear left down a peaty trough, following the right bank of a burn to reach the ruin of **Bà Cottage**. A short track now leads to the West Highland Way, where you turn right.

Return 7km

With superb views of the hills you've just traversed, this is one of the best stretches of the **West Highland Way**. The path here treads the course of a military road built to pacify the Highlands in the aftermath of Culloden. The centuries-old cobbles have survived almost intact – a quiet rebuke to less durable modern construction methods. Victoria Bridge may seem distant, but it's easy walking that quickly eats the miles.

Stob Ghabhar from Stob Coire Sgreamhach (Walk 28)

Glen Etive hills

*B*en Starav has the carved grace of an archetypal mountain, rising more than a kilometre out of Loch Etive in one great rush. Its sharp twin peaks radiate ridges that cup rugged corries, providing the meat of an airy traverse of the hill. Although often done in isolation, Starav is best combined with its neighbours – mysterious Beinn nan Aighenan, one of the least accessible of local 3000-ers; steep-sided Glas Bheinn Mhor; bipolar Stob Coir' an Albannaich; and dome-headed Meall nan Eun. Following the high crests between canyon-like Glen Etive and the wild boggy country to the south, this long, satisfying ridge walk gives a respectable tally of five Munros. Merging it with Walk 29 would create a grand traverse of the entire Etive/Black Mount range, a major challenge for motivated runners or weekend backpackers.

↑ *Ben Starav (left), Loch Etive and Ben Cruachan (Walk 31) from Stob Coire Sgreamhach (Walk 28)*

ROUTE INFORMATION

Start/finish	Layby near the turnoff for Coileitir (NN 136 468)
Distance	26km (16 miles)
Ascent	2400m
Time	11hrs
Terrain	Occasional light scrambling on the ridges of Ben Starav, and elsewhere some steep rocky sections in ascent and descent. The ground can be soggy in glens Etive and Ceitlein.
Summits	Ben Starav 1078m (obscure); Beinn nan Aighenan 957m ('hill of the hinds'); Glas Bheinn Mhor 997m ('big green-grey hill'); Stob Coir' an Albannaich 1044m ('peak of the corrie of the Scotsman'); Meall nan Eun 928m ('hill of the birds')
Maps	OS Landranger (1:50,000) 50; OS Explorer (1:25,000) 377 & 384; Harvey British Mountain Map (1:40,000) Ben Nevis and Glen Coe – does not cover Beinn nan Aighenan
Public transport	Buses run on the A82, but none go down the long Glen Etive road
By bike	One way to get around the lack of public transport in Glen Etive
Accommodation	Glencoe YH (01855 811219); Clachaig Inn (01855 811252)
Sleeping out	High cols and corries provide many camping options
Seasonal notes	A feasible one-day winter round given firm conditions underfoot. The north ridge of Ben Starav has mountaineering interest in snow, while the east ridge running to Stob Coire Dheirg gives a short entertaining grade I winter scramble (avoidable on the south side). Take care descending from the east ridge of Stob Coir' an Albannaich, particularly if corniced and/or icy.
Short cuts	Both Beinn nan Aighenan and Meall nan Eun are easily omitted. The cols between the Munros provide get-out routes, and descent is also possible from Stob Coir' an Albannaich, over Beinn Chaorach and then parallel with the obvious straight burn-cutting down to Coileitir.

↑ Ben Starav's east ridge, leading out to Stob Coire Dheirg

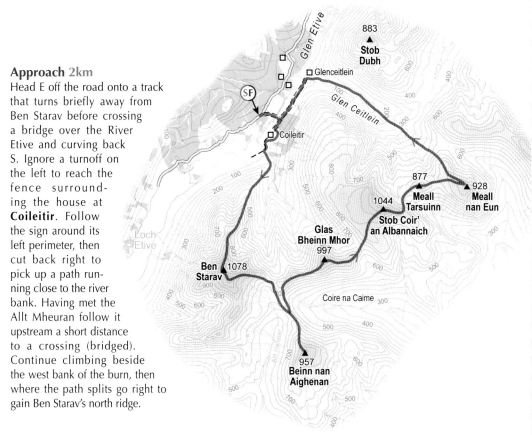

Approach 2km

Head E off the road onto a track
that turns briefly away from
Ben Starav before crossing
a bridge over the River
Etive and curving back
S. Ignore a turnoff on
the left to reach the
fence surround-
ing the house at
Coileitir. Follow
the sign around its
left perimeter, then
cut back right to
pick up a path run-
ning close to the river
bank. Having met the
Allt Mheuran follow it
upstream a short distance
to a crossing (bridged).
Continue climbing beside
the west bank of the burn, then
where the path splits go right to
gain Ben Starav's north ridge.

On the hill 20km

This is a brutal ascent, redeemed by rapid height
gain and a magnificent outlook over the depths
of Glen Etive. The upper section of the ridge thins
dramatically above Coire an Fhir Leith, rearing to a
sudden steep finish on **Starav's** pointy tip. From the
summit cairn follow flat ground around the corrie
edge (caution if corniced) to the beguilingly narrow east ridge, from where a short descent and a
moderately scrambly climb lead to the sharp peak
of Stob Coire Dheirg. Killjoys can bypass the crest
on its south flank. Continue E down the ridge, now
easier, to a pronounced bealach at 766m or 767m
(sources vary).

Look for a faint path that makes a descending
traverse across the rough southwest flank of Meall
nan Tri Tighearnan to a lower col between Coire na
Caime and the glen of the Allt Hallater. From here
a broad rocky ridge leads to **Beinn nan Aighenan's**
isolated summit. Return to the lower bealach, then
climb steeply N through outcrops onto the summit
ridge of Meall nan Tri Tighearnan.

Glen Etive and the Glen Coe peaks (Walk 28)
from the north ridge of Ben Starav

Pass over this minor top, cross a dip and continue up to **Glas Bheinn Mhor**. The east ridge gives a pleasant easy descent at first, then from a very slight summit veer NE, descending steeper rocky ground to reach the next bealach (spot height 738m; possible get-out route to Glen Etive). Plough straight on, climbing a short steep slope, crossing a shallow bowl, then continuing up the dull grassy southern flank of **Stob Coir' an Albannaich**. At the summit cairn a different side to the hill's character is unveiled with a flourish – a spectacular open corrie dropping away towards Glen Ceitlein.

At first glance reaching the next col seems improbable, and while easier than it looks it does need care in winter conditions. From the east Stob Coir' an Albannaich appears as a sharp cone, and the initial descent of the east ridge is indeed very steep. About 500m distance from the summit the ridge levels out, and a small cairn marks the point at which to leave it. Here drop N, picking a grassy way among outcrops; for once the administrative boundary marked on OS maps is a useful guide rather

than a messy distraction. Straightforward ground is reached on the bealach, and it's now a gentle stroll over the intervening bump of **Meall Tarsuinn** and on up to the rounded top of **Meall nan Eun**.

From the cairn head WNW over the plateau, then follow a vague ridge NW along the edge of the mountain's rocky northeast flank. A descent to the Lairig Dhochard, the bealach connecting Meall nan Eun with the Stob Ghabhar group (Walk 29), is fraught with crags, so it's better to hold the NW line, where rough going soon gives way to the grassy tussocks of upper **Glen Ceitlein**. Continue down-glen to pick up a boggy path on the north bank of the Allt Ceitlein.

Return 4km

Follow this for 2km, the path becoming a sketchy track before meeting a better used track at right angles. Turn left onto this, going parallel with the River Etive for just over 1km to another junction. Go right for the bridge back over the river to the road.

Stob Coir' an Albannaich (left), Glas Bheinn Mhor and the distant Achallader hills from Stob Core Dheirg

Ben Cruachan, Beinn Eunaich
and Beinn a' Chochuill

*R*ising in splendid independence between the glinting ribbons of Loch Etive and Loch Awe (Scotland's longest), Ben Cruachan is instantly recognisable from afar. Its sharp spine links a row of pyramid peaks, throwing down spurs on both sides to enclose rocky corries. The south flank drops steeply to Loch Awe, starting point for the ever-popular skyline walk around the central corrie. The corrie houses the Cruachan reservoir, part of an ambitious pumped storage power station whose turbines hide in a vast cavern. This side of the mountain may be well trodden, but in contrast the northern flank overlooking empty Glen Noe feels inaccessible, and it's well worth exploring. In order to do so, the walk described here starts with neighbouring Beinn Eunaich and Beinn a' Chochuill, characterful hills in their own right, before progressing to the clustered peaks of Cruachan proper and a classic ridge-walking finish.

↑ *Ben Cruachan and Loch Etive from Ben Starav (Walk 30)*   167

Start/finish	Layby on B8077 just west of the bridge over Allt Mhoille (NN 135 287)
Distance	26km (16 miles)
Ascent	2270m
Time	11hrs
Terrain	The slopes on either side of the Lairig Noe are steep, crag-scattered and virtually pathless. From Sron an Isean to Stob Dearg is an extended series of narrow and at times rocky ridges. The way is well trodden and easily followed, but made more interesting by the occasional scrambly step. After a long eroded descent to the reservoir dam, it's tarmac all the way home.
Summits	Beinn Eunaich 989m ('fowling hill'); Beinn a' Chochuill 980m ('hill of the cowl'); Stob Diamh 998m ('peak of the stag'); Drochaid Ghlas 1009m ('grey bridge'); Ben Cruachan 1126m ('heaped mountain'); Stob Dearg 1104m ('red peak'); Meall Cuanail 918m ('hill of the flocks')
Maps	OS Landranger (1:50,000) 50; OS Explorer (1:25,000) 377; Harvey British Mountain Map (1:40,000) Southern Highlands
Public transport	Glasgow to Oban trains stop at both Lochawe and the Cruachan power

	station; fit your walk around the timetable to save tarmac walking between the two at the end of the day
By bike	Leave a bike at the power station on the A85 for an easy post-hill return to the car; if only there was a way to pre-stash it at the reservoir
Accommodation	Oban YH (01631 562025); Bridge of Orchy Hotel (and bunkhouse) (01838 400208); Crianlarich YH (01838 300260); Inveroran Hotel (01838 400220)
Sleeping out	The Lairig Noe and the northern corries of Cruachan have camping potential
Seasonal notes	With a pre-dawn start and a sense of urgency the hill stage of this walk can be fitted into a single winter day, while the tramp from the Cruachan reservoir is feasible after dark. Both flanks of the Lairig Noe demand care in ice or deep snow. Cruachan's narrow crests and scrambly steps take on a mountaineering flavour under snow, and are best suited to competent winter walkers with a head for heights.
Short cuts	Treat the route as two separate day walks, breaking at the Lairig Noe

Approach 2km

From the layby head briefly NE along the road to pick up the track signed for Castles Farm. Pass under a pylon line, then branch left onto the track that heads for the Lairig Noe (a possible way to bypass the first two peaks). About 1km further on look out for a cairned path on the right.

On the hill 15km

The cairned path is easily missed, but it is just as practical to head up the steep grassy slopes leading onto the broad crest of Beinn Eunaich's south ridge. A long and fairly gentle ascent now leads up the ridge to the summit cairn on the edge of **Eunaich's** little eastern corrie. Descending WNW over bouldery ground a ridge soon takes shape, with a well-trodden path dropping onto the bealach at the head of Coire Glas. A steep initial pull, then an easier angled ascent

lead on up an extended grassy ridge (often corniced in winter) to the top of **Beinn a' Chochuill**.

A path descends SW, skirting right of a little crag and then fading into very steep grassy slopes above the **Lairig Noe**; continuing down to this pronounced col, it is worth trending slightly left to avoid craggy ground. Above the Lairig looms the rocky northeast flank of Sron an Isean, with no paths and no obvious breach. Go straight up the lower spur, following a partly underground burn into the mouth of a shallow rock-scattered corrie. Climb its left flank, weaving up steep slippery grass between granite outcrops to reach the crest of the ridge not far east of **Sron an Isean**. Here a clear path is met, leading quickly to this easternmost top on the Cruachan crest. A well-defined ridge drops into a dip and continues on up to the broader peak of **Stob Diamh**.

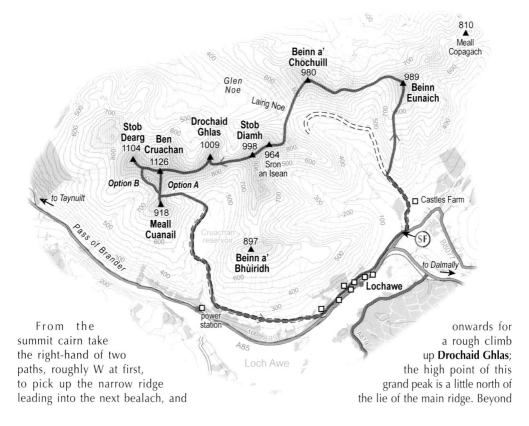

From the summit cairn take the right-hand of two paths, roughly W at first, to pick up the narrow ridge leading into the next bealach, and onwards for a rough climb up **Drochaid Ghlas**; the high point of this grand peak is a little north of the lie of the main ridge. Beyond

Left to right – Meall Cuanail, Ben Cruachan and Stob Dearg from Drochaid Ghlas

another bealach is the east ridge of Ben Cruachan itself, rising in a series of rocky prows. The first notable scramble is a downclimb of a slabby step; the rough granite provides good friction, but care is needed if it's wet or icy. The blocky ridge above offers more scrambly fun if sticking to the crest – or follow easier ground just to its left. As befits the highest point of the hill **Cruachan's** main summit is sharp and rocky, and crowned with a frost-shattered trig point.

Escape to the dam is now close at hand, but in good conditions it is worth staying high for the dead-end detour to the westernmost top, **Stob Dearg** (aka Taynuilt Peak). Despite missing Munro status, this pointed summit has an independent character and offers unrivalled views west towards the sea (shame about the windfarm). The down-and-up to Stob Dearg is steep and rocky, although less hands-on than Cruachan's east ridge.

Returning to the Stob Dearg / Cruachan col there's now a choice. **Option A** Reclimb Cruachan before descending a stony path S to the bealach at the head of Coire Dearg. **Option B** contour across Cruachan's south side to reach the same place. The latter is more complex, since seeping rock slabs and broken outcrops bar the traverse. If taking Option B, first descend S until roughly level with the target col, so that the contouring route leads below rather than through the slabs.

Once on the col it would seem rude not to quickly climb the outlying top of **Meall Cuanail** for the perspective it offers on the main Cruachan ridge. It's best then to backtrack to the col, from where a path leads down into Coire Dearg. Steep and rubbly at first, the trail becomes boggy lower down. Height is rapidly lost, and the reservoir track soon met.

Return 9km

On reaching the impressive dam the track becomes a surfaced road. Cross the dam and stay left at a junction (turning right allows a direct descent to the power station) for the long gradual descent around the hillside into **Lochawe** village. Pavements now lead all the way along the A85 to the B8077 turnoff.

Ben Cruachan (left) and Drochaid Ghlas from Stob Garbh

Achallader's five Munros

*B*einn Dorain is an icon of the Southern Highlands, its huge coned bulk dwarfing the main road and railway at its foot. Its less famous neighbours – Beinn an Dòthaidh, Beinn Achaladair and Beinn a' Chreachain – are scarcely less imposing, forming a continuous steep wall buttressed with craggy corries facing out over the waterlogged plain of Rannoch Moor. Beinn Mhanach hides behind their protective barricade, an undistinguished lump that's nevertheless worth the effort for its atmosphere of seclusion. Although they are generally climbed in twos or threes, these five Munros are best walked in a single extended round, as described here, with the Auch Gleann track giving good access to the heart of this great arc of mountains.

Approach 4km

Follow the private road downhill past **Auch**, crossing a bridge to meet a track crossroads (the West Highland Way). In distance terms the shortest way to Beinn Dorain's summit is via the relentless southern spur, but the following is far more enjoyable. Go straight on, pass a cottage, ford the Allt Coralan (may prove tricky in flood) and continue into Gleann Ach'-innis Chailein (Auch Gleann). At a track junction beneath the **railway viaduct** stay left, following the Allt Kinglass upstream beneath the steep face of Beinn a' Chaisteil (Walk 33), crossing and recrossing the river. After 2km leave the track at a small pine plantation.

↑ *Beinn Dorain (right) and the Black Mount (Walk 29) from Beinn Odhar (Walk 33)* 171

ROUTE INFORMATION

Start/finish	Small layby on the A82 by the private road to Auch (NN 317 353); further parking spaces available fairly nearby
Distance	31km (19½ miles)
Ascent	2200m
Time	11hrs
Terrain	Trails on the main hill crests are easily followed, but there are rougher pathless sections on Meall Tionail, Beinn Mhanach and Coire nan Clach
Summits	Beinn Dorain 1076m ('mountain of the streamlets', possibly); Beinn an Dòthaidh 1004m ('mountain of scorching'); Beinn Achaladair 1038m ('mountain of the farm by the hard water'); Beinn a' Chreachain 1081m 'mountain of the clamshell', possibly); Beinn Mhanach 953m ('hill of the monks')
Maps	OS Landranger (1:50,000) 50; OS Explorer (1:25,000) 77
Public transport	The start of the walk is midway between Bridge of Orchy and Tyndrum, both served by train and bus routes from Glasgow
By bike	About 8km of walking can be saved by cycling the Gleann Ach'-innis Chailein (Auch Gleann) track
Accommodation	Bridge of Orchy Hotel (and bunkhouse) (01838 400208);

Crianlarich YH (01838 300260; Inveroran Hotel (01838 400 220)

Sleeping out Grassy Gleann Ach'-innis Chailein (Auch Gleann) is suitable for camping. Gorton bothy (NN 375 481) is quick to access and convenient for Beinn a' Chreachain, but not for the round as described here.

Seasonal notes A long walk for a single winter day (see Short cuts, below), although a bike would help. Under snow there are no technical difficulties, but care may be needed on the ascent of Meall Tionail and the steep descents from Beinn Achaladair and Beinn Mhanach (in the latter case, retracing the ascent is gentler). In poor visibility the descent from Beinn an Dòthaidh also needs attention. River crossings may be dicey in spate conditions.

Short cuts Low cols between each of the hills make it simple to miss any out. If returning to Gleann Ach'-innis Chailein (Auch Gleann) from the east end of Beinn an Dòthaidh drop to the bealach mentioned in the walk description, then continue E down to the track in order to avoid the crags of Coire a' Ghabhalaich.

Beinn an Dòthaidh (left), Beinn Achaladair and Beinn a' Chreachain from Beinn Dorain's northeast ridge

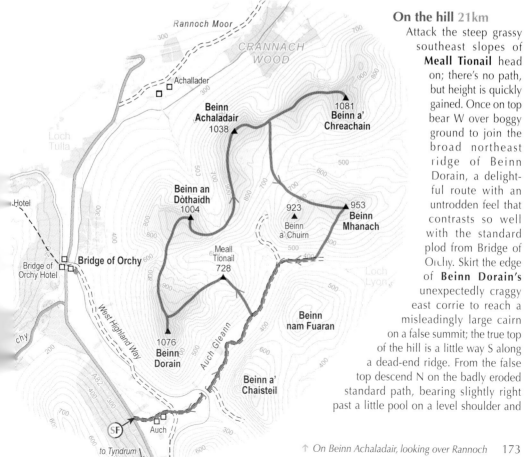

On the hill 21km

Attack the steep grassy southeast slopes of **Meall Tionail** head on; there's no path, but height is quickly gained. Once on top bear W over boggy ground to join the broad northeast ridge of Beinn Dorain, a delightful route with an untrodden feel that contrasts so well with the standard plod from Bridge of Orchy. Skirt the edge of **Beinn Dorain's** unexpectedly craggy east corrie to reach a misleadingly large cairn on a false summit; the true top of the hill is a little way S along a dead-end ridge. From the false top descend N on the badly eroded standard path, bearing slightly right past a little pool on a level shoulder and

↑ On Beinn Achaladair, looking over Rannoch Moor to distant Ben Alder (small snow patches)

Map labels:
Rannoch Moor
CRANNACH WOOD
Achallader
Beinn Achaladair 1038
Beinn a' Chreachain 1081
Loch Tulla
Beinn an Dòthaidh 1004
Beinn a' Chuirn 923
Beinn Mhanach 953
Hotel
Meall Tionail 728
Loch Lyon
Bridge of Orchy
Bridge of Orchy Hotel
Beinn nam Fuaran
West Highland Way
Beinn Dorain 1076
Auch Gleann
Beinn a' Chaisteil
A82
SF
Auch
to Tyndrum

then dropping down steeper ground onto the saddle at the head of Coire an Dòthaidh.

The path up **Beinn an Dòthaidh** veers NE across the grassy scoop of its southern flank to reach the summit plateau and cliff edge overlooking Coire Achaladair (substantial cornices common in winter). Of three summits, the middle one is fractionally the highest. Follow the rim to the sharper eastern top, then descend the wide southeast spur, bearing left to avoid the crags of Coire a' Ghabhlaich and reach the bealach at the head of Coire Daingean. A path now climbs the well-defined southern ridge of **Beinn Achaladair** onto its first top, from where the ground curves up to the level summit crest, the high point of which is at the near end. With precipitous slopes dropping unbroken to Rannoch Moor the sense of space is exhilarating.

Continue to the far end of the summit crest and then descend around the rim of the dramatic northeast corrie, the path weaving through steep rock outcrops to gain level ground at a saddle. A grassier ascent gives access to the minor top of Meall Buidhe, and another enjoyable level ridgetop. Descend to the col above Coire an Lochain, then climb stony ground to the edge of **Beinn a' Chreachain's** little northeast corrie and its domed summit. From this furthest extremity of the day retrace your steps to the saddle below Beinn Achaladair.

Cut S across the pathless lower slopes of Coire nan Clach to reach the peaty bealach between Beinn Achaladair and Beinn a' Chuirn. Now make a grassy ascent ESE, roughly following a fence line to skirt **Beinn a' Chuirn** and reach the saddle between this top and its parent Munro **Beinn Mhanach**. Pass between old gate posts to climb E onto the beachball summit. A 600m descent SSW leads down the mountain's steep southern flank into Srath Tarabhan. Meet the track about 1km west of Loch Lyon.

Return 6km

Head back down Gleann Ach'-innis Chailein, passing a sheep shed at Ais-an t-Sidhean that was once home to the poet Duncan Ban MacIntyre. It is an oft-quoted irony that he was no fan of the woolly usurpers for which Highland communities were cleared, but he did have a soft spot for the magnificent Beinn Dorain.

Beinn Achaladair and Rannoch Moor from the northern corrie of Beinn an Dòthaidh

Tyndrum's five Corbetts

The Tyndrum Five is a rewarding challenge for connoisseurs of the quality walking to be found below the 3000ft threshold. This is one of the only Corbett groupings that allows so many to be climbed in a feasible single day. It's a well-known route, yet far less threadbare than the more heavily used multi-Munro rounds. Paths are faint and crowds unlikely, and this peace is very appealing. Although ringed by higher ranges these hills offer fantastic views, and the best of them have qualities to match many Munros – conical Beinn Odhar, with its airy outlook over Tyndrum; Cam Chreag's knobbly seclusion; and split-sided Beinn a' Chaisteil, half turfy grazing and half precipitous rampart. This is prime sheep country, and the going is generally grassy. But such is the nature of Corbetts that each of the five stands distinct, and a lot of steep upping and downing is needed to link them all. For an extended two-day trip combine this route with Walk 32.

Approach 4km

As for Walk 32 to the railway viaduct; here take the right-hand track up **Glen Coralan**. Having passed some way above an attractive waterfall, the track fizzles into rough pastures.

On the hill 16km

Continue briefly up-glen, staying N of the burn in its water-worn cutting, then curve N for the climb onto **Beinn a' Chaisteil's** long southeast ridge. With an outlook over the precipitous face above Glen Coralan

↑ *Looking down Gleann Ach'-innis Chailein (Auch Gleann) to Beinn a' Chaisteil (left), Beinn Odhar and the Ben Lui hills (Walk 34)*

ROUTE INFORMATION

Start/finish	Small layby on the A82 by the private road to Auch (NN 317 353); further parking spaces available fairly nearby	**By bike**	About 8km of walking can be saved by cycling into Glen Coralan, although the track is fairly bumpy in places
Distance	24km (15 miles)		
Ascent	2100m	**Accommodation**	Bridge of Orchy Hotel (and bunkhouse) 01838 (400208); Crianlarich YH (01838 300260); Inveroran Hotel (01838 400220)
Time	10hrs		
Terrain	Pleasant grassy walking on the tops of the hills, but the flanks are steep and lower ground can be boggy. Paths are sketchy in some places and non-existent in others.		
		Sleeping out	This would be an enjoyable round from a secluded base camp in Glen Coralan
Summits	Beinn a' Chaisteil 886m ('castle mountain'); Beinn nam Fuaran 806m ('mountain of the springs'); Cam Chreag 884m ('crooked crag'); Beinn Chaorach 818m ('sheep mountain'); Beinn Odhar 901m ('dun-coloured mountain')	**Seasonal notes**	No technical difficulties under snow, but the descents from Beinn Chaorach and Beinn Odhar need careful footing. The uniformly grassy slopes may be hazardous in avalanche-prone conditions. The round would make a fantastic ski tour.
Maps	OS Landranger (1:50,000) 50; OS Explorer (1:25,000) 377	**Short cuts**	Any of the tops can be easily omitted, although that is not playing by the rules
Public transport	The start of the walk is midway between Bridge of Orchy and Tyndrum, both served by train and bus routes from Glasgow		

Beinn Odhar and the Ben Lui hills (Walk 34) from Beinn a' Chaisteil

Early morning on the Beinn nam Fuaran – Beinn a' Chaisteil col, with the Achallader hills (Walk 32) in the background

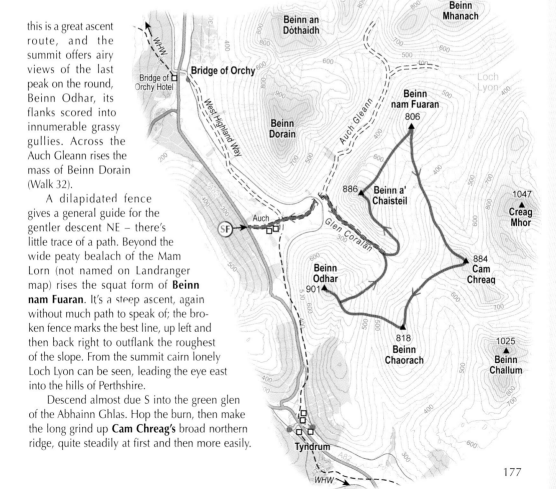

this is a great ascent route, and the summit offers airy views of the last peak on the round, Beinn Odhar, its flanks scored into innumerable grassy gullies. Across the Auch Gleann rises the mass of Beinn Dorain (Walk 32).

A dilapidated fence gives a general guide for the gentler descent NE – there's little trace of a path. Beyond the wide peaty bealach of the Mam Lorn (not named on Landranger map) rises the squat form of **Beinn nam Fuaran**. It's a steep ascent, again without much path to speak of; the broken fence marks the best line, up left and then back right to outflank the roughest of the slope. From the summit cairn lonely Loch Lyon can be seen, leading the eye east into the hills of Perthshire.

Descend almost due S into the green glen of the Abhainn Ghlas. Hop the burn, then make the long grind up **Cam Chreag's** broad northern ridge, quite steadily at first and then more easily.

A cairn marks the highest of several rocky knobbles above the craggy eastern face of the hill. The setting is remote, with views of nearby Munros Ben Challum and Creag Mhor. Descend roughly WSW through rocks and bogs to meet a disused electric fence, a weird low-lying double row of wooden posts that approximates to the northern perimeter of Loch Lomond and The Trossachs National Park and the Argyll–Stirling county line.

A path follows the posts onto the next saddle (beware snares of abandoned rusty wire), past the remains of a generator that once powered the fence, and then on up the northern slopes of **Beinn Chaorach**. The name means 'sheep mountain', and it would be tempting to say that's all this dull grassy lump is good for, were it not for the views.

From the summit trig bear very slightly N of W to descend the relentlessly steep slope into the glen below Beinn Odhar; the double fence line is still visible, although following it exactly is of no advantage. Still with the fence, more or less, continue W up the similarly uncompromising flank of **Beinn Odhar** to emerge with relief on its gentler southeast spur. Climb this, past a level shoulder, to reach a tiny pool below the stony summit dome. A short steep climb now gains the cairn on top, with some of the best views of the day as a reward for the hard graft. Go back past the pool to the shoulder, then descend a vague grassy spur ENE into **Glen Coralan**.

Return 4km

Regain the north bank of the Allt Coralan and retrace your steps (or tyre tracks) back to **Auch**.

Loch Lyon from Beinn nam Fuaran

Ben Lui, Ben Oss and Beinn Dubhchraig

*I*n both size and grace Ben Lui stands head and shoulders above its neighbours, its distinctive twin peaks rising at the hub of five radiating ridges. Seen from the east Lui's symmetry is striking, with the high scoop of Coire Gaothach hugged by the outstretched arms of two sharp ridges. Although long, the walk-in from this side is visually exciting, Ben Lui growing ever larger above the Cononish glen. Under snow Coire Gaothach and its precipitous edges have the look of something Alpine, and there is a mountaineering flavour to any ascent on this side of the hill.

On this walk Ben Lui is combined with adjacent Ben Oss and Beinn Dubhchraig, pleasant Munros too. The views span the crowded peaks of Arrochar and Crianlarich, Cruachan and the Black Mount, the length of Loch Lomond and even, on clear days, the distant heights of Arran and Jura. For the very keen there's a fourth Munro, Beinn a' Chleibh, nearby, although it entails a lengthy detour or a linear route with associated transport shenanigans.

↑ *Ben Lui from the Cononish glen*

Start/finish	Dalrigh car park (NN 343 291)
Distance	22km (14 miles)
Ascent	1560m
Time	8hrs
Terrain	A good track leads quickly from Dalrigh to the foot of Ben Lui; paths on the hills are generally well trodden, if a little intermittent and boggy in places
Summits	Ben Lui (Beinn Laoigh) 1130m ('mountain of the calf'); Ben Oss 1029m ('elk mountain', possibly); Beinn Dubhchraig 978m ('mountain of the black rock')
Maps	OS Landranger (1:50,000) 50; OS Explorer (1:25,000) 364; Harvey British Mountain Map (1:40,000) Southern Highlands
Public transport	Train or bus from Glasgow to Tyndrum
By bike	A quick easy cycle along the length of the Cononish track, although this entails varying from the route as described here
Accommodation	Bridge of Orchy Hotel (and bunkhouse) 01838 (400208); Crianlarich YH (01838 300260); Inveroran Hotel (01838 400220)
Sleeping out	Upper Cononish glen, the bealach above Coire Laoigh and the shores of Loch Oss on the south side of Beinn Dubhchraig all offer good wild camps
Seasonal notes	Since much of the walk is low level and do-able in the dark, this route suits winter's brief days. Under snow, technical difficulties are confined to the ascent of Ben Lui from Coire Gaothach. There are three obvious choices here. **1** Hardest is Central Gully, a magnificent grade I snow climb up the headwall; beware avalanche risk. **2** The ridge bounding the south side of the corrie is a gentler grade I climb. **3** Those without relevant competence should avoid both and stick to the less formidable north rim of the corrie; even this is steep enough to demand respect. Large cornices may be encountered on any of these routes. If in doubt contour W from the north rim of Coire Gaothach to ascend via Ben Lui's northwest ridge.
Short cuts	The bealach at the head of Coire Laoigh separates Ben Lui from its two neighbours, offering a handy bad-weather escape into the Cononish glen

↑ *Ben Lui from Ben Oss*

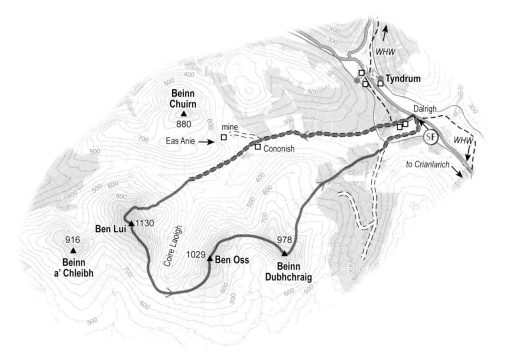

Approach 6.5km

From the car park take the track signed for Ben Lui, heading W past two houses. Cross a bridge over a burn, pass a turnoff signposted for the West Highland Way, then go under the railway. The track continues up the glen between spruce plantations and the broad stony River Cononish, entering the Ben Lui National Nature Reserve (famous for its saxifrages). Beyond **Cononish** farm the track climbs gently below a working gold mine and the prominent waterfall of Eas Anie (a superb ice climb in a cold snap), then traverses the hillside for about 1km before descending to the Allt an Rund, where it terminates.

On the hill 14km

Cross the burn, then take an earthy path steeply uphill beside the Allt Coire Ghaothaich to pass between the twin peaks framing the mouth of the corrie. From the sloping corrie floor there are three main ascent possibilities depending on conditions and inclination (see Seasonal notes, above, for the options). In either summer or winter the least problematic choice is the ridge forming the north rim of the corrie – more a walk than a scramble. To reach this, climb quite steeply W to a little saddle between the minor top of Stob Garbh and Ben Lui, then take the path up the defined crest leading to **Ben Lui's** NW top. The short summit ridge runs from here to the main peak; beware cornices along the edge.

Climbing out of Coire Gaothach onto Ben Lui's north ridge

Descend the SE ridge – steep at first, although the incline soon relents – to the boggy bealach at the head of Coire Laoigh. An intermittent path now makes a long ascent on grass and boulders to the cairn on top of **Ben Oss**. This hummocky terrain can be confusing in mist, but in clear weather Ben Lui looks particularly imposing from here. From the summit of the day's second Munro stay with the high ground, descending NE and then E onto a minor top (spot height 941m on OS maps) and from there to the Bealach Buidhe, which divides Coire Buidhe and Coire Garbh. A path now zigzags quite steeply uphill onto a shoulder at about 900m, scattered with little lochans. From here a gentle ascent ESE gains the summit of **Beinn Dubhchraig**, your reward a distant view along the length of Loch Lomond.

Head briefly down the broad NE spur before trending left from about the 900m contour into the shallow scoop of Coire Dubhchraig (unnamed on 1:50,000 map). Here pick up a boggy path which runs downhill beside the Allt Coire Dubhchraig, passing through spruce plantations to enter a beautiful open wood of Scots pine on the lower slopes.

Return 1.5km

Once back in the Cononish glen cross a footbridge over the Allt Coire Dubhchraig, then bear right over marshy ground to join a track. This runs towards the A82, crossing first the railway then an old stone bridge over the River Cononish to regain the car park at **Dalrigh**.

Ben Lui and Beinn a' Chleibh from the Ben Cruachan range (Walk 31)

Crianlarich hills

*T*he hills south of Crianlarich form an attractive rumpled skyline running west–east from the tangle of tops and ridges above Glen Falloch to the smooth cones of Ben More and Stob Binnein. These twins are giants of the area, and from below they certainly look the part; there are no higher mountains further south in Britain. In distant views the ground may appear grassy, but flanks and summits are liberally studded with rock, beautifully weathered mica schist outcropping in a chaos of craggy knolls that makes for interesting route finding.

Separated in places by deep glens, the group's seven Munros are generally climbed only in twos or threes – yet this more ambitious extended traverse really repays the extra effort. Runners or overnighters could start with Beinn Chabhair, with its purgatorial labyrinth of hummocks and hollows; but excluding it gives the neater and more manageable circuit described here.

Approach 1km
Cross a stile and a boggy field to pass under the railway. Take a track which crosses a bridge and then follows the River Falloch upstream. At a little ford peel right onto a clear path (cairn).

On the hill 20.5km
Climb S up the boggy slope onto the north ridge of An Caisteal, known as Twistin Hill. Make an enjoyable ascent of this long ridge, passing over several mini-summits and a curious rock crevasse to reach

↑ Left to right – Ben More, Stob Binnein and Cruach Ardrain from Beinn Dubhchraig (Walk 34)   183

ROUTE INFORMATION

Start/finish	Car park off the A82 in Glen Falloch, about 2km southwest of Crianlarich (NN 369 238)
Distance	27km (17 miles)
Ascent	2910m
Time	12hrs
Terrain	Clear trails on all the tops, but sections both west and east of Cruach Ardrain are pathless. Steep ground abounds throughout, scattered with little crags that make route finding circuitous at times.
Summits	An Caisteal 995m ('the castle'); Beinn a' Chroin 942m ('mountain of the sheepfold'); Beinn Tulaichean 946m ('mountain of the hillocks'); Cruach Ardrain 1046m ('the high-stacked heap'); Stob Binnein 1165m ('conical peak', possibly); Ben More 1174m ('big mountain')
Maps	The route cuts across OS Landranger (1:50,000) 50, 51 & 56 and OS Explorer (1:25,000) 364 & 365; since it covers the lot on one sheet Harvey British Mountain Map (1:40,000) Southern Highlands is best
Public transport	Buses and trains from Glasgow to Fort William both stop at Crianlarich
By bike	Leaving bikes near Benmore Farm (A85) would cut out the end-of-day road plod
Accommodation	Bridge of Orchy Hotel (and bunkhouse) 01838 (400208); Crianlarich YH (01838 300260); Inveroran Hotel (01838 400220)
Sleeping out	The complex humps and hollows provide many sheltered campsites, particularly the low glens either side of Cruach Ardrain
Seasonal notes	Likely to be too long and strenuous for a single winter day. Several sections require care in winter – the descent S from An Caisteal; the west face of Beinn a' Chroin; and the very steep descent NE from Cruach Ardrain. The smooth profile of Ben More belies its winter danger. Closely skirting a small but very steep corrie (most clearly seen on the Harvey map), the descent of the northwest spur demands attentive navigation – and careful footing in icy conditions. Avalanches have been known here too.
Short cuts	The hills neatly divide into three separate groups with low cols between each; shorter variations covering just one or two groups are easily made. The most obvious places that permit this are Glen Falloch, the northwest ridge of Cruach Ardrain (Meall Damh) and Benmore Glen.

the cairns on top of **An Caisteal**. Continue down the south ridge, an intricate descent through rocks with one or two very easy scrambly moments – slippery when wet. Beyond the Bealach Buidhe the path flirts briefly with the craggy west face of Beinn a' Chroin, weaving up right and then back left through rock tiers with one short steep scrambling step.

Beinn a' Chroin forms an extended ridge of grassy knobbles – a cairn marks top 938m but the high point is actually the next lump to the east, roughly midway along the summit ridge. At a saddle below the most easterly summit cut left on a path that descends gently across the hillside to rejoin the main trail on the blunt north spur. To avoid the crags of Coire Dhonnacha (not named on 1:50,000 map) follow this spur downhill to about the 550m contour, where it is possible to cut E to the boggy valley floor just downhill of the bealach between **Coire Earb** and **Ishag Glen**.

Bearing left of the crags climb steep, pathless rough ground onto Stob Ghlas, a complex area of many rocky lumps and boggy dips. Skirt just right of the highest knobble, passing tiny pools to reach secluded Coire Earb (which confusingly shares a name with its near neighbour). Contour around the back of the corrie, staying below a row of outcrops, to gain a well-trodden path in the grassy dip on the ridge between Cruach Ardrain and Beinn Tulaichean. Turn right for the quick easy climb onto **Tulaichean**, then return to the saddle and continue more steeply onto **Cruach Ardrain**, a grand peak and arguably the best in the group.

The descent NE is precipitous and eroded. From the saddle below, a path weaves through crags on complicated ground to reach a cairn on the high point of **Stob Garbh** ('rough peak' – well named). Here, leave the trail and head roughly E to pick a

Ben More (left) and Stob Binnein from Cruach Ardrain →

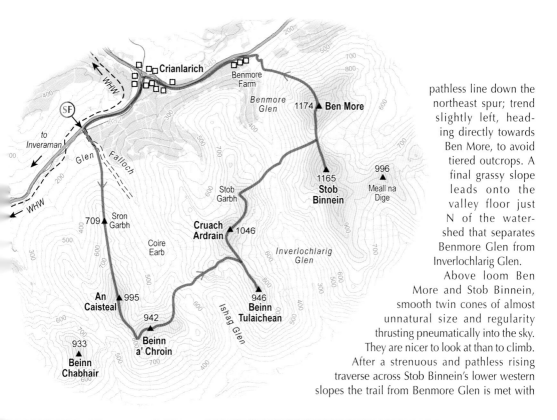

pathless line down the northeast spur; trend slightly left, heading directly towards Ben More, to avoid tiered outcrops. A final grassy slope leads onto the valley floor just N of the watershed that separates Benmore Glen from Inverlochlarig Glen.

Above loom Ben More and Stob Binnein, smooth twin cones of almost unnatural size and regularity thrusting pneumatically into the sky. They are nicer to look at than to climb. After a strenuous and pathless rising traverse across Stob Binnein's lower western slopes the trail from Benmore Glen is met with

relief. Although not marked on OS maps this well-used path ascends directly to the Bealach-eadar-dha Bheinn, the cleavage between the two peaks.

Consider leaving extraneous gear beside a prominent boulder before completing the long grind onto **Stob Binnein** – recommended even if your legs are now protesting, for the expansive southward views. Return to the col and continue N for the steep and similarly drawn-out slog onto **Ben More**. With the flats of Strath Fillan stretched out far below, this peak conveys a sense of scale even greater than its neighbour's. The disadvantage soon becomes clear – it's a long way down.

Invisible on the maps but clear on the ground, a path descends the north-west flank. In snow or poor visibility particular attention is needed to stay safely right of a treacherous crag band just below the summit area, more a shallow scoop than a defined corrie. The trail is eroded and unremittingly steep, but at least height is quickly lost (not too quickly, hopefully). The path is easily misplaced on the lower slopes, but keep dropping WNW and the Benmore Glen track is eventually met. Turn right onto this, zigzagging through pastures to the A85 near **Benmore Farm**.

Return 5.5km

Those who haven't left a car or bike here now face a trudge along the verge into **Crianlarich**, and on down the A82 to the car park in **Glen Falloch**; as it'll probably be dark by now, watch out for speeding traffic.

Stob Garbh (left), Ben More and Stob Binnein from Beinn Tulaichean

Ben Vorlich and Stuc a' Chroin from Beinn Tulaichean

Arrochar 'Alps'

*T*he roughest range in the Southern Highlands, the Arrochar 'Alps' are also among the most accessible, rising just west of Loch Lomond and in sight of Glasgow's tower blocks. Although close-
packed the hills stand isolated from one another, steep-sided and scattered with countless outcrops.
Compared to the real thing these Alps have been rather over-promoted, bar one. Its neighbours may
be bigger, but The Cobbler is the star attraction – a triple-topped rock peak with the jagged profile (if
not scale) of a mini Chamonix Aiguille.

This classic circuit combines this most impressive of Scotland's Corbetts with the four Munros
of the range. The walk centres on Coiregrogain, a pretty glen despite the best efforts of commercial
foresters and electricity generators. The hills rise far above the mess of power lines. The Mont Blanc
range this ain't, but who needs crevasses and altitude sickness anyway?

Approach 2km

Follow the pavement outside the **power station**,
then a footpath parallel with the A82, to reach the
surfaced access road for Loch Sloy. Go through a
gate, under a railway bridge, and then cut a corner on a path to rejoin the access road, which is
followed uphill beside Inveruglas Water. Pass
beneath a power line to a junction by a large electricity **substation**.

Going right here, the road curves back on itself
to climb across the lower slopes of Ben Vorlich.
Leave the road just before a second junction.

↑ *Ben Vane (right) and Beinn Ime from Ben Vorlich*

Lochs Lomond, Arklet and Katrine from Ben Vane

ROUTE INFORMATION

Start/finish	Car park at Inveruglas (NN 322 099)
Distance	26km (16 miles)
Ascent	2700m
Time	10½hrs
Terrain	Steep, knobbly and rough. Given the popularity and accessibility of the range the pathless sections on Ben Vorlich, Ben Vane and Beinn Ime may come as a surprise. The only scramble is optional – 15m of exposed grade 3 onto the topmost rock of The Cobbler's Centre Peak.
Summits	Ben Vorlich 943m ('mountain of the bay'); Ben Vane 915m ('middle mountain'); Beinn Ime 1011m ('butter mountain'); The Cobbler 884m; Beinn Narnain 926m ('mountain of the notches', possibly)
Maps	OS Landranger (1:50,000) 56; OS Explorer (1:25,000) 364; Harvey British Mountain Map (1:40,000) Southern Highlands
Public transport	Glasgow to Fort William buses will stop on the A82. With minor variations this walk is also possible as a linear route between the train stations at Ardlui and Tarbet.
By bike	If Ben Vorlich is omitted it is worth cycling to the bridge over Inveruglas Water (NN 298 095)
Accommodation	Crianlarich YH (01838 300260)
Sleeping out	The many hollows give endless camping possibilities. One of the best and most remote spots is Lag Uaine between Beinn Ime and Ben Vane.
Seasonal notes	As a one-day winter round this is perhaps best curtailed (see Short cuts, below). If Ben Vorlich is included, care will be needed on the descent to Loch Sloy, the steepest of the day. The final short summit scramble on The Cobbler becomes a technical winter climb for which a rope would be advisable.
Short cuts	Missing out Ben Vorlich gives a much easier day, starting with the well-used path up the southeast spur of Ben Vane. Either The Cobbler or Beinn Narnain can also be omitted.

On the hill 17km

Attack steep pathless ground scattered with schist outcrops to gain the long, undulating south ridge of **Ben Vorlich**. This eventually leads to the broad summit area; pass a trig point to reach the cairn that marks the highest point. Unfortunately most of the hard-won height gain now has to be lost.

From the cairn backtrack for approximately 1km down the ridge, passing just left of a rocky mini-summit. At the vague saddle beyond this cut directly downhill towards the Loch Sloy dam, a steep rough descent with no clear path. Cross the **dam** and from the far side head W on another challenging pathless leg, skirting right of a craggy knoll to climb through outcrops onto a boggy levelling below the rugged upper slopes of **Ben Vane**. A burn leads SW towards the skyline; follow this into a vague gully, then turn left for the final climb onto the summit, a knobble overlooking the big south face.

Descend W, bearing slightly right whenever you are met with a crag band, for the easiest line into the low bealach between Ben Vane and Beinn Ime; again there's no path. The secluded hollow of the Lag Uaine is a far cry from the bagger's trails on these popular Munros. Two burns run down the hillside above, close together. Go between them – a steep path-free ascent at first, easing onto the soggy Glas-Bhealach. Turn S for the long climb onto **Beinn Ime**; finally there's a path (of sorts). The summit view ranges from Ben Nevis to Ben Lomond, the Arran skyline to the Ochils. Fans of wind turbines may be pleased to see clusters like giant mushrooms further west in Argyll.

A more heavily worn path descends SE towards the lip of Beinn Ime's craggy eastern corrie, then curves S down a gentle grassy incline onto the spongy Bealach a'Mhaim, a major col at the hub of three hills. Cross a fence via a stile and continue on the path to the saddle between Beinn Narnain and The Cobbler, where bags may be left. It's worth climbing both, but if you have to miss one don't make it the latter.

The Cobbler path begins as a staircase of stone blocks, then becomes more eroded as it skirts the North Peak to reach the higher Centre Peak. The mountain's true summit is a free-standing rock, infamous among height-averse walkers and only reachable by a short sharp scramble that can be unnerving in adverse weather. The route starts with a squeeze through the obvious window-like cave, then follows an exposed ledge overlooking a drop on the west flank to finish up well-polished blocks. The way off is to reverse the way up. Although lower, The Cobbler's

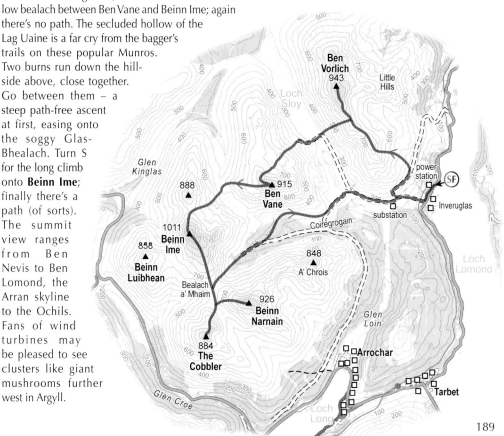

189

WALK 36 ARROCHAR 'ALPS'

The summit block of The Cobbler's Centre Peak – a short sharp scramble – and, to the left, Ben Lomond

other tops are more dramatic still – the massive rock molar of the South Peak (only for climbers) and the North Peak with its improbable overhanging fins.

Return to the saddle and take the obvious path up **Beinn Narnain**, a little eroded and steep in places but soon over. The broad stony summit plateau offers a superb view of The Cobbler. On paper, closing the circuit with the minor top of A' Chrois might look attractive, but this late in the day the forestry that swathes its lower slopes is unlikely to appeal. It is less hassle to return to the Bealach a'Mhaim, from

where a vague path follows the fence down a steep grassy slope into the head of **Coiregrogain**. Cross a stile and plunge into dense new-growth pines. After a couple of minutes the path veers slightly left. Cross two little burns to reach a vehicle track.

Return 7km

This leads down through the woods of Coiregrogain, with dramatic views of the craggy flanks of A' Chrois and Ben Vane. Meet the Loch Sloy access road, which is followed back downhill to the A82.

← *Loch Long and the South Peak of The Cobbler from Centre Peak*

191

Ben Lawers group
and the Tarmachan Ridge

*B*en Lawers has a sense of solid scale befitting the highest Scottish peak outside the Cairngorms
and Lochaber. The overused tourist path, ignoring the good bits in its beeline for the topmost
point, is a poor way to climb a grand hill. Lawers is best treated as a range rather than a single summit, a clutch of big Munros on a high ridge that snakes between Loch Tay and Glen Lyon to provide
the superb multi-topped traverse described here. But let's go larger still.

   To the west a pronounced bealach and road divides Lawers from the adjacent Tarmachan
Ridge, defining each as distinct hill groups. Although less massive, the knobbly Tarmachan peaks
contrast nicely with their rolling neighbours. With a high (and early) start from the Lochan na Lairige
road both groups can be incorporated into one logical round. While determined baggers could fea-
sibly scalp nine Munros, the walk described misses two outliers.

↑ *Ben Lawers (left) and An Stùc from Meall Garbh in spring*

ROUTE INFORMATION

Start/finish	Pay and display car park off the high road between the Lawers and Tarmachan ranges, formerly the NTS visitor centre (NN 609 379)		descent from Creag na Caillich to Killin less so.
Distance	29km (18 miles)	**By bike**	Leaving a bike at Killin before starting is a good way to turn this into a linear walk without being tied to the bus timetable
Ascent	2400m		
Time	12hrs	**Accommodation**	Braveheart Backpackers, Killin (01567 829089)
Terrain	Clear paths on largely grassy hills; vague hints of scrambling on An Stùc and Meall Garbh, but insignificant in dry snow-free conditions	**Sleeping out**	Good camping on the An Stùc – Ben Lawers saddle and the Beinn Ghlas – Meall Corranaich col. Cunning souls unwilling to abide by the spirit of the game might leave camping gear in their car for evening use prior to finishing the walk the following morning.
Summits	Meall Garbh 1118m ('rough hill'); An Stùc 1118m ('the peak'); Ben Lawers 1214m ('loud mountain', possibly); Beinn Ghlas 1103m ('grey-green mountain'); Meall Corranaich 1069m ('crooked hill', possibly); Meall nan Tarmachan 1044m ('hill of the ptarmigans'); Meall Garbh 1026m ('rough hill'); Creag na Caillich 916m ('crag of the old woman')		
		Seasonal notes	These hefty inland hills hold snow well. Under deep snow this walk would be ambitious for a single day, although magnificent over two. In icy conditions three sections require particular care – the ascent of the steep east flank of An Stùc; the slopes either side of the Beinn Ghlas – Meall Corranaich col; and the Meall Garbh crest and descent from its western end.
Maps	OS Landranger (1:50,000) 51; OS Explorer (1:25,000) 378; Harvey Superwalker (1:25,000) Ben Lawers		
Public transport	Using infrequent Killin to Aberfeldy buses on the A827, this route can be turned into a shorter linear walk. If doing this, the initial ascent from Lawers along the Lawers Burn to Coire nan Cat is obvious; the final	**Short cuts**	Do either Lawers or Tarmachan, rather than both; the road between the two makes this a rather too easy option

Approach 8km

The whole Lawers/Tarmachan range is a National Nature Reserve with an unrivalled collection of arctic/alpine plants and fascinating prehistoric archaeology. From the car park follow a boardwalk and then a footpath signed for Ben Lawers, ascending into a fenced area of regenerating vegetation. Just after the path crosses a burn split off right, stepping through a gap in a locked gate onto the grassy slopes below Beinn Ghlas. Make a gradually rising traverse on sheep tracks to reach a pronounced shoulder at about 660m altitude overlooking Loch Tay. Continue contouring beside a line of dilapidated fence posts, descending slightly and crossing the Allt an Tuim Bhric in its deep cutting to meet a water-works access track. This hugs the 600m contour for nearly 4km, eventually ending at a small dam in the mouth of Coire nan Cat. Cross the **Lawers Burn** here.

On the hill 16km

Head N on an occasional path past some old shielings, ascending steeply just left of a fenced-off conservation area to reach the hummocky Meall Greigh – Meall Garbh col (the unremarkable Munro Meall Greigh is easily bagged from here). Bear left to meet the main path along the skyline, which is followed strenuously uphill onto the knobbly top of **Meall Garbh**. A rough descent now leads to the high saddle below the most formidable obstacle in the range, the ragged cone of **An Stùc**. Despite impregnable appearances a worn trail winds uphill through the outcrops, initially slightly left of centre. There is some scrappy scrambling and a degree of exposure, but little to write home about in summer. If in doubt it's possible to traverse rightwards below the rocks to come at An Stùc via its grassier north ridge.

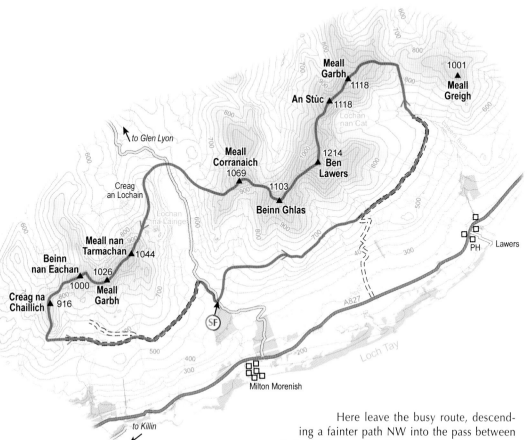

From the airy summit an easier path drops to the low bealach above the head of **Lochan nan Cat**. The loch is named for its fancied feline resemblance (although 'Lochan nan Splodge' would be more appropriate). There follows a long grind up to **Ben Lawers** itself, initially quite rugged skirting the mini-peak of Creag an Fhithich, then on a gentler slope beside the corrie rim, where fat cornices can form. Lawers's summit sports two trig points, but no trace remains of the famous cairn built by number-fixated Victorians to artificially boost the mountain into the exclusive 4000ft club.

Descend the eroded tourist trail down the east spur to the next col. (From here a get-out path avoids Beinn Ghlas, skirting its northern slopes before cutting down Coire Odhar back to the car park.) Staying with the ridge crest, however, a painless ascent leads quickly to the attractive summit of **Beinn Ghlas**.

Here leave the busy route, descending a fainter path NW into the pass between Beinn Ghlas and Meall Corranaich. Broken crags just above the pass are avoided by bearing slightly left. Cross a path to follow a less trodden route that attacks the rocky southeast flank of **Meall Corranaich** head on, weaving a cunning course through crags up to the grassy summit. The southwest ridge is an obvious quick route back to the road, but stay with it only briefly. After the initial steep descent look out for a path cutting right beside an old fence line, which leads gently down to the boggy ground above **Lochan na Lairige**.

With the start/finish point now so close the assault on the Tarmachans may require willpower, but it's worthwhile. Cross the road at its high point near a prominent cairn a little north of the loch, then make a long easy ascent over **Creag an Lochain**. Bumpy, soggy ground leads to the north ridge of **Meall nan Tarmachan**, and thence the summit.

The famous Tarmachan Ridge traverse awaits, a complex and fascinating route that twists and turns over a succession of rugged summits. Although a

← *Approaching the summit of Meall Garbh*

tiring way to round off a long day, it ranks in its own right among the best ridge walks in the Southern Highlands.

First descend a well-trodden path onto confusing hummocky ground above the buttresses of Cam Chreag. A sharp pull now gains the impressive peak of **Meall Garbh**. Now comes the best bit, a short scrambly descent onto a spectacular level arête. Despite the airy feel there is no difficulty, and it's over in moments. The ridge soon broadens as it drops westwards towards the next major col. The final descent to this saddle is on steep broken rock, and likely to cause problems if icy or wet; easier a little north of the worn path.

Beyond the col the path leads over two pronounced minor peaks before reaching the summit of **Beinn nan Eachan** – potentially confusing in mist.

In descent from here skirt slightly right to avoid a crag before gaining hummocky ground below. After a short final climb the grassy summit of **Creag na Caillich** will be greeted with relief; it's almost all downhill from here. A direct descent from the end of the south ridge runs into cliffs, so again bear right for the safest line to the col beyond. Turning E, pick down scree and boulders to reach an old vehicle track on the slopes below the Tarmachan peaks.

Return 5km
By now your legs could be forgiven for wobbling, but the track gives a quick easy finish.

Loch Tay from the Meall Garbh arête

Beinn a'Ghlo, the Tarf and the Tilt

The twisting ridges and high peaks of Beinn a'Ghlo give a classic (if perennially popular) single-day hill walk, which is especially good when combined with Glen Tilt. This trench-like fault is carved along the base of the massif from barren uplands to forested lower reaches, the rushing River Tilt a constant companion. While the Tilt cuts a strikingly straight swathe through the hills, its upper tributary, the Tarf Water, meanders in a broad ill-defined basin, its surrounding hills a rolling sprawl of bog and moorland. What this landscape may lack in scenic distinction it makes up for with challenging terrain and an inspiring sense of emptiness.

Although the walk as described could be substantially shortened with no reduction in the summit tally, following the circuit as far as the Tarf Water is highly recommended. It will entail an overnight stay for most – and, as luck has it, the Feith Uaine bothy is ideally placed. For dedicated baggers the walk might be stretched further to also encompass remote Beinn Dearg to the west.

↑ *Beinn a'Ghlo from Ben Vrackie – Carn Liath is the rounded peak on the left, with the Carn a' Chlamain hills half-hidden behind it*

ROUTE INFORMATION

Start/finish	Glen Tilt car park above Blair Atholl (NN 874 663)
Distance	41km (25½ miles)
Ascent	1960m
Time	16hrs (best over 2 days)
Terrain	Eroded paths link Beinn a'Ghlo's main peaks. Estate tracks run from Glen Tilt to the Tarf Water, and from the summit area of Carn a' Chlamain all the way down Glen Tilt to Blair Atholl; elsewhere the going can be boggy and practically pathless.
Summits	Beinn a'Ghlo ('mountain of the veil'); Carn Liath 975m ('grey hill'); Bràigh Coire Chruinn-bhalgain 1070m ('height of the corrie of round blisters'); Carn nan Gabhar 1129m ('hill of goats'); Carn a' Chlamain 963m ('hill of the kite')
Maps	OS Landranger (1:50,000) 43; OS Explorer (1:25,000) 394
Public transport	Train or bus to Blair Atholl followed by a short road walk to the start of the walk as described
By bike	Although cycling the length of Glen Tilt is quick, it's hard to devise a circular route of any great length that exploits this
Accommodation	Pitlochry YH (01796 472308)
Sleeping out	Grassy camping in upper Glen Tilt. The Feith Uaine bothy (aka Tarf Hotel) (NN 926 789) is an oasis of 'civilisation' in a desert of bog and heather, and well worth the long walk. There are several rooms, each with a fireplace, so space should usually be available even at weekends. Bring your own comestibles and combustibles.
Seasonal notes	A snowy Beinn a'Ghlo traverse is a must for competent winter walkers; by contrast the Tarf hills offer a different sort of challenge, navigating through bleak tundra-like terrain.
Short cuts	The Glen Tilt track allows the walk to be split neatly into two separate shorter routes. Carn a' Chlamain can also be climbed from near Forest Lodge in Glen Tilt via a zigzagging stalker's path, although this means missing out on the Tarf stage.

The hills of the Tarf from Carn nan Gabhar

Approach 5km

Walk right along the road, crossing the bridge over the Tilt by some houses, then turning left to follow the road uphill. Keep right at a fork, climbing steadily to the end of the public road beside **Loch Moraig**. There's parking here for the standard one-day round of Beinn a'Ghlo. Take the right fork in the continuation track, gently climbing over moorland to reach a little tin-roofed barn.

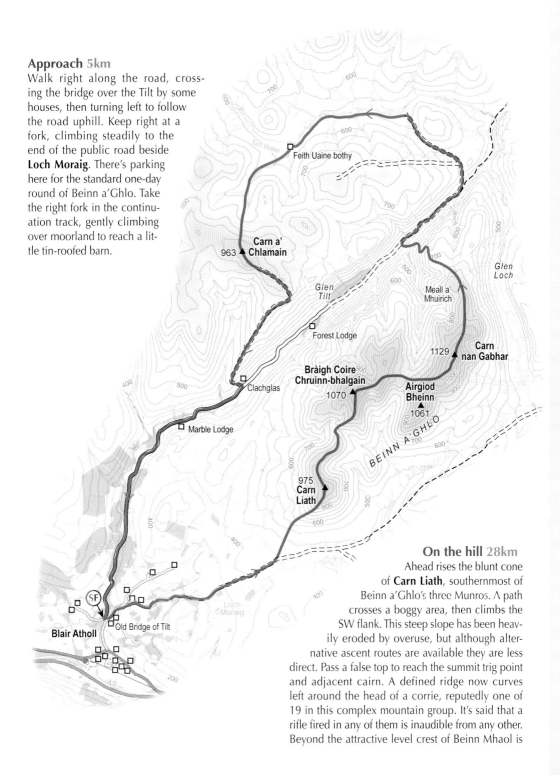

On the hill 28km

Ahead rises the blunt cone of **Carn Liath**, southernmost of Beinn a'Ghlo's three Munros. A path crosses a boggy area, then climbs the SW flank. This steep slope has been heavily eroded by overuse, but although alternative ascent routes are available they are less direct. Pass a false top to reach the summit trig point and adjacent cairn. A defined ridge now curves left around the head of a corrie, reputedly one of 19 in this complex mountain group. It's said that a rifle fired in any of them is inaudible from any other. Beyond the attractive level crest of Beinn Mhaol is

199

Looking south from Carn Liath

an abrupt descent into a tight notch, where the path kinks rightwards.

Slog uphill, first E and then N along a stony crest onto **Bràigh Coire Chruinn-bhalgain**. Now stay with high the ground, descending a little E over a slight rise to pick up the obvious path down to the grassy saddle at the head of Glas Leathad. From here the path makes a rising traverse leftwards onto the skyline between Airgiod Bheinn and **Carn nan Gabhar**. Turn left, climbing past a cairn on a stony false summit, and then a trig point, to reach the cairn marking the top spot on Beinn a'Ghlo's highest mountain.

Crowds and path erosion will now be left behind as you descend N beside the craggy bowl of Coire Cas-eagallach, with a distant view ahead over rolling lesser hills to the high Cairngorms, arrayed in a row from Sgor Gaoith (Walk 39), Braeriach, Cairn Toul and Ben Macdui (Walk 40) to Beinn a' Bhuird and Ben Avon (Walk 41). A vague path leads over an unnamed top to the heathery hump of **Meall a' Mhuirich**. Bear N from here to descend quite steeply onto the hill's northwest shoulder, where a decent stalker's path (not marked on OS maps) zigzags down heathery slopes to the floor of **Glen Tilt**. Cross a small footbridge over a side-stream, then follow the path through a pasture to a bridge over the River Tilt itself (fording this elsewhere is safely possible only in low water).

On the far bank of the river is a 4WD track; follow this upstream for 2km to a fork. Take the left-hand track, which zigzags up the steep glen wall onto open moorland above, then stay right at another junction to climb over a saddle into the basin of the Tarf Water, which is met at a steading. A vehicle track runs for some distance along the north bank, but for the **Feith Uaine bothy** (aka the legendary Tarf Hotel) stay on the south side, where a vague boggy path leads along the river bank for about 3km to the bothy. Most people will call it a night here.

Leave the bothy and the Tarf Water behind and head WSW along the Feith Uaine Mhòr, staying right where the burn first divides and then left at the second fork to ascend the desolate glen west of Meall Tionail. There's no real path, just the occasional boot print. When the stream dwindles into peat bogs continue S, climbing grassy slopes onto **Carn a' Chlamain**. From the north top cross a 4WD track to reach the rocky hump of the main summit, with an excellent view of Beinn a'Ghlo.

Descend steeply ESE along the edge of the south face to join the vehicle track. Once on easier angled ground the trail splits; stay right. On reaching the steep rim of **Glen Tilt** the stony track cuts right before following a pronounced spur downhill towards the glen; a final leftwards kink leads to the house at **Clachghlas**.

Return 8km
Glen Tilt's woods and rapids make for an idyllic walk-out. Various side-paths are available, but it's easiest to stay with the main track all the way.

The high Cairngorms (Walks 40 and 41) from Carn nan Gabhar

Munros of Glen Feshie

G len Feshie's two Munros make a fine pair. Sgor Gaoith has a polarised character. The bland slopes bulging above the woods of Glen Feshie promise little, yet on its hidden side lurks one of the grandest faces in the Cairngorms, a complex expanse of tottering ribs and gullies dropping over 500m into lonely Loch Einich.

    While Sgor Gaoith only pretends to be a nondescript lump, Mullach Clach a' Bhlàir is the real thing, the high point (by a fraction) of the green, gently rolling table land of Mòine Mhòr – an emptiness with few equals in Scotland. Here's a second Munro tick for those who are keeping score, and a long stride with a sense of lonely spaciousness for others who favour the journey over the destination. With its broad river meandering through boulder banks, open meadows and copses of ancient Scots pines, the final stretch down Glen Feshie is a soothing contrast to the heights above.

↑ Sgoran Dubh Mor (right) and Sgor Gaoith from Gleann Einich at dawn

ROUTE INFORMATION

Start/finish	Car park 1km from Auchlean at the Glen Feshie road-head (NN 851 985) or any of several laybys further north
Distance	29km (18 miles)
Ascent	1150m
Time	9½hrs
Terrain	Gentle inclines, generally grassy ground and predominantly clear paths and tracks
Summits	Sgor Gaoith 1118m ('windy peak'); Mullach Clach a' Bhlàir 1019m ('summit of the stone of the plain')
Maps	The walk straddles OS Landrangers (1:50,000) 36 and 43, so OS Explorer (1:25,000) 403 is more convenient; Harvey British Mountain Map (1:40,000) Cairngorms and Lochnagar also covers the entire walk
Public transport	Train or intercity coach to Kingussie or Aviemore; local buses run no closer than Kincraig near Feshiebridge
By bike	A bike left for retrieval at the end of the day could save a few kilometres of tarmac walking
Accommodation	Glenfeshie Hostel (01540 651323); Aviemore YH (01479 810345)
Sleeping out	Reasonably sheltered grassy spots beside the burns that meander over the Mòine Mhòr, although perhaps not in stormy weather. A pitch in upper Glen Feshie would be idyllic. Alternatively, the Ruigh-aiteachain bothy (NN 847 928) is one of the most palatial of MBA-maintained huts.
Seasonal notes	With long stretches at low level this is a suitable walk for the short days of winter. The east face of Sgor Gaoith may carry substantial cornices, while in the wrong conditions Mòine Mhòr can become a featureless desert of billowing spindrift (see Short cuts, below). In a snowy spell the route is ski friendly.
Short cuts	Miss out Mullach Clach a' Bhlàir by descending the clear path from Carn Bàn Mòr

Coire Garbhlach

Approach 4.5km

Walk back N along the road, passing the Glenfeshie Hostel, to reach a wide junction with a forest track; turn right here to follow a clear path uphill through the woods. At another junction continue straight on, staying N of the Allt Ruadh and climbing more steeply through stands of old Scots pines. Just before the main path crosses a side-stream (the Allt nam Bò – not named on all maps) quit it for a narrower left turnoff.

On the hill 19km

This trail ascends through scattered woods and then open heathery ground, leading to a little bealach between Geal-chàrn and Creag Mhigeachaidh, where there is a tiny stone-walled wind shelter. Now leave the path and head SE, weaving up a steep rubble-strewn slope. From a substantial cairn on the ridge crest it's easier going to the summit of **Geal-chàrn**. Stay with the high ground, descending slightly to cross a pronounced gap in the ridge before climbing again to a vague saddle under Meall Buidhe (not named on Landranger map). A traverse path skirts left of this top to reach the boggy saddle under the dome of Sgòran Dubh Mòr – there's a spring here for drinking water. Bear SE up to the col between **Sgòran Dubh Mòr** and Sgor Gaoith, from where the former may be quickly visited for the sake of completeness.

For **Sgor Gaoith** head to the edge of the huge face overlooking

the glacially gouged trough of Loch Einich, a marked change on the rolling ground encountered so far. Follow the cliff rightwards up to the surprisingly dramatic summit, a suitable spot to pause and contemplate Braeriach on the far side of the gulf. A well-trodden path descends SSW, soon leaving the edge of the crags to cross a broad saddle before climbing gently onto **Carn Bàn Mòr**.

Just beyond the summit cairns a path is met at right angles (see Short cuts, above). A direct course

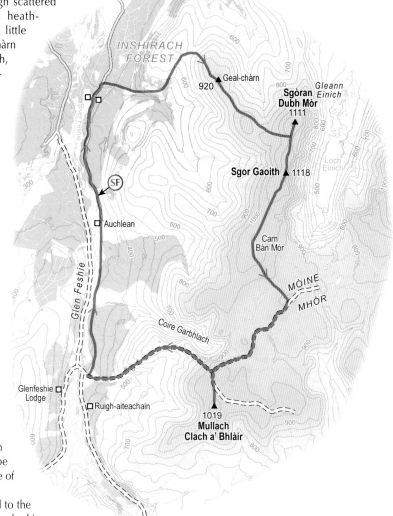

← Sgor Gaoith (left) and Sgoran Dubh Mor from Braeriach

from this junction to the distant hummock of Mullach Clach a' Bhlàir runs into an intractable peaty hollow at the heart of Mòine Mhòr; instead go left on this path, which veers SE for nearly 2km on a gradual descent and reascent, looping wide of the bogs to join a track carved starkly into the soft green hills.

Head right along this track, which winds circuitously over the plateau, eventually coming to a parting of the ways on the slopes above Coire Garbhlach. Turning S, the track arcs towards **Mullach Clach a' Bhlàir**. An obvious well-trodden line cuts the corner in the main track, before crossing the track and climbing onto the summit ripple. This may be one of the least distinctive Munros in Scotland, but the wild open setting is worth it. Return to the junction above Coire Garbhlach, from where a stony track descends steeply NW beneath the rim of this dramatic craggy bowl. A final descent through pines and juniper thickets gains a path junction in a meadow on the floor of Glen Feshie, not far north of **Ruigh-aiteachain** bothy.

Return 5.5km

Paths back N along the wooded floor of the glen are not quite as straightforward as may be supposed, especially after dark. Each of the maps covering the area has a different take on things, and the situation on the ground seems different to them all (OS Explorer is probably the clearest). Follow the path right through the meadow to join a track on the east bank of the wide **River Feshie**. Heading downstream, the track soon climbs into a forestry plantation. After about 1km bear slightly right on a narrower footpath, crossing a forest track at right angles to meet the Allt Garbhlach beyond the edge of the woods. Hop the burn a little distance upstream and continue N over open ground to rejoin the **River Feshie** near a footbridge. Do not cross. In a marshy area near an old cottage there's a choice of route; stay slightly right for the path leading to the road at **Auchlean Farm**.

Braeriach from Sgor Gaoith

Cairngorms 4000-ers

B *ritain's largest national park is a place like no other. The Cairngorms are hills of great stature, their sprawling plateaux and grand ice-gouged corries contrasting with the softer beauty of the pine woods lower down. The climate and wildlife recall the sub-arctic far north, as if an ice age island had been left high and dry by subsequent climate change. Boasting the second, third, fourth, fifth and sixth highest mountains in Scotland – all 4000-ers – the central massif of the Cairngorms comprises the most extensive area of high ground in the British Isles. The hills are split in two by the deep trench of the Lairig Ghru, a famous through-route linking Speyside with Deeside.*

This wild area is ideally suited to overnight backpacking trips, and this long circuit starting from the Cairngorm ski centre is the neatest way to link the five 4000-ers. Strong contenders might pack the lot into a single mega-day, but adding an overnight en route allows you to savour the special character of the Cairngorms.

↑ *Sgor an Lochain Uaine (left) and Braeriach from Ben Macdui*   207

ROUTE INFORMATION

Start/finish	Coire Cas car park, Cairngorm Mountain ski centre (NH 989 061)
Distance	34km (21 miles)
Ascent	2300m
Time	14hrs
Terrain	The gravel and stunted vegetation of the high plateaux give easy going. Rougher ground is crossed on the descent from Ben Macdui, around the summit of Cairn Toul, on Sròn na Lairige and in the Chalamain Gap. Well-trodden paths predominate – some too much so and badly eroded.
Summits	Cairn Gorm 1245m ('blue mountain'); Ben Macdui (Beinn MacDuibhe) 1309m ('MacDuff's mountain'); Cairn Toul (Carn an t-Sabhail) 1291m ('peak of the barn'); Sgor an Lochan Uaine (aka Angel's Peak) 1258m ('peak of the green lochan'); Braeriach (Am Braigh Riabhach) 1296m ('grey/drab/brindled upland')
Maps	OS Landranger (1:50,000) 36; OS Explorer (1:25,000) 403; Harvey British Mountain Map (1:40,000) Cairngorms and Lochnagar
Public transport	A regular bus service runs from Aviemore to the ski centre
Accommodation	Cairngorm Lodge YH (01479 861238); Aviemore YH (01479 810345); Fraoch Lodge hostel, Boat of Garten (01479 831331)
Sleeping out	Good camping (or snow holing) on the plateau between Cairn Gorm and Ben Macdui – in benign weather. The col between Macdui and Carn a' Mhaim offers well-drained ground close to running water. In the Lairig Ghru, at the mid-point of the walk, is Corrour bothy (NN 981 958). It's small and busy. The nearby Garbh Coire 'bothy' is a dank hovel sleeping three or four at a push – camping is preferable here.
Seasonal notes	It is hard to overstate the potential severity of winter weather in the high Cairngorms, the coldest and snowiest mountains in Scotland. Sweeping unchecked over the rolling terrain the winds can be ferocious (speeds in excess of 170mph have been recorded). In settled weather this walk is feasible over two winter days. Navigation on the featureless plateaus demands close attention, particularly when cairns and paths are buried under snow and the many corrie edges corniced. In really snowy spells touring skis can be the most practical mode of transport, and this route is one of the all-time classic tours of Scotland.
Short cuts	The route readily splits into two separate walks – Cairn Gorm and Ben Macdui followed by a descent via the west side of Coire an Lochain; and Cairn Toul / Braeriach via the Lairig Ghru

On the hill 34km

From the unlovely ski centre buildings take the track that runs beside the funicular railway for several hundred metres before passing under the line and zigzagging up the slopes of Coire Cas. Just beyond the third tight bend in the track a stone-paved path cuts right, climbing onto Fiacaill a' Choire Chais, the corrie's west-bounding ridge (when the pistes are open follow this ridge from lower down to avoid skiers). This leads to a prominent cairn on a level shoulder dividing Coire Cas from Coire an t-Sneachda. A short detour E up **Cairn Gorm's** stony dome gains the walk's first 4000-er.

Head back down past the cairn on the shoulder before tracing the rim of **Coire an t-Sneachda's** crags (often teeming with climbers) over a broad summit to the saddle at the top of Coire Domhain. The most direct path to Ben Macdui now skirts well left of **Cairn Lochan**, passing the meandering stream of Feith Buidhe in its broad basin and the lochan of the same name. Now on stonier ground the cairned path turns S, ascending gently over the bulging plateau before a short steeper pull up the flank of Macdui's north top. Staying right of this summit, cross a little scoop at the head of Allt a' Choire Mhóir to reach **Ben Macdui's** summit dome. The top of Scotland's

*The Lairig Ghru, Devil's Point and
Beinn Bhrotain from Ben Macdui*

second highest mountain has a trig point, a stone-walled windbreak and a panorama plaque – and what a view! Lower ranks of hills roll out in brown and purple waves, while over the gulf of the Lairig Ghru stands the deep-scalloped mass of Cairn Toul / Braeriach.

Descent requires attention, since the slope immediately south is steep and prone to avalanche; follow the plateau edge ESE for about 800m to find the Allt Clach nan Taillear (may be concealed under snow). Descend the vague spur SE of the stream – there's a sketchy path and some bouldery ground – to reach the wide col between Ben Macdui and Carn a' Mhaim. The slope leading from here into the **Lairig Ghru** is awkward in places, so alternatively stay with the path close to the Allt Clach nan Taillear initially before curving S to meet the main trail running along the base of the Lairig. Head S on this path for a little over 1km to cross a footbridge over the Dee before following

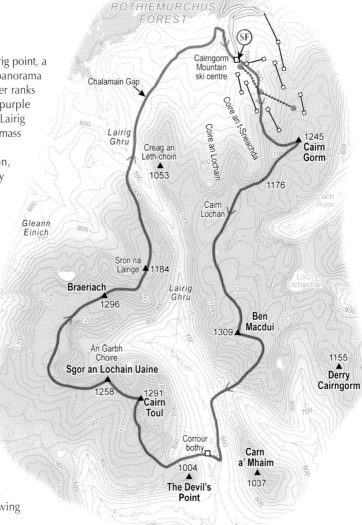

209

Ben Macdui from Braeriach

a clear trail through the bogs to **Corrour bothy**.

The path continues uphill into Coire Odhar, zigzagging up the steep headwall to boggy ground on the saddle above. From here the **Devil's Point** can be quickly mounted (isn't it time to reinstate its less euphemistic original Gaelic name, 'penis of the demon')? Continuing N the sometimes sketchy path climbs rocky slopes to the rim of Coire an t-Saighdeir, which is followed to the Stob of the same name, an offshoot of Cairn Toul. Stay with the edge as it curves up to **Cairn Toul** itself. The high point is the northern peak overlooking cavernous An Garbh Choire, perhaps the grandest corrie complex in the land.

Cairn Toul (left) and Sgor an Lochain Uaine from Braeriach

A short bouldery descent and reascent gain the neighbouring summit of **Sgor an Lochan Uaine**, famous for the scramble up its northeast ridge and arguably an even better viewpoint than Cairn Toul. Head W from here around the edge of Garbh Choire Mor. Rotting cornices generally plaster the rim well into summer, while sheltered beneath the crags is a snow patch that rarely melts at all. Once up on the Braeriach plateau the ground is easier underfoot, a gravelly expanse with a uniquely spacious feel. Cross the baby River Dee in a shallow hollow above its impressive falls, then leave the edge of the escarpment to strike directly for the summit of **Braeriach**, where the plateau edge is bitten into by the cliffy bowl of Coire Bhrochain.

Having now met the most popular and best-trodden route on Braeriach, follow the path E along the cliff edge before descending leftwards onto the broad ridge of **Sròn na Lairige**. The path stays just E of the high ground initially before descending the boulder-strewn lower crest, with a steep eroded section at the finish. Once down on more accommodating ground stay right at a fork for the easiest path into the base of the **Lairig Ghru**, where the trail soon crosses the burn as it bubbles up from a pile of boulders. Here turn right onto an eroded mess of a path for a last leg-sapping climb into the **Chalamain Gap**, a dry gulch carved by glacial meltwater. Clamber over boulders in the gap to reach a better-engineered trail that runs downhill to cross a burn before following a moraine ridge, from where a short descent leads into the wooded gorge of the Allt Mor. Cross a footbridge and turn right to follow a path upstream to the **ski centre**.

Braeriach from the Ben Macdui – Carn a' Mhaim col

Beinn a' Bhuird
and Ben Avon

*E*ven compared to their higher neighbours Ben Avon and Beinn a' Bhuird look big. These eastern heartlands of the Cairngorms combine considerable height with a sort of topographical obesity, their bulbous plateaux sprawling over miles of rolling ground. The effect may not be subtle, yet these massive bodies exert an attraction like gravity, and each is special in a different way. Ben Avon's upper slopes bristle with weathered granite tors, an array of natural castles. From many angles Beinn a' Bhuird looks gentle and grassy, but its inner recesses hide a series of epic rock-walled corries. The scale and remoteness of the country makes an adventure of any trip here, and all possible approaches are long. Those with a bike and a spare weekend might come in from the north along the length of Glen Avon; from the south it's a choice of Gleann an t-Slugain or Glen Quoich. The latter is quicker, and its Scots pine woods are easy on the eye.

↑ *Ben Avon's summit tor from Carn Eas*

ROUTE INFORMATION

Start/finish	Linn of Quoich car park (NO 118 911)
Distance	33km (20½ miles)
Ascent	1330m
Time	11hrs
Terrain	Straightforward tracks in the lower glen, with a clear path up Beinn a' Bhuird and easy striding on the tops – but navigation across the plateaux needs attention in mist. Descent from Carn Eas is steep and pathless, and there's some rough boggy ground if following the south bank of Quoich Water en route back down-glen.
Summits	Beinn a' Bhuird 1197m ('mountain of the table'); Ben Avon 1171m (probably after the River Avon)
Maps	OS Landranger (1:50,000) 36 & 43; OS Explorer (1:25,000) 404; Harvey British Mountain Map (1:40,000) Cairngorms and Lochnagar
Public transport	Regular buses from Aberdeen to Braemar via Ballater, but none beyond Braemar
By bike	Cycle to the ford in Glen Quoich to save over 10km of track trudging
Accommodation	Braemar YH (01339 741659)
Sleeping out	Good camping on the meadow where Glen Quoich divides, and idyllic sites elsewhere in the woods. The high corries of Beinn a' Bhuird offer many options, including various howffs secreted under boulders; a small one that's common knowledge is found in the eastern corries at (NO 097 995).
Seasonal notes	The unsheltered high plateaux are featureless in a white-out, and the heavily corniced corrie headwalls a lurking danger. Beware cornice and possible avalanche risk on lower slopes too, such as Alltan na Beinne on the ascent of Beinn a' Bhuird and when descending Carn Eas from Ben Avon. The Glen Quoich track is fine pre-dawn or post-sunset, but bikes, fitness and friendly conditions would be essential for a one-day winter walk; in deep snow expect to take 2 days. In heavy rain or thaw the river crossing in Glen Quoich may be best further upstream.
Short cuts	Either of the hills can be done alone. Between Beinn a' Bhuird and Ben Avon, The Sneck offers a quick escape to lower ground.

Garbh Choire of Beinn a' Bhuird from The Sneck

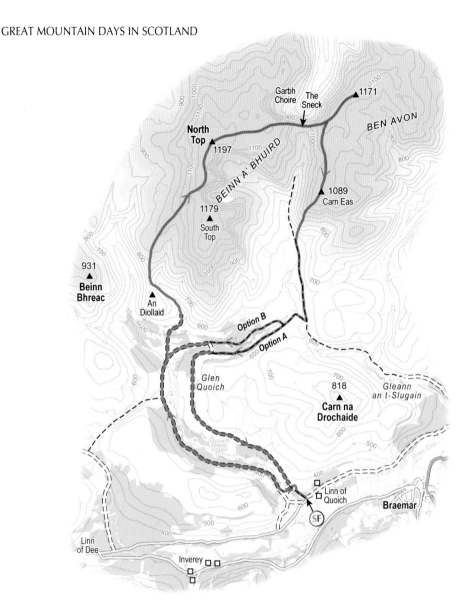

Approach 7km

Take the riverside path past a boarded-up cottage and through woods to a second cottage, where a footbridge crosses the river above an interesting natural 'waterslide' (don't try this at home). Ascend briefly to a vehicle track, which is followed up-glen through scattered Scots pines. After nearly 5km the glen broadens and divides around the bulging southern end of Beinn a' Bhuird. Ford the river (be

Woods in Glen Quoich

Ben Avon and Slochd Mor from the eastern top of Beinn a' Bhuird

circumspect in spate) then take the left branch where the track splits, continuing past a grassy meadow into a band of woods. The track now becomes a narrower footpath.

On the hill 16km

This climbs out of the trees and around the flanks of **An Diollaid** above a burn-cutting to reach the saddle between this satellite peak and the main body of the mountain. Continuing up the broad shoulder of Beinn a' Bhuird, views open across a boggy expanse to hulking Ben Macdui (Walk 40) and the distant blunt pyramids of Beinn a'Ghlo (Walk 38). Height is gained easily, and the rim of craggy Coire an Dubh Lochain is soon met. Head N across the plateau past the edge of equally dramatic Coire nan Clach; Beinn a' Bhuird's high point, **North Top**, is marked by a simple cairn set a little back from the cliffs.

Leaving the summit and the corrie edge, strike across the open plateau to the little rocky top of Cnap a' Chlèirich. From here drop almost due E

to the pronounced saddle of **The Sneck**; where the descent becomes eroded bear slightly left close to the edge of **Garbh Choire** to avoid steeper ground on the right. Continue E out of the col, ascending a steep stony path beside the rim of more crags onto Ben Avon. The view back into Garbh Choire reveals the full magnificence of this rocky cirque, home to some of the best remote climbs in the country. It's an easy stroll over undulating gravelly ground to **Ben Avon**'s high point, a distinctive granite tor. The topmost rocks require a bit of basic scrambling. Given time, other of Ben Avon's many tors are worth exploring too.

The following little-trodden leg affords stunning views of Beinn a' Bhuird's eastern corries. Return towards the plateau edge overlooking The Sneck, then bear S for nearly 2km on a gentle descent and gradual reascent to a cairn marking point 1089m, or **Carn Eas**. Now descend roughly SE to pick up the vague spur that divides the hill's western and southern aspects. The ground soon steepens, and although it's not difficult in summer conditions a lot of snow can build up here. From about the 900m contour bear S to meet a very clear path in the barren upper reaches of Glen Quoich.

Return 10km
Follow this down-glen for approximately 2km, and just before the main path veers towards Gleann an t-Slugain turn right onto a rougher trail to the Quoich Water. The path immediately turns away from the water, heading in the downstream direction to rejoin the burn after a few hundred metres. Here there's a choice.

Option A Stay with the path on the south side of the burn – rough and boggy; occasionally disappears under heather. This is a safer option after a day or

rain or snowmelt and preferable for novelty later on. The path eventually meets a vehicle track which continues down the east side of lower Glen Quoich to reach **Linn of Quoich** after a further 6km.

Option B Ford the burn to gain a clearer path on its north bank. This then meets a track on the north side of the burn, which leads to the ford described in the approach section of the walk. Recross here, and retrace your steps back down the west side of Glen Quoich.

Either way, you get to enjoy some of the prettiest native pine woods in the Cairngorms. Unless new growth is encouraged here and deer strictly controlled, this priceless fragment will slowly die out.

Lochnagar (Walk 42) from Beinn a' Bhuird's Coire Dubh Lochain

Lochnagar via The Stuic

With its bulky shoulders swelling over the forests of Deeside, Lochnagar is a mountain of regal bearing (with a royal owner, incidentally). The northeast cirque is one of Scotland's greatest corries and a crucible of classic climbing – an amphitheatre of 'steep frowning' cliffs scored by dark gullies that shelter ribbons of snow into most summers. The standard walker's ascent follows a track from Glen Muick, but although it rims the all-important corrie it misses much of this complex massif.

Instead, this walk approaches from Deeside, giving a much longer and more varied route that visits quieter corners and offers a little light scrambling. It starts in one of the finest Scots pine woods in the country before climbing into remote Coire Lochan nan Eun, with its scattered boulders and lochans. Above is The Stuic – an exciting taste of ridge scrambling for beginners, and for old hands a pleasant ascent off the beaten track. Once the main corrie has been duly marvelled at and the popular summit visited, enjoy the long rough walk-out over obscure foothills.

↑ *The Stuic from Coire Loch nan Eun* 217

ROUTE INFORMATION

Start/finish	Pay and display car park at Keiloch (NO 188 912)
Distance	23.5km (14½ miles)
Ascent	1070m
Time	9hrs
Terrain	A bit of everything – clear forest tracks, pathless boggy ground, steep bouldery descents and an easy grade 1 scramble
Summits	Carn a' Choire Bhoidheach 1110m ('cairn of the beautiful corrie'); Lochnagar ('loch of noise/laughter'); Cac Carn Beag 1155m ('little shit cairn', possibly, or 'little cairn of the slope')
Maps	OS Landranger (1:50,000) 44 covers most of the walk, but the start is on Landranger 43; OS Explorer (1:25,000) 388; Harvey British Mountain Map (1:40,000) Cairngorms and Lochnagar

Public transport	Regular buses from Aberdeen to Braemar via Ballater
Accommodation	Braemar YH (01339 741659)
Sleeping out	Coire Lochan nan Eun is ideal for wild camping, and there won't be much passing traffic; the little glen of the Blackshiel Burn is a good alternative
Seasonal notes	Lochnagar can hold a lot of snow, and its undulating plateau feels exposed in poor weather; the corrie rims may carry substantial cornices. An easy summer scramble, The Stuic becomes a short but steep grade I winter climb under snow, and should be considered only by the appropriately equipped and experienced.
Short cuts	Avoid the extra distance and rough ground on Cnapan Nathraichean by returning to the glen via Sandy Loch, using the approach route described

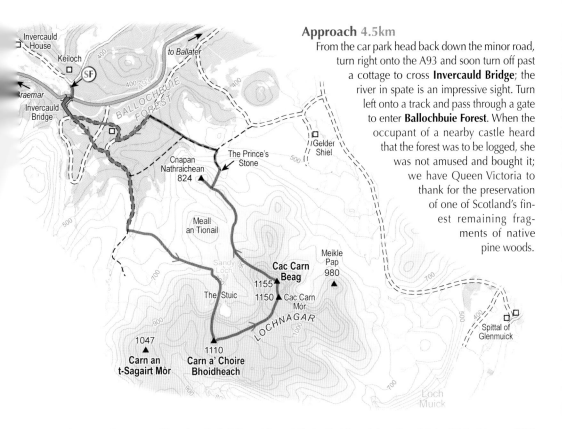

Approach 4.5km

From the car park head back down the minor road, turn right onto the A93 and soon turn off past a cottage to cross **Invercauld Bridge**; the river in spate is an impressive sight. Turn left onto a track and pass through a gate to enter **Ballochbuie Forest**. When the occupant of a nearby castle heard that the forest was to be logged, she was not amused and bought it; we have Queen Victoria to thank for the preservation of one of Scotland's finest remaining fragments of native pine woods.

At a three-way junction take the middle course, then after 1km go straight on at a crossroads; pass through another gate, and at the next junction branch right. The track winds uphill to a bend overlooking the falls of Garbh Allt – worth a quick detour. Staying with the track, turn away from the water, then go left at a junction and continue uphill. As you climb, the trees thin and become more stunted; beyond a deer fence at the upper edge of the forest the track continues over heather moorland beside the Feindallacher Burn.

On the hill 12.5km

At a little corrugated iron shelter leave the track, hop the burn and head roughly E over rough boggy ground with intermittent traces of a path. The Allt Lochan nan Eun is soon met, leading to the shores of **Sandy Loch** in the mouth of Lochnagar's remote and beautiful Coire Loch nan Eun. To the left rounded slopes bulge up to Cac Carn Beag, the mountain's high point, but attention is dominated by the formidable rocky prow of The Stuic ahead, your route out of the corrie. A path threads through the boulders to reach a level shoulder at the foot of the prow,

overlooking Loch nan Eun. Follow your nose (and occasional crampon-scratched rocks) directly up the front of The Stuic; it is not as hard as appearance might suggest but does call for some basic scrambling on blocky granite.

Once safely on the plateau above **The Stuic** a quick detour S wins you the unremarkable Munro summit of **Carn a' Choire Bhoidheach**; the similarly dull tick of Carn an t-Sagairt Mòr out to the W may be a ridge too far for all but the most enthusiastic baggers. Continuing ENE a clear path shadows the rim of Coire Lochan nan Eun before making a fairly gentle climb onto the summit area of **Lochnagar** itself, giving a bird's-eye perspective on the massive crags of its eponymous corrie. Heading N along the cliff edge, descend slightly from the broad top of **Cac Carn Mòr** ('big' in Gaelic, although actually the lower of the two Cac Carns), passing the deep slot of Black Spout Gully before reascending to reach the summit trig point of **Cac Carn Beag**.

Descend roughly WNW down a broad, gently angled rock-strewn shoulder; from about the 1070m contour the slope steepens appreciably (take

Looking back at The Stuic from the northwest spur of Lochnagar

Beinn a' Bhuird and Ben Avon (Walk 41) from Lochnagar's northwest spur

care if it is snowy), then gradually eases off as you approach the saddle between Lochnagar and the rounded hummock of **Meall an Tionail**. It's easy to cut the walk short here by retracing the approach via Sandy Loch, but in clear weather the little-trodden lower foothills are worth exploring.

Before reaching the low point of the saddle cut N across the boggy upper glen of the Blacksheil Burn to gain the low rocky ridge on its far side. Follow the high ground over two unnamed tops before a rough descent and reascent gains **Cnapan Nathraichean**, an outlying summit worth climbing for its outlook over the woods of Deeside. Direct descent NW from here leads to shenanigans with deer fences and trees, so instead return to the col SE of Cnapan Nathraichean and descend steeply NNE to pick up a path near **The Prince's Stone**, which marks the spot where a royal once kipped in a hut.

Return 6.5km

Go left (W) at a path junction to enter **Ballochbuie Forest**, and just into the woods stay right at another junction to descend through the woods beside Ballochbuie Burn, crossing and recrossing the stream. Once down in the glen turn left onto a forest track, then follow the network of tracks back to **Invercauld Bridge** – there's a choice of exact route, all clearly marked on OS maps.

221

Glen Clova circuit

A rippled expanse of heather and peat, the high plateaux of The Mounth, south of the Cairngorms, make ideal backpacking country. Although they're relaxing on a fine day when the melodious song of moorland birds drifts on a balmy breeze, these open heights can feel distinctly challenging in foul weather. There are few distinctive summits here, one rounded hump being very much like the next – the attraction is their spacious emptiness. For scenic grandeur the glens and corries take first billing, craggy glacial trenches scored deep into the landscape. Glen Clova is arguably the prettiest in the area, and certainly the most accessible for visitors from central Scotland and all points southwards.

Clova and adjacent Munros Driesh and Mayar attract weekend crowds, yet the hinterland beyond has an air of real remoteness, and this circuit of all six watershed Munros ringing the head of the glen gets away from it all. This walk is a tough single day out, but could easily be enjoyed over a more leisurely two with a night spent in the shelter of Davie's Bourach (otherwise known as Lunkard bothy). It's short on facilities (and headroom) – but location, location, location.

↑ *Woods in upper Glen Clova*

Start/finish	Paying car park by the ranger centre at the head of Glen Clova (NO 283 761)
Distance	30km (19 miles)
Ascent	1440m
Time	13hrs
Terrain	A mix of forest tracks, clear hill paths and a long pathless section. The ground is boggy, so gaiters are worth wearing at any time of year. Plenty of remote terrain exposed to the worst of the weather.
Summits	Broad Cairn 998m; Cairn Bannoch 1012m ('peaked hill'); Tolmount 958m ('hollow mountain'); Tom Buidhe 957m ('yellow hill'); Mayar 928m ('high plain', possibly); Driesh 947m ('bramble')
Maps	OS Landranger (1:50,000) 44; OS Explorer (1:25,000) 388; Harvey British Mountain Map (1:40,000) Cairngorms and Lochnagar covers most but not all of the walk; Harvey

	Superwalker (1:25,000) Lochnagar covers the whole thing
Public transport	Infrequent buses from Kirriemuir to Glen Clova
Accommodation	Glen Clova Hotel bunkhouse (01575 550350, www.clova.com)
Sleeping out	Although the ground tends to bogginess there are any number of secluded hollows between the hills. However, perhaps the most obvious overnight option is a 'bothy' rather than a camp; Davie's Bourach (NO 233 778) is cramped, dingy and more of a howff than a hut, but at least it's weathertight.
Seasonal notes	An arduous trip in winter, and given the limited available daylight it might be best as an overnighter. The high featureless summits would be very serious in a white-out. Under deep soft snow the full round might only be practicable on touring skis.
Short cuts	Follow Jock's Road into Glen Doll to cut the walk roughly in half

Glen Callater from Tolmount

The River South Esk in upper Glen Clova

Approach 6km

Beyond the picnic area a woodland path leads along the west bank of the river. After nearly 1.5km cross a footbridge, soon meeting a forestry track. Turn left to pass **Moulzie** farmstead. Where the track bends left continue straight on (muddily), skirting riverside woods, and then a while later cross a footbridge to the west bank. The glen now kinks left between impressive craggy bluffs. Continue on the stony track parallel with the river, passing a natural waterslide (with reluctance on a scorcher) and the oddly named cliff of Juanjorge, and then climbing steadily into open woodland. Look out for a turnoff on the right, which leads to a footbridge over a little gorge before zigzagging uphill onto the heathery saddle between Glen Clova and Glen Muick.

On the hill 22km

Just before an estate hut (not a good night-time option) turn left onto an eroded path for the long ascent onto **Broad Cairn**. There are excellent views of the huge Creag an Dubh Loch, Eagles Falls and Lochnagar (Walk 42). From the little summit tor continue roughly west skirting Cairn of Gowal and passing over an unnamed hummock to reach the rocks of **Cairn Bannoch**, the walk's high point. The path now curves left across Fafernie (care in mist), becoming vaguer underfoot as it descends the broad south-southeast spur to the boggy col above Glen Callater. Cross **Jock's Road** (indistinct here among all the peat) – a famous historic through-route linking Braemar with the Angus glens – then ascend easily onto **Tolmount**, a great viewpoint looking down the length of craggy Glen Callater. Descend S into another hollow before bearing left for the gentle ascent onto **Tom Buidhe**.

> **Detour for overnighters** If intending to spend a night in Davie's Bourach then from Tom Buidhe it's best to strike SE and then E into the boggy upper reaches of Glen Doll, crossing White Water (care in spate) and hummocky ground to pick up Jock's Road, which leads to the 'bothy' – a sort of shed dug into the hillside. This was built following the death of five walkers here in a blizzard in 1959, and although very spartan (earth floor, no headroom, no windows) its shelter is certainly very welcome.

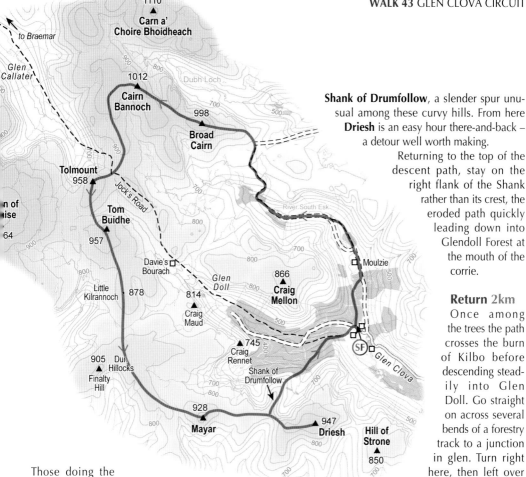

1110
▲
**Carn a'
Choire Bhoidheach**

to Braemar

Glen
Callater

1012
▲
**Cairn
Bannoch**

Dubh Loch

998

**Broad
Cairn**

River South Esk

Tolmount
958 ▲

Jock's Road

**Tom
Buidhe**

957

Davie's □
Bourach

Glen
Doll

866
▲
**Craig
Mellon**

□ Moulzie

n of
ise

64

Little
Kilrannoch

878

814
▲

**Craig
Maud**

▲ 745
**Craig
Rennet**

**Shank of
Drumfollow**

905 Dun
▲ Hillocks

Finalty
Hill

928

Mayar

647
Driesh

**Hill of
Strone**
▲
850

(SF)

Glen Clova

Shank of Drumfollow, a slender spur unusual among these curvy hills. From here **Driesh** is an easy hour there-and-back – a detour well worth making.

Returning to the top of the descent path, stay on the right flank of the Shank rather than its crest, the eroded path quickly leading down into Glendoll Forest at the mouth of the corrie.

Return 2km

Once among the trees the path crosses the burn of Kilbo before descending steadily into Glen Doll. Go straight on across several bends of a forestry track to a junction in glen. Turn right here, then left over a bridge, then right again, passing a house and a farm to reach the **ranger centre**.

Those doing the walk over one day should head roughly S from Tom Buidhe over **Little Kilrannoch** to **Dun Hillocks**, from where a short detour would lead to the unremarkable top of Finalty Hill. Stay with the high ground onto **Mayar's** domed summit. This entire stretch is featureless and boggy, calling for pinpoint navigation in poor visibility.

From Mayar's summit cairn descend a well-used stony path NNE and then E along an open grassy crest. Meet and follow a decrepit fence; nearing the rim of Corrie Sharroch you're joined by a second, higher fence that protects the rare plants of the Corrie Fee nature reserve from overgrazing. The ridge soon narrows as you reach the top of the descent path down the

Craig Maud from Jock's Road near Davie's Bourach   225

Galloway hills

*S*urprisingly, perhaps, great mountain days can be found south of the Central Belt. The rolling expanse of the Southern Uplands benefits from a comparative neglect, and crowds are generally conspicuous by their absence. Counter to the general smooth-sloped theme hereabouts, the hills at the heart of the Galloway Forest Park are rugged – scattered with rock knobbles and sandy-shored lochans and defended by a winning combination of man-eating bog, ankle-twisting tussock and impenetrable conifers.

This skyline walk around the parallel ranges the Rhinns of Kells and the Awful Hand shows this area at its uncompromising best and visits three Corbetts, including Merrick, highest summit in the south. The terrain feels as demanding as most in the Highlands, yet the setting is subtly different; views range from Arrochar, Arran and Ailsa Craig to the Antrim coast, Northern Ireland's Mourne mountains and the Lake District. There's linguistic novelty too – the Gaelic of the north here being heavily anglicised and often giving way to hill names in picturesque old Scots.

↑ *Merrick and the Dungeon Hills from Corserine*

ROUTE INFORMATION

Start/finish Forest Drive – laybys at about (NX 446 939)

Distance 34km (21 miles) minimum (longer finish possible)

Ascent 1850m minimum

Time 13hrs

Terrain Bogs, tussocks, bracken and dense forestry plantations characterise the lower slopes; higher up the going is generally easier, with the smoothest turfy ground on the Rhinns of Kells ridge. Paths can be faint to non-existent in places and route finding tricky, particularly near Loch Enoch and Dungeon Hill.

Summits Shalloch on Minnoch 775m ('middle heel or middle forge', possibly); Tarfessock 697m ('grassy hill'); Merrick 843m ('branched/fingered'); Corserine 814m ('cross of the Rhinns')

Maps OS Landranger (1:50,000) 77; OS Explorer (1:25,000) 318; Harvey Superwalker (1:25,000) Galloway Hills

Public transport Not great; bus from Ayr or Castle Douglas to Dalmellington, then hitchhike or a long walk to Loch Doon

Accommodation Newton Stewart YH (01671 402211)

Sleeping out Loch Enoch and the Dungeon Hill – Craignaw col offer excellent camping. Backhill of Bush bothy (NX 480 842) is ideally placed mid-walk, but thanks to too easy vehicular access this once pleasant hut has been blighted by anti-social litter louts. Its long-term fate remains unresolved (as of summer 2010). Tunskeen bothy (NX 425 906) would be convenient if starting the circuit from the south instead of the north.

Seasonal notes Being southerly and of modest size these hills attract severe conditions less often than most, but don't bank on that. Although there are no particular winter difficulties, snow and short daylight hours would make a single-day circuit unlikely.

Short cuts Avoid the Rhinns of Kells by heading N through the woods from Backhill of Bush bothy to Loch Doon; not all tracks and fire breaks are marked on the maps, so improvisation helps

Corserine from the Dungeon Hill – Craignaw col

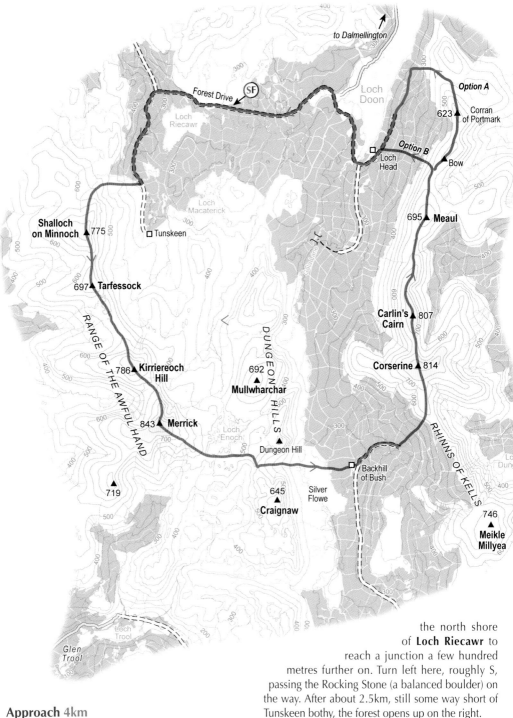

Approach 4km

Cars can be parked at many points by the unsurfaced Forest Drive that runs between the tarmac roads at lochs Doon and Bradan. Continue walking W along the track, passing a children's playground above the north shore of **Loch Riecawr** to reach a junction a few hundred metres further on. Turn left here, roughly S, passing the Rocking Stone (a balanced boulder) on the way. After about 2.5km, still some way short of Tunskeen bothy, the forest opens up on the right.

On the hill 25km

Leave the track for an intermittent path that ascends W, weaving among outcrops on rough tussocky ground. As height is gained curve gradually left to ascend the north flank of **Shalloch on Minnoch**, reaching its spacious twin-topped summit with relief. The trig point sits on the slightly lower-looking western top. From the eastern top descend SSE, then pass over the smaller hump of **Tarfessock**. Scattered with rocks and little pools, Tarfessock's broad southeast ridge runs down to a low col below the abrupt northern flank of **Kirriereoch Hill**. Cross a fence and attack the slope head on, the ground steepening and becoming quite rocky higher up before easing in the final walk to the summit cairn.

Beyond the next dip rises the bulk of Merrick. A largely grassy ascent leads to the outlying spur of Little Spear, from where a sculpted ridge arcs around a shallow corrie up to **Merrick** itself. From the summit trig point descend SE towards Loch Enoch. The ground soon runs into the rocky knobbles and boggy hollows that characterise the Dungeon Hills, a low range squeezed between the Awful Hand and the Rhinns of Kells. This remote granite heartland is arguably the most interesting part of the Galloway hills, and the only bit to offer quality rock climbing.

A sketchy path winds along the rough southern shore of **Loch Enoch**, whose pale sandy beaches are inviting on a warm day. At the southeast corner of the loch peel right to pass S of Craignairny. Skirt above a steep little crag overlooking the head of the

Little Spear from Merrick

glen of Loch Neldricken, then descend rock steps to a pronounced col at the northern end of **Craignaw**, the rockiest of all local hills – worth a there-and-back detour.

Just below the col a cairn marks the descent path (rough and easily misplaced) E into a pronounced corrie. Pass between the craggy bluffs of **Dungeon Hill** and Craignaw onto level ground, the wide marshy trough of the **Silver Flowe**, and continue E between two small lochs with some bog-related entertainment to reach Saugh Burn and a forest boundary. A muddy path follows the right edge of a clear-felled area to reach **Backhill of Bush**, a scruffy bothy in a pretty burnside setting. It was here that the notion of a Mountain Bothies Association was first mooted in the 1960s, and it would be sad if this historic hut were lost to vandalism.

Beyond the bothy go left on a forest track beside **Downies Burn**. The track soon veers away from the burn, then passes a junction with a downhill track. At the next junction go right, the track curving uphill through the woods for about 2km. Look out on the left for a muddy path that cuts NE directly uphill along a burn at the edge of a clear-felled area. Above the trees grassy slopes lead to **Corserine's** south ridge, and from there onto the expansive domed summit, bowling green smooth. Continuing N along the spine of the Rhinns of Kells, where a drop and reascent gain the pronounced top of **Carlin's Cairn**. A 'carlin' is an old hag or witch, and although it's unclear which witch we're talking about, she seemingly merited a huge summit cairn.

With views of Loch Doon ahead, continue over **Meaul** to the col below **Bow**. There is no trouble-free way from the Rhinns of Kells to Loch Doon, so here there are two choices.

Option A Long, scenic and loopy. Stay high over **Bow** and **Coran of Portmark** to descend a path towards Loch Doon as marked on the map. Since the loch shore is extremely rough, stay up in the woods, where a muddy forest track runs parallel to the shore, descending gradually to the head of the loch (only the second half of the track is marked on the OS Landranger map).

Option B Direct but pine-infested. From the **Meaul–Bow col** drop NW to the forest boundary at about NX 500 926, then cut downhill through the forest, using burns and fire breaks to meet the lower track near the loch head.

Return 5km

Beyond the buildings at **Loch Head** go right at a track junction to cross a bridge over the river of Gala Lane; this heads back N to meet the **Forest Drive** in a little under 2km; a 30min jog west along this should regain the car.

230   *Backhill of Bush – easy vehicular access has left this historic bothy vulnerable to littering and vandalism*

Glen Rosa circuit, Arran

*S*mall but perfectly composed, the hills of Arran's northeast quarter are as striking as any in Scotland. The peaks huddle together like the towers of a rocky fortress, their turreted tors and battlement ridges rising high out of the wide blue Firth of Clyde. The crystalline granite weathers into shelving slabs and giant jumbles of curvy blocks, a monumental rock architecture with countless possibilities for climbers and scramblers. Walkers, too, are spoilt for choice.

Two main glens slice the heart of these hills, each providing a classic skyline circuit. The Glen Sannox horseshoe is shorter and more scrambly, while the Glen Rosa circuit described here covers more ground. A detour from the round allows Caisteal Abhail to be incorporated, giving a full hand of the island's main peaks. The walk described involves a minimum of hands-on clambering, but mountaineers can make an entirely different day of it by including the traverse of A' Chir, a Moderate-grade ridge climb with few equals outside Skye.

↑ Caisteal Abhail (left) and the Witch's Step from North Goatfell   231

ROUTE INFORMATION

Start/finish	Ferry pier, Brodick (NS 022 359)		**By bike**	Cycling from the ferry at Brodick saves some road walking
Distance	25km (15½ miles)		**Accommodation**	Lochranza YH (01770 830631); camping in the mouth of Glen Rosa
Ascent	2000m			
Time	10hrs		**Sleeping out**	The many corries provide atmospheric camps, although generally rough. Summits such as Caisteal Abhail and Beinn Tarsuinn have softer grass, but no water. The Saddle between Cir Mhòr and North Goatfell has both good pitches and running water, plus a handy mid-walk location.
Terrain	Well-trodden paths throughout – in places a little too well trodden and badly eroded. If A' Chir is avoided then scrambling is very limited, but the rough ground can still be hard going. The A' Chir traverse is a Moderate-grade rock climb, a description of which is beyond the scope of a walking guide (see Appendix 3).			
Summmits	Goatfell 874m; North Goatfell 818m; Cir Mhòr 799m ('big comb'); Caisteal Abhail 859m ('castle of the fork'); A' Chir 745m ('the comb'); Beinn Tarsuinn 826m ('transverse hill'); Beinn Nuis 792m ('hill of the fawn')		**Seasonal notes**	Southerly, insular and of modest altitude, these hills attract less snow and ice than mainland ranges. As a winter round this is a long day (see Short cuts, below) with slight hints of mountaineering.
Maps	OS Landranger (1:50,000) 69; OS Explorer (1:25,000) 361; Harvey Superwalker (1:25,000) Arran		**Short cuts**	The low cols either side of Cir Mhòr offer quick escape paths into Glen Rosa. Caisteal Abhail can be easily missed out; so too can Beinn Tarsuinn and Beinn Nuis, by following a clear path over Beinn a' Chliabhain from the Bealach an Fhir-bhogha.
Public transport	Calmac ferries from Ardrossan and Claonaig to Brodick and Lochranza respectively. Regular buses between Brodick, Sannox and Lochranza.			

Approach 3.5km

Drivers can park at Cladach (NS 013 376) for the Goatfell path. Pedestrians should follow Brodick's seafront W to head out of town on the A841. At a junction go right, over a bridge, then turn left onto a gated private drive. This leads N through pastures, climbing slightly and curving right to cross the Cnocan Burn, and soon meets the popular Goatfell path.

On the hill 16.5km

Follow this uphill through Cnocan Wood, then over boulder-scattered slopes above the treeline. The ground steepens as it rises onto Meall Breac, curving left for a final rough climb up the east ridge of **Goatfell**. Although Arran's highest peak is overshadowed in quality by its near neighbours, the broad summit offers excellent views over Brodick Bay to the Galloway hills (Walk 44) and into the rugged heart of the range;

Ben Cruachan (Walk 31), Antrim and the Paps of Jura can sometimes be spotted.

Continuing N the summit hordes soon thin out. On Stacach, the crest leading to North Goatfell, a row of rocky tors can either be scrambled direct

The Witch's Step from The Saddle at dawn

Left to right – Cir Mhòr, A' Chir and Beinn Tarsuinn from Caisteal Abhail

or skirted via a path on the east flank. At **North Goatfell** the deep trough of Glen Sannox suddenly yawns below, its head dominated by a trio of striking mountain features – spear-sharp Cir Mhòr, among the most spectacular of Scottish peaks; tor-studded Caisteal Abhail; and the formidable notch of Ceum na Caillich (aka the Witch's Step).

Descent of the northwest ridge is steep and unpleasantly eroded in parts. An obvious rock pinnacle on the crest is bypassed to the left (there's no direct way off its top), and thereafter the ground gradually becomes less onerous as the path winds down to **The Saddle**, the major bealach between glens Rosa and Sannox.

The continuation up Cir Mhòr was formerly both steep and badly eroded; thanks to recent path upgrades it is now merely steep. The path attacks the climb

233

head on before trending a little left to pass through a gap between the main summit and the blocky top of the Rosa Pinnacle, famous for some of Britain's finest rock climbs. Once through the gap cut back right for a short easy scramble onto **Cir Mhòr's** airy summit at the apex of the mountain's huge north face.

Descend briefly W, then bear right along the cliff rim for the rocky path down to the bealach below **Caisteal Abhail**. The curving ridge up Arran's second highest peak gives grassier going; the high point is a blocky tor that can be scrambled direct at grade 2 (there's an easy way round the back).

Return to the bealach and climb slightly back towards Cir Mhòr to pick up a cairned traverse path cutting across the mountain's rock-scattered west flank onto the bealach north of A' Chir. The full traverse of this ridge is a rock climb, with the section north of the mountain's summit being particularly exciting. Walkers should miss it out. To do so, head briefly along the ridge towards this, but soon cut right onto an obvious path that first descends slightly, then threads among the rocks under **A' Chir's** craggy west face before climbing a little onto

the Bealach an Fhir-bhogha at the southern end of the A' Chir spine. Competent scramblers might consider a detour along the easier southern section to A' Chir's summit, with some tricky slabs and involved route finding; note that this will be harder in reverse.

Continuing up **Beinn Tarsuinn** the eroded path veers a little left overlooking Ealta Choire to pass left of a mass of rock, then cuts back right onto the northeast ridge, leading steeply to the summit. Delightfully grassy ground leads S into a little col and on to the broad summit of **Beinn Nuis**, the final top of the day. Stay with the cliff edge to descend SSE, the path steep and badly worn in places. Cross the bogs of Coire a' Bhradain, hop over the Garbh Allt and pass through a gate to follow the muddy trail on the left bank of the gorge down into Glen Rosa.

Return 5km

Follow the track down-glen to reach a tarmac road at some houses just beyond the campsite; this leads back to the A841 and **Brodick**.

Cir Mhòr and the Witch's Step from lower Glen Rosa

Cuillin Traverse, Rum

A ridge-walking classic on a unique island, Rum's Cuillin Traverse is a worthy counterpart to its infamous namesake on nearby Skye – easier but no less memorable. Rising straight out of the sea the hills form a close-packed group that dominates the southern half of Rum, their distinctive saw-toothed outline prominent from many points on the mainland and surrounding islands. These sharp peaks seem ancient and vaguely exotic, their evocative Norse names only adding to the romance. Depending on whether the most difficult sections of ridge are scrambled direct or skirted around, the traverse can be treated either as a walk or a mini-mountaineering expedition.

The Cuillin stand tall among Scotland's finest small ranges – thanks, in no small part, to their setting. Having been run as a National Nature Reserve for many decades Rum is the closest thing Scotland has to a wilderness island; there are no surfaced roads and only a handful of permanent residents. Visitors should strongly consider extending their stay to explore beyond the Cuillin.

Approach 4.5km

From Kinloch take a path in the castle grounds signed for the Cuillin through old woods, which soon thin into new growth as height is gained. Follow the Allt Slugain a'Choilich into Coire Dubh. Here cross the burn via an old dam and either make a bee-line for the **Bealach Bairc-mheall** or trend left onto the rock-strewn shoulder of Cnapan Breaca to reach the broad gravelly northwest ridge of Hallival, first of the five main peaks.

Askival and Eigg from Trollaval

ROUTE INFORMATION

Start/finish	Ferry slipway on Loch Scresort (NM 411 991), or nearby Kinloch Castle or campground
Distance	22km (14 miles)
Ascent	2050m
Time	10hrs
Terrain	Rough, with many steep ascents and descents and several sections of exposed narrow ridge. Scrambling opportunities abound, spanning the full range of difficulty up to Moderate-grade rock climbing on the Askival Pinnacle; all these sections can be easily avoided. For a full scrambler's route description see *Scotland's Mountain Ridges* (Cicerone). The return path from Dibidil is often boggy.
Summits	Hallival 723m ('ledge mountain', Norse); Askival 812m ('spear mountain', Norse); Trollavall 702m ('troll mountain', Norse); Ainshval 781m ('rocky ridge mountain', Norse); Sgurr nan Gillean 764m ('peak of the young men' or possibly 'ghyll peak', Norse/Gaelic)
Maps	OS Landranger (1:50,000) 39; OS Explorer (1:25,000) 397
Public transport	Several Calmac ferries from Mallaig to Rum every week, although timetables may necessitate a long weekend
By boat	Accomplished sea kayakers might relish arriving under their own steam; Elgol, on Skye, is a popular starting point. This is a serious open crossing.
Accommodation	Hostel at Kinloch Castle (01687 462037); camping beside Loch Scresort (facilities; small fee)
Sleeping out	A camp in Atlantic Corrie or upper Glen Dibidil would be great; the excellent Dibidil bothy (NM 393 928) is also well placed for the Cuillin Traverse
Seasonal notes	In full winter conditions the Cuillin Traverse offers genuine mountaineering, up to grade III if the more difficult sections are included. In heavy rain or thaw, burn crossings on the Dibidil–Kinloch path may be hazardous, and there have been accidents. In summer Rum's voracious midges can make camping a nightmare – come prepared.
Short cuts	It's possible (although a shame) to avoid the long coastal return walk by backtracking from Sgurr nan Gillean over Ainshval and down to the Bealach an Fhuarain. From here traverse under Trollaval to the Bealach an Oir, then across the head of Atlantic Corrie to the Bealach Bairc-mheall.

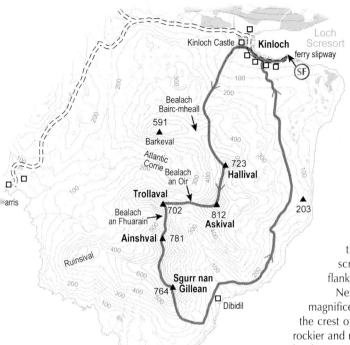

On the hill 8.5km

A rough path climbs **Hallival's** northwest flank, weaving through boulders and crag tiers. From the cairn on the domed top there's a superb view of the Skye Cuillin (Walk 47), Knoydart (Walks 20 and 21) and the peaks to come. Grassy burrows on this and other Rum summits are not rabbit holes but the nests of Manx shearwaters, seabirds that return to their nests only under cover of darkness; Rum has about 23 per cent of the world population of these birds. More crag tiers and scree await on the descent of the south flank, and there's a little light scrambling.

Next is **Askival**, Rum's highest peak and a magnificent one. Initially a narrow grassy arête, the crest of the north ridge soon becomes much rockier and more exposed. Taken direct it gives the hardest scrambling of the day, with a short section of Moderate-grade climbing on the Askival Pinnacle. Many walkers miss it all by taking the well-worn

Ainshval (left) and Trollaval from Hallival

path on the left (east) flank, requiring only some very modest scrambling to reach the summit.

In descent Askival's west ridge offers some short-lived scrambling on the true crest, although again an eroded path on the left flank avoids the difficulties. Either way it's steep, and much height is lost dropping to the **Bealach an Oir**. Non-scramblers might prefer to omit the next peak, Trollaval, by traversing around the head of Glen Dibidil to gain the Bealach an Fhuarain. To climb **Trollaval** head due W up steep grass slopes. A ridge soon takes shape, becoming narrow and scrambly near the top. There's more interesting airy scrambling between the mountain's two very sharp summits. Descent from Trollaval requires care in mist. First return from the west summit to the east, then head roughly SSE where an eroded path weaves steeply downhill between crags to reach the **Bealach an Fhuarain**.

A large buttress guards direct access to **Ainshval** from here, and while it provides an interesting high-end scramble most walkers will avoid it by cutting right to ascend a steep scree path onto Ainshval's north ridge. There's a fine rock crest on the upper ridge – this is a hard scramble, and yet again it can be entirely avoided via a well-scuffed rubbly path just on the left flank. The summit of Rum's second highest peak marks a transition from rough to grassier going.

From the wide turfy summit head S into a dip, from where a climb up a short stretch of rockier ridge leads onto a minor top. A last casual stroll, and **Sgurr nan Gillean** is in the bag. This southernmost of Rum's peaks has a remote feel and an uninterrupted sea view. Direct descent from here to Dibidil bothy is not advised. Instead head S, skirting the craggy southeast face and descending steep and quite complex ground to reach gentler slopes below. Bear E across bogs and heather to pick up the muddy coastal path leading N past the superbly located **Dibidil** bothy.

Return 9km

Having forded the Dibidil river (care in spate), the path to Kinloch takes a spectacular line across steep slopes high above the coast. It can be muddy, and there's a fair amount of ascent coming at the end of a long hill day, but the views of Eigg and Skye more than compensate. Eventually Loch Scresort comes into sight, and the path makes a gradual descent back to **Kinloch**.

Ainshval (left), Hallival, Askival and the distant Skye Cuillin (Walk 47) from Sgurr nan Gillean

Bla Bheinn,
Sgurr na Stri and Sligachan, Skye

S *kye's Cuillin are uniquely ferocious, a jagged mini-Alps in a maritime setting. The famous Cuillin Traverse is only for experienced mountaineers. Luckily the range looks as good from a distance as close up, and the outlying Munro Bla Bheinn is a superb viewpoint that rivals any summit on the Main Ridge for craggy drama. A reasonably non-technical traverse of Bla Bheinn is described here – a strenuous route to the beach at Camasunary, perhaps, but worth it. From there an adventurous coastal path leads into the fastness of Coruisk, beneath the serrated wall of the Cuillin proper. Above stands the little rock peak of Sgurr na Stri. Its ascent is optional, although with such a pivotal location it is hard to imagine a better summit panorama. After these highs, finish with the long walk-out to Sligachan, one of the great low-level through-routes of Scotland in its own right.*

↑ *Bla Bheinn dwarfs Camasunary bothy*

ROUTE INFORMATION

Start	Car park above Loch Slapin (NG 560 215)
Finish	Sligachan (NG 485 298)
Distance	21km (13 miles)
Ascent	1500m
Time	8½hrs
Terrain	Rubbly path and some modest scrambling on the ascent of Bla Bheinn; less trodden but more pleasant descending the south ridge. The optional ascent of the south side of Sgurr na Stri is a superb long grade 2/3 scramble; except for the brief grade 1/2 scramble of The Bad Step the alternative ascent via Coruisk is rugged but hands-free.
Summits	Bla Bheinn (Blaven) 928m ('blue mountain'); Sgurr na Stri 497m ('the hill of strife'); Cuillin (obscure, but possibly 'high rocks', Norse)
Maps	OS Landranger (1:50,000) 32; OS Explorer (1:25,000) 411; Harvey Superwalker (1:25,000) Skye: The Cuillin
Public transport	Broadford–Elgol bus service on B8083 to access start of the walk; Sligachan is on the Broadford–Portree route. The rightly popular Elgol boat service provides alternative access to Coruisk, except in winter (01471 866244).
By boat	A paddle from Elgol across Loch Scavaig to Camasunary and Coruisk is one of the great sea kayak trips of Scotland
By bike	A combination of bike and car would rule out reliance on limited bus services
Accommodation	Broadford YH (01471 822442)
Sleeping out	Superbly located beachside bothy at Camasunary (NG 510 187) and excellent camping as well. A camp anywhere around Coruisk, Sgurr na Stri or Glen Sligachan would be a treat too.
Seasonal notes	In winter Bla Bheinn needs competence in both ascent and descent, and the short scramble onto the south peak may be spicy
Short cuts	From Camasunary several options are available – walk S to Elgol; go directly up-glen to Sligachan, missing both Coruisk and Sgurr na Stri; coast path to Coruisk minus Sgurr na Stri; Sgurr na Stri via Option A or the corrie between it and Sgurr Hain, minus Coruisk.

↑ *Bla Bheinn (right) and the fierce little rock peak of Clach Glas from Srath na Creitheach*

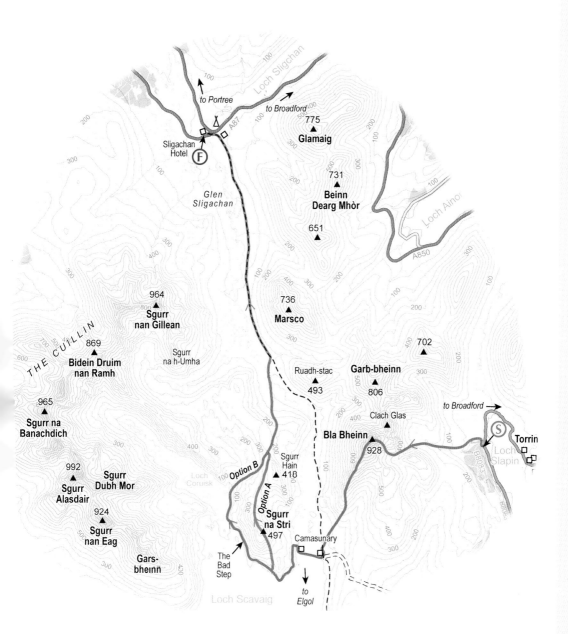

On the hill 12km

From the car park return to the road to pick up a path on the north bank of the Allt na Dunaiche. The great gully-seamed crags of Clach Glas and Bla Bheinn loom ever more imposing ahead. Ford the burn twice then make a steep eroded ascent into Coire Uaigneich to outflank the cliffs. Where the corrie opens out the path braids into several strands; bear right up scree and a short scrambly rock band to gain **Bla Bheinn's** east spur. The path now makes a steady ascent W, following the cliff edge past the top of the Great Prow, a famous rock climb. From the summit trig point the view over the broken crags to Clach Glas is stunning; there is no non-climbing route onto this fierce peak.

Coruisk and the Cuillin Main Ridge from Sgurr na Stri, with Sgurr Dubh Mor (left) and Sgurr nan Gillean (far right)

Descend into a pronounced gap, then make a short sharp grade 2 scramble onto Bla Bheinn's lower south top. Now head S onto the south ridge, a long and visually stunning descent with rotting cliffs to the right and the sea below, with Rum (Walk 46) floating on the horizon. The ridge is rocky and quite narrow in places, but not difficult. At a cairn on a low shoulder the path drops left to skirt a crag. Once on the bogs below, cut a corner on a sketchy trail to the private house at **Camasunary**, then follow the sandy shore to the bothy at the west end of the bay.

Ford the river just upstream of a broken footbridge (in spate you may have to go further) to pick up the coastal path around the steep headland of **Rubha Bàn** – watch out for a deep cleft in the sea cliff at one point. As the headland is turned there's a sudden view into Coruisk, the most impressive place in Scotland; the huge slabby pyramid of the Dubhs

Ridge is prominent. Where a burn flows through a cutting into the sea there are two options.

Option A Follow the burn steeply uphill towards Sgurr na Stri's rocky south flank, split from top to bottom by a gully from which the burn flows. Take the steep buttress right of this cleft, ad-libbing up a long series of slabs, walls and corners; this is a grade 2/3 scramble by the easiest line and a minor classic. From **Sgurr na Stri's** east top cross the gap to the main summit before descending NNW; an occasional path stays with the high ground to curve right over a minor top, then skirts left of **Sgurr Hain** to reach a cairn on a saddle to its north.

Option B is slightly longer than Option A, but with less ascent. Continue along the coast path. Just before Coruisk is The Bad Step, a short scramble that some find intimidating; stay quite low, follow the polished rock, and it's no more than grade 1/2.

The northern Cuillin from Sligachan. From the left:
Sgurr nan Gillean, Am Basteir, Sgurr a' Bhasteir and Bruach na Frithe

Now pass between knolls to reach the outflow of **Loch Coruisk**. Take the soggy path slanting uphill of the loch shore, climbing above little Loch a' Choire Riabhaich to reach the saddle north of **Sgurr Hain** (as on Option A). A detour from here onto Sgurr na Stri is hard work, but cannot be recommended highly enough.

Return 9km

From the cairned saddle to the north of Sgurr Hain a path drops into **Glen Sligachan**; it's unpleasantly eroded in parts. Cross the boggy glen floor to meet the Camasunary–Sligachan through-route. This is followed N between the crags of Marsco and the spires of Sgurr nan Gillean, a spectacular end to a day of superlatives.

Bla Bheinn (left), Clach Glas and Sgurr nan Each from Torrin on Loch Slapin

Trotternish Ridge, Skye

*S*kye's Trotternish Ridge is uniquely weird. The western slopes tilting gently into moorland contrast strikingly with the eastern side, which forms the country's longest escarpment – a rampart of sinister dark basalt cliffs that marches almost unbroken for over 25km, breaking into displays of surreal extravagance among tottery spires and gargoyles. Near the north end of the ridge are the clustered spikes of The Quiraing; further south broods the Old Man of Storr and its attendant spires. Although both are fixtures on the island's thriving tourist circuit, summer's crowds barely disturb their hallucinatory ambience, and between these two famous highlights is a great deal of deserted but equally unforgettable country. This route follows the cliff edge from end to end to create a walk of startling novelty, reaching parts that others only read about in fantasy books. It is feasible in one long day (particularly recommended for runners), but for full effect do it over two and camp with the pixies.

↑ *Bioda Buidhe (left) and the distant Quiraing from the Bealach Uige*

ROUTE INFORMATION

Start	Layby just south of Flodigarry (NG 463 709)
Finish	Portree
Distance	35km (22 miles)
Ascent	2100m
Time	13hrs
Terrain	A mix of close-cropped turf and boggy ground – a very forgiving surface for walking or running. Although the ridge-top moorland can be featureless, it's hard to go far wrong with navigation thanks to the constant presence of an enormous cliff to the east.
Summits	Quiraing ('pillared enclosure', possibly); Bioda Buidhe 466m ('yellow top'); Beinn Edra 611m ('outer mountain', Norse); Sgùrr a' Mhadaidh Ruaidh 593m ('peak of the red fox'); Hartaval 668m ('rocky fell', Norse); The Storr 719m; Ben Dearg 552m ('red mountain')
Maps	OS Landranger (1:50,000) 23; OS Explorer (1:25,000) 408 covers all but the southernmost corner of the walk, for which you need 410; Harvey Superwalker (1:25,000) Skye: Storr and Trotternish

Public transport	Bus from Portree to Flodigarry
By bike	Stashing a bike at the far end of the ridge would remove any need for post-walk buses or hitchhiking
Accommodation	Dun Flodigarry Hostel (01470 552212); Uig YH (01470 542746)
Sleeping out	Many turfy hill-top and bealach camping possibilities in calm weather. Despite the plentiful bogs there are surprisingly few running burns on the ridge, and the main issue is sourcing clean drinking water; this will have a bearing on choice of campsite.
Seasonal notes	These low, maritime hills are less likely to offer serious winter conditions than bigger mountains inland. Under snow there would be no particular difficulties, except in the ascent of Ben Dearg from the north.
Short cuts	Several major bealachs offer escape from the ridge, but it can be a long soggy slog to the nearest road either east or west. Consider finishing at The Storr for easy access to the A855.

The Storr cliffs and Old Man

On the hill 32km

For the sake of variety, the initial section of the walk runs below the escarpment; there's plenty of clifftop ground later in the day. Just south of **Flodigarry** look out for a path signed for The Quiraing, starting from a parking layby. The path leads SW, passing two small lochans then climbing quite steeply towards the base of the cliffs.

Once on a level continue S beneath the crags to enter **The Quiraing**. On rounding a bend at an overhung rock the path runs between the sinister Prison on the left (the traverse of which is an exciting scramble) and a cluster of spires overhead on the right that includes the remarkable Needle. An optional detour, right, up scree leads to The Table, a bizarre area of turf, level as a football field, hidden among the pinnacles. This alien landscape has developed as the lava of the ridge slipped over underlying sedimentary rocks, a process that is still ongoing (the road near Flodigarry needs regular repair). Where the path splits stay right, soon reaching the busy **car park** at the top of the hairpins on the Uig–Staffin road.

Continue S on a well-trodden clifftop path, soon leaving any crowds behind to ascend onto **Bioda Buidhe**. The view from the edge is spectacular, ranging over the massive rock peaks of Dun Dubh and Druim an Ruma, and acres of bog rolling to a coast dotted with whitewashed crofts. Across the water are the rumpled islands of Rona and Raasay, and, beyond, the mountains of the mainland. Head SW on marshy ground to skirt inset cliffs, descending quite steeply to the **Bealach nan Coisichean**.

Stay with the rim for the driest walking and best views – advice that holds good for the entire walk – taking care not to trip on discarded coils of rusty fence wire. Beyond Bealach Uige an uphill slog gains the cliff-edge trig point on top of **Beinn Edra**. Beyond is the **Bealach Mhoramhain**, from where escape can be made either W or E.

A series of little summits leads on down the ridge, each a variation on the bog/escarpment theme. A steep descent from **Creag a' Lain** (point 609m on Landranger map) brings you to a broad saddle with some tremendous rock scenery (and good camping); although a dead end, from here it

The Sound of Raasay from The Storr, with Raasay's Dun Caan just visible above the clouds

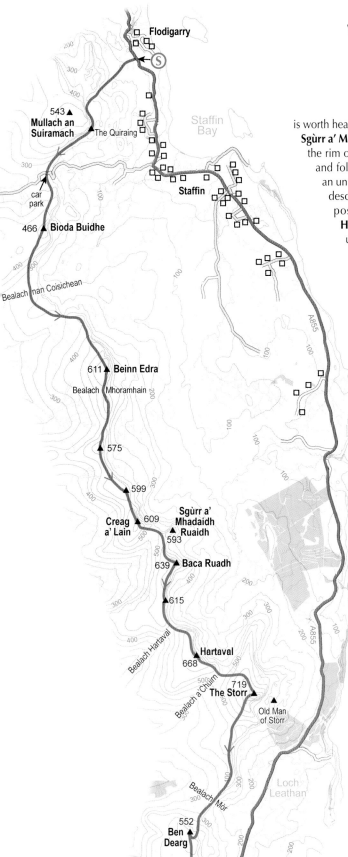

is worth heading out onto the promontory summit of **Sgùrr a' Mhadaidh Ruaidh**. Continue uphill around the rim of Coir' an t-Seasgaich onto **Baca Ruadh** and follow the gently sloping ridge SSW over an unnamed minor top to make a steeper final descent to the **Bealach Hartaval** (another possible bad-weather escape point). **Hartaval** itself is easy enough on the way up, although steeper on the far side. On approaching the **Bealach a'Chuirn** bear slightly S to avoid craggy ground.

Above this major pass looms **The Storr**, highest point on Trotternish and a superb hill by any standards. Slog painfully E up its dull side to reach the crest of the north ridge, turning right to follow a popular ascent path onto the grassy tabletop summit. On clear days the outlook is enormous – the hills of Harris, the saw-toothed Cuillin, and prominent peaks of Scotland's western seaboard from An Teallach to Kintail. Peer over the giddy gulf of the east face to the Old Man of Storr and its attendant spires far below. To descend loop W around the head of a gully, then drop straight down a long grassy slope to the **Bealach Beag**. Yet more clifftop entertainment leads to the **Bealach Mòr**, a pronounced low point from which a quick escape is possible E to the A855.

Ben Dearg is now all that remains, a cliff-guarded hill that looks daunting from below. Ascend easily until below the final steepening. There are now three choices – head straight up the eroded slope directly above (care required); alternatively, bear a good distance right to gain the skyline ridge more easily; or cut left and follow an exposed traverse

map continues on page 248

247

path that crosses a crumbly face to reach a weird landslipped gulch between the main hill and some pinnacles. Climb very steep grass on the right to emerge on the summit plateau. From this final worthwhile summit on the ridge cross a fence and head S, staying with the boggy high ground over the lumps of **A' Chorra Bheinn** and **Pein a' Chleibh** to eventually hit a minor road at **Achachork**.

Return 3km
On joining the A855 it's a 20min downhill stroll into **Portree**.

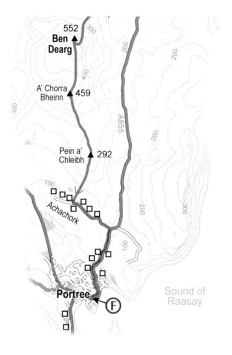

Bla Bheinn (Walk 47) and the Cuillin from Ben Dearg

An Cliseam range, Harris

*T*he rugged hills of North Harris are among the most extensive of any Hebridean range, an *elemental wilderness of rock, loch and sky. Rising between the turbulent Atlantic and the windswept bogs of Lewis these are distinctly maritime hills, and moisture is a constant companion either underfoot or overhead (often both). Deep glens running north–south slice the principal massif into four distinct tranches, making a full traverse over every major summit an overnight backpacking challenge.*

This more manageable single-day outing concentrates on the two eastern groups. As the highest point in Harris and the only Western Isles Corbett, An Cliseam (or Clisham) receives the lion's share of attention, and a circuit of the main peak and its satellite summits is a superb ridge walk that fully deserves its comparative popularity. By contrast, the Uisgneabhal Mòr group to the west seems almost untrodden, and seekers of solitude will find it hugely inspiring. Just don't leave home without your gaiters.

↑ *The North Harris hills from Losgaintir – from the right, An Cliseam,*
Mulla-Fo-Dheas, Uisgneabhal Mòr and Oireabhal

ROUTE INFORMATION

Start/finish	B887 at Bun Abhainn Eadarra (NB 131 042)	**Sleeping out**	Waterlogged, uneven ground that doesn't lend itself to comfortable camping; the best bet is either up high, or down near the Abhainn Langadail at the midway point of the walk

Distance 21km (13 miles)

Ascent 1950m

Time 9hrs

Terrain Very tough. Boggy ground predominates low down, while the hills are invariably rough and steep. Some basic ridge scrambling on Mulla-Fo-Dheas, mostly avoidable. Path is clear on the crests of the An Cliseam range, but less so on the Uisgneabhal Mòr hills; long pathless sections to start and finish.

Summits An Cliseam (Clisham) 799m ('rocky cliff'', possibly); Mulla-Fo-Dheas 743m ('south summit'); Mulla-Fo-Thuath 720m ('north summit'); Tèileasbhal 697m (obscure); Uisgneabhal Mòr 729m ('big oxen peak', Norse/Gaelic)

Maps OS Landranger (1:50,000) 13 or 14; OS Explorer (1:25,000) 456

Public transport Tarbert–Hushinish bus stops at Bun Abhainn Eadarra

Accommodation Hostel at No.5 Drinishader (01859 511255); Rhenigidale YH (no advance bookings)

Seasonal notes Limited altitude and the Atlantic influence make winter conditions less reliable than on mainland hills, and plenty of wind and rain is generally more likely than snow in any season. But given snow, this is a magnificent round, the ridges of Mulla-Fo-Dheas calling for basic mountaineering skills.

Short cuts With appropriate transport an alternative high start from the A859 will save some distance and ascent. Although all stages of the walk are worthwhile, the An Cliseam range is the truly unmissable bit; a shorter day is to do the classic Scaladail horseshoe from the east, leaving the western hills for another trip. The glen between the An Cliseam range and Uisgneabhal Mòr offers a low-level retreat in bad weather, but it is only a 'soft' option in the sense of being abnormally boggy (and largely pathless, incidentally).

Looking north to Loch Langabhat and the watery hinterland of west Lewis

The cliffs of Sgurr Scaladail and Loch Mhisteam from Mullach an Langa

On the hill 21km

From the driveway of a house just right of a little burn take the old stalker's path as marked on OS maps, a rough and muddy route onto the shoulder of Cleit nan Uan. Leave the path at its high point and climb quite steeply onto Creag Ghreinebridh. Boggy terrain leads on to the minor summit of Tarsabhal, with the bulk of An Cliseam now prominent to the north. Stay with the high ground along a vague shoulder, then skirt a little right of **An Cliseam's** stone-strewn south face to pick up a path up its southeast flank. The rocky summit ridge is surprisingly narrow.

From the trig point and large circular wind break continue briefly along the summit ridge, then turn off left at a cairn to descend a stony slope almost due W onto a pronounced bealach. Continue over a steep minor summit to another little col, then follow the narrow east ridge of **Mulla-Fo-Dheas** – there's a little entertaining scrambling on the crest, which can be avoided via a path just on the north flank.

From the rocky summit pick a way down the scrambly northwest ridge to another col, and continue more easily onto **Mulla-Fo-Thuath**. Take the broad northeast shoulder, bearing left on stony slopes to avoid the broken crags at its northern termination. After the next col it's a short easy climb onto **Mullach an Langa**, a good viewpoint on the An Cliseam horseshoe.

Descend quite steeply NE, soon losing any trace of path in the bogs of Cnoc a' Chaisteil. Here cut left, dropping down a steep pathless slope between two burns to reach the spongy levels of the Abhainn Langadail, a wild and secluded spot despite the intrusive bulldozed estate track.

Hop over the river (in flood this may be best slightly upstream) and climb the rough slope beside the burn named Gil Slipir on the map; look closely and an old stalker's path can be found, easing the ascent with a couple of wide zigzags. At the boggy col above, the still sprightly might detour up **Stulabhal** – but most will happily ignore it and turn left for the path-free ascent onto the broad shoulder above the cliffs of Gleann Stuladail. Follow the high ground, veering left onto the long northern ridge of

Tèileasbhal; this proves an enjoyable way up the hill, and there's even a vague path at times. The boulder-heaped summit is sharper than might be expected.

Descend the obvious southwest ridge to a col slung between precipitous corries, then continue quite steeply up to the stony summit of **Uisgneabhal Mòr**, an excellent viewpoint (if you're lucky). Drop S, where a long ridge soon takes shape. Follow this, curving a little SSW lower down, to the shallow col before Creag na Speireig, and from here cut left onto the minor top of Brunabhal. Stay with the soggy high ground, heading S to meet the B887 just west of **Bun Abhainn Eadarra**.

Uisgneabhal Mòr and Tèileasbhal (left) and the An Cliseam range from the south

Uig hills, Lewis

Quality is not necessarily proportional to size, and Lewis proves the point. The limits of height-oriented hillwalking are rarely more apparent than in southwest Lewis, a remote area of immaculate sand beaches and intriguing gnarled rock peaks that would fall far below the radar of anyone fixated solely on Munros or Corbetts. Despite very modest elevations, this secretive little upland poses a considerable challenge, its summits outdoing some twice their height for sheer uncompromising character.

The hills are ploughed into two parallel chains by the north–south trench of the Bealach Raonasgail. Each is separated from its neighbours by low cols, bristling crags and scattered with numerous tiny lochans; this circuit of both sides of the central glen inevitably involves a lot of ascent. Walking here is an effort well worth making – but few do, and eagles seem as common as people. Yet this is a place with a unique atmosphere, shining seascapes below and vast skyscapes above; and between the two is a waterlogged land, its peaty skin pulled back to reveal the gneiss bones beneath.

↑ *The Uig hills from the north on a stormy evening*   253

ROUTE INFORMATION

Start/finish	Track off the road to Mangurstadh (Mangurstadh) (NB 032 313) – park unobtrusively
Distance	21km (13 miles)
Ascent	1420m
Time	7½hrs
Terrain	Track provides easy access, but the hills themselves are steep and pathless, with a challenging mix of bogs and rock outcrops
Summits	Tahabhal 515m (obscure); Teinneasabhal 497m (obscure); Tamanasbhal 467m (obscure); Cracabhal 514m ('crow hill' or 'creviced hill'); Mealaisbhal 574m ('lumpy hill hill', possibly Norse/Gaelic combination)
Maps	OS Landranger (1:50,000) 13; OS Explorer (1:25,000) 458
Public transport	Daily bus from Stornoway to Mangersta (Mangurstadh)
By bike	The stony Bealach Raonasgail track is ideally suited to mountain bikes, and about 8km of walking can be saved by cycling to the outflow of Loch Raonasgail
Accommodation	Uig Sands campsite (01851 672248); Kershader YH (0845 293 7373)
Sleeping out	Few flat pitches of any size; the shore of Loch Raonasgail is a good spot, and there are numerous possibilities higher up among the many lochans and hollows
Seasonal notes	Full winter conditions are rare, but if encountered then the steep ascent of Tahabhal and the descent from Cracabhal both require care. The burn crossing at the outflow of Loch Raonasgail may prove tricky in very wet weather; if so, detour around the head of the loch. For access information in stalking season call 01851 672421.
Short cuts	The Bealach Raonasgail track neatly bisects the hills, so it's possible to do either half of the circuit in isolation. Note that direct short cuts into the central glen are not advisable from any summit thanks to numerous crags.

Teinneasabhal from the Cracabhal–Mealaisbhal col

watery wilderness of the Harris/Lewis badlands. The huge but little-known climber's cliff of Creag Dubh is seen in profile. An ascent of **Tamanasbhal** is a fairly easy extension worth making. This done, return to the hummocky col and drop W to the high point of the **Bealach Raonasgail**.

The northeast buttress of Mealaisbhal and Loch Raonasgail

Approach 4km

Start from the road to Mangurstadh, just above the famous Uig sands. The rough private track can't be driven (locked gate at Abhainn Stocaill), but gives an easy walk or cycle, with the hills rearing out of the boggy moor as you near lonely **Loch Raonasgail**. Just before the loch outflow leave the track to ford the burn beside a big boulder.

On the hill 12km

Make a rising traverse over rough ground on the western flank of **Tarain** to reach a boggy hollow just below the col between this outlying hill and the steep mass of **Tahabhal**. The latter is the highest peak east of the Bealach Raonasgail, and presents steep craggy faces both north and west. From the boggy hollow, a line of weakness can be seen running straight up the hill's northwest aspect; climb this on steep grass, weaving among scattered outcrops and staying just right of the biggest crag. Luckily it's not a huge hill, and the angle soon eases. A cairn marks the high point of the broad summit area.

Descend SSE to avoid steep rocky ground, crossing the bealach just left of some pools and continuing in the same line for the easiest way up the lower slopes of **Teinneasabhal**. Above this steep slope turn right for an easier stroll to the summit cairn. Now head S to a long hummocky col at the head of Coire Dhiobadail, with intriguing views down remote Loch Diobadail to the

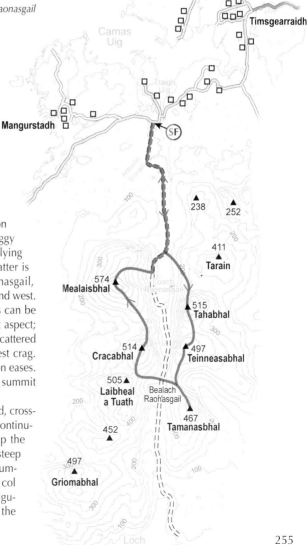

255

Cross the track at a prominent cairn, from where a vague and soon-to-disappear trail climbs W to the rocky col between **Laibheal a Tuath** and Cracabhal. Turn right, weaving uphill through slabby gneiss outcrops onto the knobbly summit of **Cracabhal**; the high point is at the northern end. Both the north and east faces are cliffy; between them is the rugged northeast spur, and with some attentive route finding this can be descended (minimal scrambling, but care needed in mist). (A more circuitous alternative is to descend the mountain's easier west spur before cutting back E past Loch Clibh Cracabhal.)

The next bealach is a complex area of knobbles and pools; cross this, passing just right of the biggest lochan. Now attack the southeast flank of **Mealaisbhal**, where grassy ground soon gives way to an extensive summit boulder field. This is the highest of the Uig hills, and the views are far ranging. To descend pick a way roughly NNE down the boulder field, reaching easier ground at a vague col before a mini-summit. To outflank the hill's precipitous north face turn E here, descending a broad depression – steep and rough at first, but gradually easing as a burn is followed down to the access track on the shore of **Loch Raonasgail**.

Return 5km
Go back the way you came.

Storm clearing west from the Cracabhal–Mealaisbhal col

APPENDIX 1
Walk summary table

	WALK	DISTANCE KM (MILES)	ASCENT	TIME	SCRAMBLING GRADE	WALKED
1	Ben Hope and Ben Loyal	33.5 (21)	1800m	12hrs	1	
2	Ben Klibreck	26 (16)	1200m	9½hrs		
3	Foinaven	27 (17)	1600m	11hrs		
4	Ben More Assynt, Conival and Breabag	34 (21)	1660m	12hrs	1/2	
5	Suilven and Canisp	25 (15½)	1790m	10hrs	optional: 3	
6	Seana Bhraigh and Càrn Bàn	31.5 (19½)	1350m	12hrs	optional: 1/2	
7	Beinn Dearg four	24.5 (15)	1600m	9½hrs		
8	Traverse of the Fannaichs	28 (17½)	2200m	11hrs		
9	An Teallach and the Beinn Deargs	37 (23)	2610m	17½hrs	optional: 3	
10	Fisherfield Six	37 (23)	3000m	16hrs		
11	Beinn Eighe	25.5 (16)	2000m	10½hrs	1	
12	Liathach and Beinn Alligin	28.5 (18)	2750m	13hrs	optional: 2	
13	Coulin Forest	28 (17½)	2150m	11hrs		
14	Circuit of Loch Monar	43 (27)	2940m	18hrs	1/2	
15	Loch Mullardoch hills	29 (18)	1840m	10hrs		
16	Carn Eighe, Sgurr nan Ceathreamhnan and more	46 (28)	2220m	16hrs		
17	Cluanie horseshoe from Glen Affric	32 (20)	1990m	11hrs	optional: 1	
18	Beinn Fhada, The Brothers and the Five Sisters	35 (22)	3870m	18hrs	1	
19	South Glen Shiel Ridge to The Saddle	31 (19)	2660m	15hrs	optional: 2	
20	Ladhar Bheinn and Loch Hourn	33 (20½)	2030m	13hrs	optional: 1	
21	Sgurr na Ciche range	37 (23)	2740m	14hrs	1	
22	Glen Finnan circuit	25 (15½)	2150m	9½hrs		
23	Beinn Odhar Bheag and Rois-Bheinn group	25 (15½)	2600m	12hrs	1 (brief)	
24	Creag Meagaidh	20 (12½)	1280m	7hrs		
25	Ben Alder and Geal-chàrn group	40 (25)	1880m	16hrs	1	
26	Lochaber Traverse	32 (20)	2800m	15hrs	1	

	WALK	DISTANCE KM (MILES)	ASCENT	TIME	SCRAMBLING GRADE	WALKED
27	The Mamores	29.5 (18½)	2615m	13hrs	optional: 1	
28	Glen Coe circuit	41 (25½)	4200m	20hrs	2	
29	Black Mount Traverse	27 (17)	1700m	10hrs		
30	Glen Etive hills	26 (16)	2400m	11hrs		
31	Ben Cruachan, Beinn Eunaich and Beinn a' Chochuill	26 (16)	2270m	11hrs		
32	Achallader's five Munros	31 (19½)	2200m	11hrs		
33	Tyndrum's five Corbetts	24 (15)	2100m	10hrs		
34	Ben Lui, Ben Oss and Beinn Dubhchraig	22 (14)	1560m	8hrs		
35	Crianlarich hills	27 (17)	2910m	12hrs		
36	Arrochar 'Alps'	26 (16)	2700m	10½hrs	optional: 3 (brief)	
37	Ben Lawers group and Tarmachan Ridge	29 (18)	2400m	12hrs		
38	Beinn a'Ghlo, the Tarf and the Tilt	41 (25½)	1960m	16hrs		
39	Munros of Glen Feshie	29 (18)	1150m	9½hrs		
40	Cairngorms 4000ers	34 (21)	2300m	14hrs		
41	Beinn a' Bhuird and Ben Avon	33 (20½)	1330m	11hrs		
42	Lochnagar via The Stuic	23.5 (14½)	1070m	9hrs	1	
43	Glen Clova circuit	30 (19)	1440m	13hrs		
44	Galloway hills	34 (21)	1850m	13hrs		
45	Glen Rosa circuit, Arran	25 (15½)	2000m	10hrs		
46	Cuillin Traverse, Rum	22 (14)	2050m	10hrs	optional: up to moderate	
47	Bla Bheinn, Sgurr na Stri and Sligachan, Skye	21 (13)	1500m	8½hrs	optional: 1/2 (brief) or 2/3	
48	Trotternish Ridge, Skye	35 (22)	2100m	13hrs		
49	An Cliseam range, Harris	21 (13)	1950m	9hrs		
50	Uig hills, Lewis	21 (13)	1420m	7½hrs		

APPENDIX 2
Key Summits and Ranges

Areas and major ranges are shown in **bold**

KEY SUMMITS / RANGES	WALK NO(S)
A' Chailleach	8
A' Chir	45
A' Chràlaig	17
A' Mhaighdean	10
Ainshval	46
Am Bodach (Mamores)	27
Am Bodach (Glen Coe)	28
Am Fasarinen	12
An Caisteal	35
An Cliseam (Clisham)	49
An Riabhachan	15
An Socach (south Loch Mullardoch)	16
An Socach (north Loch Mullardoch)	15
An Stac	23
An Stùc	37
An Teallach	9
Angus glens	43
Aonach air Chrith	19
Aonach Beag (Central Highlands)	25
Aonach Beag (Lochaber)	26
Aonach Eagach	28
Aonach Meadhoin	18
Aonach Mòr	26
Arran, Isle of	45
Arrochar	36
Askival	46
Assynt	4, 5

KEY SUMMITS / RANGES	WALK NO(S)
Beinn a' Bhuird	41
Beinn a' Chaisteil	33
Beinn a' Chochuill	31
Beinn a' Chreachain	32
Beinn a' Ghlo	38
Beinn a' Chlaidheimh	10
Beinn a' Chroin	35
Beinn Achaladair	32
Beinn Alligin	12
Beinn an Dòthaidh	32
Beinn Chaorach	33
Beinn Dearg Bheag	9
Beinn Dearg Mòr	9
Beinn Dearg	7
Beinn Dorain	32
Beinn Dubhchraig	34
Beinn Edra	48
Beinn Eibhinn	25
Beinn Eighe	11
Beinn Eunaich	31
Beinn Fhada	18
Beinn Fhionnlaidh	16
Beinn Ghlas	37
Beinn Ime	36
Beinn Liath Mhòr Fannaich	8
Beinn Liath Mhòr	13
Beinn Mhanach	32

KEY SUMMITS / RANGES	WALK NO(S)	KEY SUMMITS / RANGES	WALK NO(S)
Ciste Dhubh	18	Goatfell	45
Clach Leathad	29	**Grey Corries**	26
Cona' Mheall	7	Hallival	46
Conival	4	**Harris, Isle of**	49
Corserine	44	**Kintail**	18
Coulin Forest	13	**Knoydart**	20
Cracabhal	50	Ladhar Bheinn	20
Creag a' Mhàim	19	**Lewis, Isle of**	50
Creag Meagaidh	24	Liathach	12
Creag na Caillich	37	**Loch Broom and Easter Ross**	6, 7
Creag nan Damh	19	Lochnagar	42
Creise	29	Lurg Mhòr	14
Cruach Ardrain	35	Màm Sodhail	16
Cuillin	47	**Mamores**	27
Deeside	41, 42	Maoile Lunndaidh	14
Driesh	43	Maol Chean-dearg	13
Drochaid Ghlas	31	Maol Chinn-dearg	19
Druim Fiaclach	23	Mayar	43
Druim Shionnach	19	Mealaisbhal	50
Eididh nan Clach Geala	7	Meall a' Bhuiridh	29
Fannaichs	8	Meall Corranaich	37
Fisherfield and Dundonnell	9, 10	Meall Cuanail	31
Foinaven	3	Meall Dearg	28
Fuar Tholl	13	Meall Garbh	37
Ganu Mòr	3	Meall nan Ceapraichean	7
Garbh Chioch Mhór	21	Meall nan Con	2
Geal-chàrn	25	Meall nan Eun	30
Glas Bheinn Mhor	30	Meall nan Tarmachan	37
Glen Coe and Lochaber	26–28	Merrick	44
Glen Shiel	18, 19	**Moidart and Glen Finnan**	22, 23

KEY SUMMITS / RANGES	WALK NO(S)
Shalloch on Minnoch	44
Skye, Isle of	47, 48
Skye Cuillin	47
Southern Highlands	29–37
Southern Uplands	44
Spidean a' Choire Leith	12
Spidean Coire nan Clach	11
Stob Ban	27
Stob Binnein	35
Stob Choire Claurigh	26
Stob Coir' an Albannaich	30
Stob Coire a' Chairn	27
Stob Coire an Laoigh	26
Stob Coire Easain	26
Stob Coire Leith	28
Stob Coire Raineach	28
Stob Coire Sgreamhach	28
Stob Dearg (Buachaille Etive Mòr)	28
Stob Dearg (Ben Cruchan)	31
Stob Diamh	31
Stob Dubh	28

KEY SUMMITS / RANGES	WALK NO(S)
Stob Gabhar	29
Stob na Bròige	28
Stob Poite Coire Ardair	24
Streap	22
Suilven	5
Sutherland	1–3
Tahabhal	50
Tamanasbhal	50
Tarfessock	44
Tèileasbhal	49
Teinneasabhal	50
The Cobbler	36
The Saddle	19
The Storr	48
Tolmount	43
Tom Buidhe	43
Tom na Gruagaich	12
Torridon	11, 12
Trollavall	46
Uisgneabhal Mòr	49

APPENDIX 3
Further Reading

Guidebooks for walks and scrambles

100 Best Routes on Scottish Mountains
Ralph Storer (Sphere 1997): a classic book of hill walks, most attractive in the original hardback format – if you can find it

Highland Scrambles North
Iain Thow (SMC 2006): route info on scrambles from Kintail northwards, including the Western Isles (but not Skye)

Scotland
Chris Townsend (Cicerone 2010): not a route guide, more a comprehensive resource for information on all the major mountain regions

Scotland's Best Small Mountains
Kirstie Shirra (Cicerone 2010): for easier trips; a good complement to the harder routes in *Great Mountain Days in Scotland*

Scotland's Mountain Ridges
Dan Bailey (Cicerone 2010): scrambles, rock and winter climbs on classic ridges across the country

Scottish Canoe Touring
Eddie Palmer (ed.) (Pesda Press 2005): info on over 100 places to explore by kayak or open canoe, on inland and tidal water, including the waterborne hill approaches covered in this book

Scrambles in Lochaber
Noel Williams (Cicerone 2002): does what it says on the tin

Skye Scrambles
Noel Williams (SMC 2000): similarly self-explanatory title

Cicerone's range of Scottish titles is probably unrivalled, providing routes coverage of the whole country for hill-goers of all persuasions. See www.cicerone.co.uk.

Skills and general interest

Avalanche!
Roberto Bolognesi (Cicerone 2007)

Hill Walking:
The Official Handbook of the Mountain Leader and Walking Group Leader Schemes
Steve Long and John Cousins (UKMTB 2003): although tailored towards those seeking an ML qualification there's plenty of skills advice for recreational walkers too

Hostile Habitats – Scotland's Mountain Environment
M. Wrightham and N Kempe (eds.) (SMT 2006): a fascinating and detailed field guide to upland landforms, habitats and wildlife aimed squarely at hillwalkers

Map and Compass – The Art of Navigation
Pete Hawkins (Cicerone 2008)

Mountain Weather
David Pedgley (Cicerone 2006)

Scotland's Mountains Before the Mountaineers
Ian Mitchell (Luath 1998): a fascinating prehistory of peak bagging

Scottish Hill and Mountain Names
Peter Drummond (SMT 1991): it's nice to know what the name of the peak you're climbing actually means, even if it's a struggle to pronounce it

APPENDIX 4
Useful Contacts and Websites

Transport

For public transport information and journey planning see www.travelinescotland.com

First Scotrail runs Scotland's trains – visit www.scotrail.co.uk

Caledonian MacBrayne enjoys a monopoly of ferry services to the Hebrides and Arran – see www.calmac.co.uk

Scottish Citylink runs the majority of the country's long-distance buses; several routes are of interest to hillwalkers – visit www.citylink.co.uk

Postbus services can be particularly useful in the northwest, where there are limited public transport alternatives – see www.postbus.royalmail.com

Weather forecasts, conditions reports and general hill information

The most detailed hilltop weather forecasts are provided by the **Mountain Weather Information Service a**t www.mwis.org.uk

The **Met Office** also offers an online mountain forecast at www.metoffice.gov.uk

In winter don't leave home without consulting the forecasts provided by **Scottish Avalanche Information Service** – www.sais.gov.uk – although they only cover certain key areas, and only for a set period each season (it may snow outside these dates)

Hillwalkers may glean useful information about current snow conditions, the state of footpaths, the prevalence of midges and all things hill related from

the news pages and forums at www.UKHillwalking.com and its sister site, www.UKClimbing.com

Stalking

Details of **Hillphones** stalking information service and the online version, Heading for the Scottish Hills, can be found at www.outdooraccess-scotland.com/hills. Although it currently covers only a sad fraction of the country, this website is the best available source for estate contacts.

Accommodation

The **Scottish Youth Hostels Association** runs a network of properties across the country, most in locations popular with hillwalkers – visit www.syha.org.uk

Details of dozens of independent backpacker's hostels can be found at www.hostel-scotland.co.uk

For accommodation providers who've signed up to **Visitscotland's Walkers Welcome** scheme, see www.visitscotland.com/walking

Organisations

Scottish Natural Heritage (SNH) is the government-funded body charged with protecting and promoting landscape, wildlife and natural habitats – see www.snh.gov.uk

Mountaineering Council of Scotland (MCofS), the representative body for climbers, mountaineers and hillwalkers, is very active in promoting access and conservation – www.mcofs.org.uk

Ramblers Scotland, another national body representing walkers' interests, access and conservation – www.ramblers.org.uk/scotland

Mountain Bothies Association (MBA), a charity that maintains about 100 unlocked shelters across the UK, the bulk in Scotland. Maintenance work is done by teams of volunteers. Details of bothy locations are now available on their website – see www.mountainbothies.org.uk.

National Trust for Scotland (NTS), Scotland's largest conservation charity with interests in both historic and natural heritage. Substantial land holdings in both national parks and other mountain areas, including the Cairngorms, Tayside, Torridon, Kintail, Affric and Glen Coe. The NTS manages 46 of the 283 Munros, and their Highland estates form the basis of several walks in this book. See www.nts.org.uk.

John Muir Trust (JMT), a wild-land conservation charity and campaign group that actively promotes the protection and restoration of Scotland's wild landscape. The JMT own important parts of Skye, Ben Nevis and Knoydart, among other areas. See www.jmt.org.

Scottish Wild Land Group, another wild-land conservation and campaigning charity with an excellent seasonal magazine, *Wild Land News*. See www.swlg.org.uk.

For world-class courses in hillwalking skills, mountaineering, climbing and paddle sports consider **Glenmore Lodge**, Scotland's National Outdoor Training Centre – www.glenmorelodge.org.uk

Info on ticks and lyme disease is provided by the charity **Lyme Disease Action** – see www.lymediseaseaction.org.uk

INDEX

LISTING OF CICERONE GUIDES

BRITISH ISLES CHALLENGES, COLLECTIONS AND ACTIVITIES
The End to End Trail
The Mountains of England and Wales
  1 Wales & 2 England
The National Trails
The Relative Hills of Britain
The Ridges of England, Wales and Ireland
The UK Trailwalker's Handbook
The UK's County Tops
Three Peaks, Ten Tors

MOUNTAIN LITERATURE
Unjustifiable Risk?

UK CYCLING
Border Country Cycle Routes
Cycling in the Hebrides
Cycling in the Peak District
Mountain Biking in the Lake District
Mountain Biking in the Yorkshire Dales
Mountain Biking on the South Downs
The C2C Cycle Route
The End to End
The Lancashire Cycleway

SCOTLAND
Backpacker's Britain
  Central and Southern
    Scottish Highlands
  Northern Scotland
Ben Nevis and Glen Coe
Great Mountain Days in Scotland
North to the Cape
Not the West Highland Way
Scotland's Best Small Mountains
Scotland's Far West
Scotland's Mountain Ridges
Scrambles in Lochaber
The Ayrshire and Arran Coastal Paths
The Border Country
The Great Glen Way
The Isle of Mull
The Isle of Skye
The Pentland Hills
The Southern Upland Way
The Speyside Way
The West Highland Way
Scotland's Far North
Walking in the Cairngorms
Walking in the Ochils, Campsie Fells
  and Lomond Hills
Walking in Torridon
Walking Loch Lomond and the Trossachs
Walking on Harris and Lewis
Walking on Jura, Islay and Colonsay
Walking on the Isle of Arran
Walking on the Orkney
  and Shetland Isles
Walking the Galloway Hills
Walking the Lowther Hills

Walking the Munros
  1 Southern, Central and
    Western Highlands
  2 Northern Highlands and
    the Cairngorms
Winter Climbs Ben Nevis and Glen Coe
Winter Climbs in the Cairngorms
World Mountain Ranges: Scotland

NORTHERN ENGLAND TRAILS
A Northern Coast to Coast Walk
Backpacker's Britain
  Northern England
Hadrian's Wall Path
The Dales Way
The Pennine Way
The Spirit of Hadrian's Wall

**NORTH EAST ENGLAND,
YORKSHIRE DALES AND PENNINES**
Historic Walks in North Yorkshire
South Pennine Walks
The Cleveland Way and
  the Yorkshire Wolds Way
The North York Moors
The Reivers Way
The Teesdale Way
The Yorkshire Dales Angler's Guide
The Yorkshire Dales
  North and East
  South and West
Walking in County Durham
Walking in Northumberland
Walking in the North Pennines
Walks in Dales Country
Walks in the Yorkshire Dales
Walks on the North York Moors –
  Books 1 & 2

**NORTH WEST ENGLAND AND THE
ISLE OF MAN**
Historic Walks in Cheshire
Isle of Man Coastal Path
The Isle of Man
The Lune Valley and Howgills
The Ribble Way
Walking in Cumbria's Eden Valley
Walking in Lancashire
Walking in the Forest of Bowland
  and Pendle
Walking on the West Pennine Moors
Walks in Lancashire Witch Country
Walks in Ribble Country
Walks in Silverdale and Arnside
Walks in the Forest of Bowland

LAKE DISTRICT
Coniston Copper Mines
Great Mountain Days in the Lake District
Lake District Winter Climbs
Lakeland Fellranger
  The Central Fells
  The Mid-Western Fells

The Near Eastern Fells
The North-Western Wells
The Southern Fells
The Western Fells
Roads and Tracks of the Lake District
Rocky Rambler's Wild Walks
Scrambles in the Lake District
  North & South
Short Walks in Lakeland
  1 South Lakeland
  2 North Lakeland
  3 West Lakeland
The Cumbria Coastal Way
The Cumbria Way and
  the Allerdale Ramble
Tour of the Lake District

**DERBYSHIRE, PEAK DISTRICT AND
MIDLANDS**
High Peak Walks
The Star Family Walks
Walking in Derbyshire
White Peak Walks
  The Northern Dales
  The Southern Dales

SOUTHERN ENGLAND
A Walker's Guide to the Isle of Wight
London – The definitive walking guide
Suffolk Coast & Heaths Walks
The Cotswold Way
The North Downs Way
The South Downs Way
The South West Coast Path
The Thames Path
Walking in Berkshire
Walking in Kent
Walking in Sussex
Walking in the New Forest
Walking in the Isles of Scilly
Walking in the Thames Valley
Walking on Dartmoor
Walking on Guernsey
Walking on Jersey
Walks in the South Downs National Park

WALES AND WELSH BORDERS
Backpacker's Britain – Wales
Glyndwr's Way
Great Mountain Days in Snowdonia
Hillwalking in Snowdonia
Hillwalking in Wales
  Vols 1 & 2
Offa's Dyke Path
Ridges of Snowdonia
Scrambles in Snowdonia
The Ascent of Snowdon
Lleyn Peninsula Coastal Path
Pembrokeshire Coastal Path
The Shropshire Hills
The Wye Valley Walk
Walking in Pembrokeshire
Walking on the Brecon Beacons
Welsh Winter Climbs

For full information on all our guides, and to order books and eBooks, visit our website: **www.cicerone.co.uk**.

Walking – Trekking – Mountaineering – Climbing – Cycling

Over 40 years, Cicerone have built up an outstanding collection of 300 guides, inspiring all sorts of amazing adventures.

Every guide comes from extensive exploration and research by our expert authors, all with a passion for their subjects. They are frequently praised, endorsed and used by clubs, instructors and outdoor organisations.

All our titles can now be bought as **e-books** and many as iPad and Kindle files and we will continue to make all our guides available for these and many other devices.

Our website shows any **new information** we've received since a book was published. Please do let us know if you find anything has changed, so that we can pass on the latest details. On our **website** you'll also find some great ideas and lots of information, including sample chapters, contents lists, reviews, articles and a photo gallery.

It's easy to keep in touch with what's going on at Cicerone, by getting our monthly **free e-newsletter**, which is full of offers, competitions, up-to-date information and topical articles. You can subscribe on our home page and also follow us on **Facebook** and **Twitter**, as well as our **blog**.

Cicerone – the very best guides for exploring the world.

CICERONE

2 Police Square Milnthorpe Cumbria LA7 7PY
Tel: 015395 62069 info@cicerone.co.uk
www.cicerone.co.uk